S0-BTA-815

Born to
SHOP
S P A I N
AND
P O R T U G A L

Bantam Books of Related Interest
Ask your bookseller for the books you have missed.

BORN TO SHOP: France
BORN TO SHOP: Italy
BORN TO SHOP: London
BORN TO SHOP: Hong Kong
BORN TO SHOP: New York
BORN TO SHOP: Los Angeles
BORN TO SHOP: Mexico
BORN TO SHOP: England, Scotland, and Ireland
BORN TO SHOP: Spain and Portugal
BORN TO SHOP: Florida

Born to SHOP

SPAIN
AND
PORTUGAL

▼

SUZY GERSHMAN
and
JUDITH THOMAS

Introduction by
VINCENTE LLADRÓ

A
BANTAM
TRADE
PAPERBACK

BANTAM BOOKS
NEW YORK • TORONTO • LONDON
SYDNEY • AUCKLAND

This one was always for LoLo

The BORN TO SHOP Team:

authors:
Suzy Gershman and Judith Thomas
additional reporters:
Michael Gershman, Steve Thomas,
Debra Chester Kalter, M.D., Luis Idigoras
editor: Jill Parsons
executive editor: Toni Burbank
assistant to executive editor: Linda Gross

BORN TO SHOP: SPAIN AND PORTUGAL
A Bantam Book / November 1990

Produced by Ink Projects
Design by Lynne Arany
Maps by David Lindroth, Inc.

All rights reserved.
Copyright © 1990 by Suzy Kalter Gershman and Judith Evans Thomas.
Cover art copyright © 1990 by Dave Calver
No part of this book may be reproduced or transmitted
in any form or by any means, electronic or mechanical,
including photocopying, recording, or by any information
storage and retrieval system, without permission in
writing from the publisher.
For information address: Bantam Books.

ISBN 0-553-34855-8

Published simultaneously in the United States and Canada

Bantam Books are published by Bantam Books, a division of Bantam
Doubleday Dell Publishing Group, Inc. Its trademark, consisting of the
words "Bantam Books" and the portrayal of a rooster, is Registered in
U.S. Patent and Trademark Office and in other countries. Marca Registrada.
Bantam Books, 666 Fifth Avenue, New York, New York 10103.

PRINTED IN THE UNITED STATES OF AMERICA

FG   0 9 8 7 6 5 4 3 2 1

CONTENTS

Moroccan National Tourist Office, John De Rose and Nancy Caruso of Royal Air Maroc, Shelley Cohen at Hôtels Concorde, Kerry Green Zobar of Hilton International, Cynthia Fontayne of the Fontayne Group on behalf of TAP, Karen Preston of Leading Hotels of the World, Sally Rugar and Shawn Feliciano of Occidental Hotels, and Margarita Muselli and Christina Tabora of Hyatt Hotels and Resorts.

In Spain: Vincente Lladró of Lladró, Mar and Angel of the Meliá Valencia, Ricardo Castillejo of the Generalidad Valenciana, Salvador Vilches and José Mateos of the Meliá Sevilla, Felica Hernandez and Gerardo Quintana of the Sevilla Tourist Promotion Board, Juan Antonio Comín Ros of the Gaudí Association, Maria Luisa Albacar in Barcelona, Dr. Amelia in Madrid, and especially Antonio Hernan Gómez and Marisa Fernandez of the Patronato Municipal de Turismo de Madrid, Maria del Mar at the Hotel Miguel Ángel, and Rafael de la Fuente at the Hotel Villa Magna. Special thanks to Carmen and Chiquita.

In Portugal: José-Maria Soengas and Teresa de Chatillon of Le Meridien and Dr. José Lobo Antunes.

In Morocco: Alami Mejjali of the Hôtel Palais Jamai, and Lebbar Najib in Fez.

Editorial Note

The prices in this book were established at the following rates:

$1 U.S. = 140 Portuguese *escudos*
$1 U.S. = 110 Spanish *pesetas*

Although every effort was made to ensure the accuracy of prices appearing in this book, it should be kept in mind that with inflation and a fluctuating rate of exchange, prices will vary. Dollar estimations of prices were made based on the following rate of exchange: 5.5 French francs = $1 U.S.

I ▾ GOOD-BYE, COLUMBUS

Once Upon a Time

Once upon a time, there was a cultural, artistic, and social connection between Spain, Portugal, and Morocco. While Spain and Portugal together form the Iberian peninsula, this doesn't include Morocco (part of North Africa), whose sands blow across the sea each year and who for hundreds of years has influenced the growth and direction of Iberian thought.

This book is a voyage to discovery. The city of Madrid may hold its own with other international centers such as London and Paris, but once you venture outside of Madrid into the countryside—and to the nearby countries (Portugal and Morocco)—you'll discover that you have crossed over into a fantasyland of architecture, culture, and, of course, shopping. It all awaits you.

The Old World

OK, OK, so Christopher Columbus didn't like Spain enough to stay in town, settle down, and open a little shop on the plaza. Couldn't wait to get going; couldn't wait to find a New World. Who cares what Leif Eriksson found up around Newfoundland? Columbus found the Caribbean ... and just in time for the winter season.

Naturally, we're grateful.

But as we approach the 500th anniversary of

the original Columbus Day, we can't help but look at what Chris left behind and what unfolded in his wake.

The Age of Discovery unfolded, as the brave and the curious set out from Lisbon, Porto, Huelva, and Cádiz. Much of what we have in the Americas today was born in those journeys. But the Old World left behind has not turned out so badly. And visitors to Spain and Portugal will find themselves celebrating the great discoveries with discoveries of their own—whether sights or shopping delights, Spain and Portugal have some very exciting things to offer.

A Short History of the Old World

The Old World ain't so old anymore. In fact, if you lend an ear to international chitchat you may catch the phrase "the New Spain."

Indeed, Spain and Portugal are new-fashioned Old World countries—each began life anew in recent decades. The death of Franco has freed Spain from repression; also Portugal ousted a dictator. These countries are profoundly different now than they were fifty years ago. It is these very differences that make them so exciting today, this rapid change that captures the imagination of travelers and tourists who have seen plenty of the Old World and are now keen to understand the New Old World.

Welcome to Iberia

O ur friend K.T., who has spent a lot of time in both Spain and Portugal, waxes philosophical when she talks about the two countries, likening them to the male and female parts of the soul: Spain is all that is macho; Portugal is a warm, comforting bowl of soup. The two countries are very different from each other, true; the similarity between them lies in the difference between their big cities and their countrysides.

So we welcome you to Iberia, to the big cities and the small cities. We suggest you spend some time in the countryside: Drive or take a bus or roam; venture past world-class capitals into world-class villages; meet the people, and buy what they make and sell. In both Spain and Portugal there are old towns with tiny, narrow, winding roads; there are big cities with high-rise apartments and department stores and modern supermarkets; there are country fairs and crafts-men and craftswomen who work in bungalows. You want shopping malls? You can find them in the New Iberia. You want the local version of Trump Tower? Just check out the Amoreiras Shopping Center in Lisbon. There are walking streets and shopping streets and so many tourist traps (we call them TTs) that your wrist will grow tired from flipping out your credit cards.

Regional Secrets

W e remind you that Iberia is not par-ticularly unified. We're dealing with countries made up of provinces that may all belong to a specific state but that want to retain and promote their own regionalism ... particularly in Spain, where Franco forbade regional differences as he promoted his totalitarian version of a unified Spain. The New Spain wants to celebrate its diversity.

Also, Spain and Portugal are new to the EEC (they joined in 1986), and do not yet have as sophisticated a plan for marketing their locally made merchandise as other EEC countries do.

As a result, you should generally trust our Moscow Rule of Shopping (below), which insists that you buy something when you see it. Granada won't have what Sevilla has, and nobody has what Madrid has; the Algarve and Porto could just as well be in two different countries, as far as Portuguese shops are concerned.

Furthermore, the shopping opportunities can vary tremendously from city to city. You're going to have to face up to the fact that some cities just aren't shopping cities. Some cities are shoe cities; some cities are crafts cities; some cities we simply call non–fashion cities. That means they only have a few Benetton shops and have never heard of Cristóbal Balenciaga.

As you travel to each region, do a little research to find out what the local specialties (craftswise, foodwise) are, and plan to buy them.

The Moscow Rule of Shopping

The Moscow Rule of Shopping is one of our most basic rules, and has little to do with shopping in Moscow, and everything to do with shopping in Spain, so pay attention. Now then: The average shopper in pursuit of the ideal bargain may not buy an item when she first sees it for sale, because she is convinced that later on in her travels she will find the same item (or an even better version) for much less money. This is a standard thought process for a person who lives in a capitalist country ... and a worthwhile thought, indicative of a crafty shopper. But for someone who lives in an Iron Curtain country, despite *glasnost*, this is no way to go shopping. Everyone in Moscow lives by only one rule: Buy it when you see it, because you will never see it again.

This also holds true in Spain, and is somewhat true in Portugal, but bears little relation to reality when shopping in Moroccan souks. (In souks, you will almost always see it again.) For some reason, Spain and Portugal have little crossover in trade between them (that we can tell, anyway), so once you are out of the province, forget it. Yes, there is Artespaña, a national chain of shops selling crafts, but even the stock in these stores varies tremendously from city to city. If you see it in Spain and you want it, buy it immediately.

But before you pounce, ask yourself these questions:

▼ Is this a touristy item I am bound to find all over town? If yes, keep looking.

▼ Is this my only shopping opportunity in this region? Will I soon be getting on a tour bus and going off to another region? If yes, buy now.

▼ Is this an item I can't live without, so that even if I end up overpaying for it, I don't care? If yes, buy now.

▼ Is this an item I can walk away from without regrets if I never see a better (or cheaper) one? If yes, keep on walking.

▼ Is this a handcrafted item that could be one of a kind? Is it signed? Is it related to a shopping opportunity that may never repeat itself? Pounce.

▼ Is the shop I am buying from reputable? If they say the shawl is silk, can I believe them? Is there a chance I am being cheated on value even though the price appears to be fair? If something goes wrong, can I make returns or get repairs, or am I stuck? It sometimes pays to overpay for an item from a reputable store that will stand behind its merchandise.

▼ Am I in this shopping situation because my tour guide brought me? Push your guide for info, then decide. Ask directly about kickbacks. You should not feel pressured to shop where a guide takes you.

The City of Origin Axiom

Generally, an item is always least expensive and can be chosen from the widest selection in the city where it is produced, or the city closest to the main factory. After all, no shipping is involved, so prices and selection should be the best.

But wait: For the first time in all our research, we found this axiom to fail us—but only in the category of Lladró! Because Lladró is sold so extensively throughout Spain, prices are very competitive. And don't forget, if you're flying Iberia Airlines, you can even buy a few pieces of Lladró on the airplane! Lladró costs less in Spain than anywhere else in the world, but prices do vary around the country, and Valencia just may not have the best regular retail prices.

Best Buys of Iberia

I n all the countries in this volume, crafts are the single best buy. While you are probably expecting us to rant and rave about the shoes and leathergoods, the truth is that these are best bought in Madrid, then Barcelona —and best forgotten everywhere else. (Unless you get lucky.)

In terms of handcrafted items, especially ceramics, regional differences are strong and there is little cross-merchandising. Once you have left a certain region, you cannot expect to see that type of work again. While the big department stores and Artespaña (a government handcrafts store) act like they have done a good job marketing the wares of various provinces, we think they have made a rather poor showing. But there are a few things you should always keep an eye out and a dollar ready for:

CARPETS: If you buy only one thing in all Spain, Portugal, or even Morocco, it will be a carpet. Of course, you probably won't buy just one carpet. We bought a total of ten. And we were being restrained. Carpet styles vary dramatically (see Iberian ABCs, page 27), so compare prices carefully. You'll find Spanish carpets, rag rugs from the Sierra Nevada, spectacular needlepoint carpets from Portugal, and knotted carpets from Morocco. Prices range from so cheap that you won't believe you got so lucky, to fair for the value, to I-can-do-better-in-New-York. You must be an educated shopper.

SHOES AND LEATHERGOODS: Spain is the home of the brave soles. But before you break out your wallet, remember: It's only the fashion cities of Spain (Madrid and Barcelona) that have the European high-style, high-quality merchandise you're looking for. If you crave fabulous shoes for $75, your dreams can come true—but only if you have a size 9 (ladies) foot or smaller and only if you shop in the right cities. Handbag selection in the high-end, high-quality department is even more limited. You can either get a crummy bag for $40 (as you can in the U.S.), or a stunning bag for $400. There aren't a lot of steals in the $100 price range. Looking for rich Corinthian leather in Córdoba? Forget it.

CERAMICS: Forgive us if we rave, but we are fools for handpainted ceramics, for faience, for tiles, for plates you hang on the wall, for flowerpots, and, yes indeedy, for Alcázars where you can see them all in the same room. We devote much of this book to finding ceramics and tiles (*azulejos*) in Portugal and Spain. Despite the fact that Portugal has the bigger reputation in this area, we have big news: Ceramics can be cheaper in Spain. Not that you won't find fabulous stuff elsewhere (you will, you will). Not that regional differences aren't huge (they are, they are). But if you are on the grand tour and want to know where to buy your tiles and ceramics, wait for Spain, folks. And stock up when you get to Sevilla.

JEWELRY: We stopped buying good jewelry years ago after we got spoiled by the prices in Brazil. Now we stick to costume stuff. And Spain is the place to go. High-fashion costume jewelry of the kind that can compete with Chanel (and other big designer accessory pieces) is easy to find in Madrid and Barcelona. Spain is also famous for Majorica pearls, which are well priced at about $100 for a choker.

SILVER: You will go crazy for the silver plate in both Spain and Portugal. Then you'll swoon when you find out how inexpensive it is. You can be serving dinner in baronial splendor for a fraction of the cost in the U.S. or elsewhere in Europe. Of course, you have to figure out how to pack that soup tureen in your underwear; but we know you can do it.

CHILDREN'S CLOTHES: Our kids are getting too big for anything except blue jeans and baggy T-shirts, but for those of you with kids at the age where they wear what you pick, you will leave with bulging suitcases. Spain has possibly the best children's clothes in the world.

FOODSTUFFS: We can't figure out why the French have the big reputation in foodstuffs and no one else gets much credit. Sure, we like everything from French toast to French fries, but Spain and Portugal have their share of wines, sherries, ports, and dry goods that should be the delight of any gourmand. You might not be able to return to the U.S. with your own hock of Serrano ham, but there are many treats like chocolates and olive oils that you will want to bring home. And cookies—did someone say cookies?

LLADRÓ: OK, let's get this taken care of right up front. We have become mini-experts on Lladró now that we know Vincente Lladró, have toured the factory, have been to the factory outlet store (see page 59), and have touched every piece of Nao and Lladró in Spain. We have more about it (page 38), but since you want to know what's hot right now, and since we never saw a tourist in the Madrid airport who wasn't carrying at least one robin's egg–blue Lladró box, here goes: Lladró is much cheaper in Spain if you buy at the factory outlet, where you can get slightly damaged goods for 40% below Spanish retail. (This means a trip to Valencia.) Otherwise, retail prices vary from store to store and town to town, and may be the same as in the U.S. Where Lladró is concerned, our City of Origin Axiom has not held up (we found many pieces less expensive at retail in Barcelona than in Valencia), and furthermore, we've got a guy on Fifth Avenue who has one of those little shops you think are just for tourists, who sells Lladró (and will mail-order) for the same, or less, than what it costs in Spain (see page 61).

2▾IBERIAN DETAILS

Craftily Yours

The best news we can have for you about shopping in Iberia—aside from the fact that if you love crafts you're going to love it here—is that most handicrafts figure into the GSP (Generalized System of Preferences) laws, under which certain nations are given a break on import duties, so that American tourists do not have to pay duty on their purchases made abroad.

You'll have to be careful how you define handicrafts, of course. Handmade shoes still come in as leathergoods—not crafts. And we already told you about our carpet from Portugal, didn't we? Despite our best arguments, the U.S. Customs officer decided it was a floor covering, not a work of art. But you'll find that most of what you're going to be buying could very well be duty-free, and we really mean duty-free—it will not count into your $400 allowance when you return to the U.S.

With GSP it's safe to say you won't have to pay duty on a lot of goods when you return to the States . . . unless you are a carpet nut or a shoe freak.

Shoe News

And while we're on the subject of paying duty, we want you to know that the duty on shoes (and all leathergoods) is a mere 8%. Uncle Sam will insist on charging you a flat 10% on the first $1,000 worth of merchandise that you declare after your $400 duty-free allowance, but after that you go to specifics. And the duty on leathergoods is only 8%. So rejoice; if the shoe fits ... pay duty on it.

Getting There

S pain, Portugal, and Morocco all have their own national airlines, which offer the most flights, the best local transportation, and often the best prices for international fliers.

IBERIA: Iberia Airlines is owned by the Spanish government and is one of the most impressive airlines we have ever flown. The airline is equipped with a newish fleet, and gives you free movies and free wine with meals. The duty-free shop on board has excellent prices. Most tours fly with Iberia, but they are also our first choice for independent travel. Iberia also has some promotional deals that are outstanding values (800-IB-SPAIN):

Madrid Amigo. If you are going to any city that Iberia flies to in Europe (and they fly to just about all of them), you can go via Madrid and sign up for the Amigo program. To get to your destination, you connect in Madrid. On either your coming or your going, Iberia will give you a free layover in Madrid for twenty-four hours. That means you get a free hotel room (honest!), free transportation, and a dinner show!

Visit Spain. This is an airline pass that allows you unlimited travel on Iberia Airlines within Spain during a sixty-day period. You cannot take in the same city twice, however, and are only allowed a certain number of connections through Madrid. The ticket has to be written at one time (it's not an air pass), although you can arrange for open tickets on a certain route. Since you can't backtrack, you should study your map of Spain and have a route worked out carefully. This ticket costs $199 and can only be bought in the U.S. It's best to use a travel agent, since this pass can be tricky to ticket. It pays for itself almost immediately—we had two interior flights that by themselves would have cost more than $199 without the pass. We must warn you that a few things can go wrong. The pass is officially for Iberia, not for Iberia's domestic subsidiary, Aviaco. So there we were, in Granada and wanting to get back to Madrid without driving to Málaga. At first Iberia did not want to honor our tickets. After a heated bilingual debate, Iberia telexed Aviaco's offices and got permission to interline the tickets. Permission was given, but it took several hours and was a tremendous aggravation. Know exactly which airports you can fly to and from before you get stuck!

TAP: TAP is the Portuguese national carrier, operating a number of flights from New York to Lisbon and many internal flights throughout the country and also into Morocco. A Los Angeles gateway was opened in 1989. They're competitive on prices to Lisbon, especially from New York. Call (800) 221-7370.

ROYAL AIR MAROC: Although Royal Air Maroc is the obvious carrier for getting to and from Morocco in style, one of our best tips is to look at their triangular fares. Most visitors to Spain and Portugal are unaware that Morocco is just an hour away by boat or plane, or that competition between TAP, Iberia, and Royal Air Maroc can be so great that promotional deals are common. Royal Air Maroc often gives you a round-trip to Casablanca with a stop or two in Spain (or Portugal) at an unbeatable price. And no trip to Iberia is complete without a stop in Morocco (see page 49).

We have flown Royal Air Maroc several times and find it superior to a flying carpet, as well as to most other airlines we've traveled on. This is a class operation, with excellent meals, amenities, and security. Call (800) 344-6726 for more information; ask specifically abut three-point fares.

THE AMERICAN CARRIERS: As the big events of 1992 get closer, several American airlines have speeded up their entry into Spain and Portugal, either by adding direct service to Barcelona or by opening up new gateway cities in the U.S. It's easier than ever to get to the Iberian peninsula without having to go through New York airports.

TWA and American are doing the most in terms of opening new routes, but Pan Am is trying to take a small share of the market as well. *Please note this very, very important tip:* TWA is pronounced "Tu-wah" in Spanish and Portuguese. We have flown TWA several times in and out of Portugal and Spain, and have found that no one knows what we mean when we pronounce TWA in the American fashion.

Sailing There

I n 1992, some daredevils are planning on taking replicas of the *Pinta,* the *Niña,* and the *Santa Maria* across the ocean to the Dominican Republic. You can make the reverse trip, a lot more comfortably and before 1992, on many cruise lines. More and more ships are returning to the Mediterranean; more and more lines are offering transatlantic crossings, which were not considered very exciting until recently. Traditional transatlantic crossings go to Southampton (for London) or Le Havre, but the new hot city for the new hot crossing is Lisbon! Ships leave from New York or from Florida.

These crossings are most often called (in the trade) turnaround cruises—a ship must be repositioned for the season (to service the Mediterranean, first you have to get there.) Turnaround cruises are often less expensive than normal cruises, or give you more for the price. Because this area is still expanding, talk to your travel agent about the possibilities for the season you want to travel in. Turnaround crossings usually leave Florida in April and return from Europe in October.

All cruises have add-on packages, so you can spend several days in Lisbon at a package price before or after your cruise. Among those now doing big business in the Mediterranean and connecting to transportation packages in either Lisbon or Barcelona are Costa Cruise Lines, Princess P&O, Cunard, and Royal Viking.

Getting Around

F or internal air travel, you'll need to rely on the three national airlines. There is some competition among them, especially on the Iberian peninsula–to–Moroccan sands route. Morocco is usually an hour's flight from Lisbon and not much more from Madrid, so there are numerous travel packages you can book (with or without a tour) that will enable you to see it all for modest prices. We've included a special Moroccan ABCs section (see page 49) to give you a hint of the exotic treasures that await, should you decide to continue your travels from Spain onto Africa.

Should you want to rent a car, take our advice and plan ahead from the U.S. with an airline fly-drive program. We ended up spending about $200 a day for car rental in Spain! We rented from Europcar (800-223-1516; 800-252-9401 in California), the firm we always use for European rentals, and paid through the nose. We love Europcar and will continue to use them elsewhere, but in Spain the prices are very high at all three of the biggies, Hertz, Avis, and Europcar. (Hertz and Avis were more!) The car (a manual Kadett 1.6) cost $78 a day, and kilometers were 65 cents each. (Unlimited mileage programs began at $300 a day.) On top of that, the hotels charged us $10 a night to park the car, various tips were needed to park and retrieve it, and driving in city centers can only be described as hellacious.

Hertz and Iberia have a fly-drive plan; call (800) IB-SPAIN. You end up with a teeny car, but you get unlimited mileage for about $50 a day, which is a major savings.

We also found (but did not test) a lease program from Europe By Car that offers one-, two-, or three-week rentals with prices guaranteed in U.S. dollars and unlimited mileage. You must return the car with a full tank of gas, of course. Local government VAT or IVA taxes are additional (that's 12% in Spain, 16% in Portugal). They do not have a Kadett 1.6 (a medium-sized car) so we could compare prices, but they do have a Peugeot 309 at about $235 for one week, $469 for two weeks, and $689 for three weeks.

The Trains in Spain

No, we haven't taken the Marrakesh Express, but we have taken trains through much of Spain and Portugal. RENFE, the Spanish train system, has numerous promotional deals for whole families and for sightseeing trips in which you get on and off the train in one package. It's all very impressive. Call (800) 992-3976 or (203) 454-8916 for all their deals on passes and tours. For the most part, this is a great way to travel, although we have a few tips:

▼ Ask several sources, or go to the train station prior to your journey, to confirm times and schedules. No concierge ever gave us the correct time for any train in Spain!

▼ Find out the difference (pricewise and timewise) between the various trains. We've all but given up first-class travel, since we think second-class is just great, but in Portugal there are some trains for businesspeople between Lisbon and Porto that only have first class. In Portugal you'll also want the *rápido;* in Spain it's the *talgo.*

▼ The meal you are automatically served in first class in Portugal on the *rápido* from Lisbon to Porto is very nice but is not included in the price of your ticket. It's another $15, please.

▼ The Andalusian Express is the Spanish version of the Orient Express. It does Andalucía in great style, but only in season. For details, call (800) 992-3976. Note that this is not a RENFE train but a private enterprise.

▼ One of the most attractive things about the Andalusian Express, aside from the glamour of it all, is that it connects Sevilla, Córdoba, and Granada, a popular tourist triangle. Despite the popularity of this route, there is no direct RENFE train from Córdoba to Granada. You can make the trip by train, but you have to make several changes and layovers and it will take about six or seven hours—if everything is on time (which it never is). Consider the Andalusian Express as not only an extravagance, but a sensible one.

Booking Iberia / I

You shouldn't go to Iberia without reading James Michener's tome of the same name, which is nonfiction and recalls trips through Spain decades ago. It's still worth reading.

We bought a ton of guidebooks to Spain and Portugal but found the publishing world lacking in suitably splendid guides to Morocco. *Frommer's* includes Morocco in a Spain edition (sans Portugal); *Spain and Portugal in 22 Days* by Rick Steves includes some information on getting to Morocco, although it's just three pages. They are good pages, though.

We bought up a series of books in the *Spain: Everything Under the Sun* series published by Passport, and had a funny experience. We did not know there was one master volume selling for $12.95 (the Traveller's Bookstore in New York has it; call 212-664-0995), so we bought the six individual books for $6.95 each! Just when we were feeling incredibly stupid at wasting our money, we discovered that the individual books offer more information per city than the master guide. If you are going into a new city in Spain, we think the individual Passport books do a good job of getting you oriented.

We paid a whopping $22.50 for the *Guide to the Best of Spain* published by Turespaña in Spain and sold (in English as well as in other languages) in the airport in Madrid. This is a 550-page book crammed with color pictures and listings of everything from beaches and squash courts to convention facilities and trade fairs. There is a section on shopping, although our edition was already three years old when we bought it, and most of the addresses of the stores were wrong. But if you want a broad and colorful look at everything Spain has to offer, this is a good book.

For Barcelona and for Madrid there are magazine-style books called *Concept* (both from the same publisher) tailored to the city and covering shopping, eating, and cultural events. The glossy looks a lot like *Vogue*, costs about $4.50, and gives you a feel for the chic side of life. Available at all newsstands.

Booking Iberia /2

The hotel picture in Spain is changing dramatically as the country revs up for the events of 1992. Up until now, the biggest problems in picking hotels has been the lack of hotels from the chains we know and trust. Meridien has a hotel in Lisbon and one in Porto (as does Sheraton); they also have several fabulous properties in Africa. Call Meridien at (800) 543-4300. Leading Hotels of the World (800-223-6800) offers The Ritz in Lisbon (next door to the Meridien), The Ritz in Madrid, the Villa Magna in Madrid, and yet another Ritz in Barcelona. In keeping with their style, these are usually the fanciest and most expensive hotels in town.

If you like to book all your hotels in one fell swoop, or are unfamiliar with which hotels are right for you in the Iberian countryside, there are two Spanish chains with offices in the U.S. that can probably book your entire trip and keep you quite happy:

MELÍA HOTELS: A Spanish chain named Sol bought a Spanish chain named Melía and changed the names of all the hotels to Melía, and is now in business as the largest chain in Spain. They offer the Spanish version of the kind of hotel you used to expect from someone like Hilton. The hotels are mostly four- and five-star properties for business travelers; there is a concierge floor. There are hotels in twenty different Spanish cities; some cities have more than one hotel. We have not stayed in every single Melía hotel in Spain, but have stayed in enough of them to know they are always in good locations and are always one of the best hotels in town. If you must choose blindly, you can't go too wrong with a Melía hotel, especially in an urban center. Call (800) 33-MELIA in the U.S.

OCCIDENTAL HOTELS: Another chain with mostly five-star properties catering to well-heeled business travelers, Occidental may not always be on the main plaza but is always convenient to business and right in the heart of transportation centers. Occidental is more of an international chain than Melía, but they do have hotels in Lisbon, Madrid, and Sevilla, and can also book you into the Ramada Renaissance in Barcelona. Call (800) 332-4872.

Hours

The two most important things to remember about shopping hours in Iberia are that stores never open when they say they do, and that they close for siesta.

Siesta in Spain is more or less from 1:30 P.M. to 4:30 P.M. or 5 P.M.; in Portugal it is usually from 2 P.M. to 4 P.M. None of these times should be considered firm, however. Stores will close during siesta, yes, but exactly when they close is an individual thing.

Although store doors may be marked for opening hours at 9 or 9:30 A.M., few actually open before 10 (except large department stores). Stores will close punctually for siesta, unless you are inside buying up a storm. Stores close anywhere from 8 to 8:30 or 9 P.M. depending on the store and the time of year—they often stay open later at night in the summer, or if a cruise ship is in town. Malls may stay open until 10 P.M., or even later.

Big department stores do not close for siesta. Of course, the big department stores in Lisbon burned down in the huge fire of 1988, but there is the Amoreiras Shopping Center, a mall where shops are jumping until midnight! Major tourist traps (TTs), especially ones owned by non-Spanish folk, are often open during siesta. Thus there are a whole slew of TTs on Las Ramblas in Barcelona that are open from 9 A.M. to 9 P.M., nonstop.

Most stores are closed on Sundays, except for those in American-style malls and some TTs in Barcelona. There are always flea markets and street fairs on Sundays.

Some of the fancier stores in Madrid do not reopen after siesta on Saturday afternoons. This will be indicated on their front door or in a window; they are usually the swanky stores in the Salamanca district. All over Spain, generally speaking, stores are open on Saturday afternoons. In Portugal, it's hit or miss, but department stores and malls are open Saturday afternoons.

You will find that the giant siesta can take a real zing out of your day unless you can accommodate your schedule accordingly. If you are on a tour, you'll want to scan the schedule each day to see when you can sneak away to shop. Tour guides know all about siesta, but sometimes they allow time for you to shop only in the stores that they have chosen for you. So think about it ahead of time. Even if you just get to stroll through El Corte Inglés (ECI) on your own during lunchtime, you'll be a better person for the experience.

Department Stores

Spain has two competing department stores, El Corte Inglés and Galerías Preciados (GP). We usually favor ECI (as it is known), but not in every market. While these department stores pose no threat to American retailing, they have several things going for them:

▼ They do not close for lunch.

▼ They do open when they say they will.

▼ They have food counters, grocery stores, cafeterias, and sometimes fancy restaurants on the premises.

▼ They represent the best way in Spain to get a VAT refund (see page 25).

▼ They take all major credit cards and will also exchange money.

▼ They are jam-packed with merchandise and choices—which is something you may not find in the average mom-and-pop stores of the non–fashion cities.

Airport Duty-frees

Madrid has two large duty-free stores in the airport. One is a series of designer boutiques with even an Artespaña boutique area; the other is like a grocery store and sells wines, liquors, cigarettes, chocolates, and perfumes. The selection is immense (no Chanel, however); liquor prices are good. Barcelona has a large shopping area in the international departure section of the airport, including a medium-sized duty-free shop that is laid out like a grocery store and sells perfumes, liquors, cigarettes, and candy. You'll have more fun in Madrid.

Lisbon's airport duty-free is so completely, outrageously expensive that we absolutely refuse to buy much of anything in it. The wines, sherries, and liquors are much more expensive than in regular stores all over Portugal. Do not wait for the last minute to buy your port at the airport, or you'll have a sorry selection and silly prices.

Money Matters

While we have always told you to go to a bank to change your money, we had so many crazy experiences changing money in Spain that we can only suggest you make your own educated choices. All banks charge a service fee for changing your money. A higher fee is charged for cash than for traveler's checks. Now, then: Your hotel will not give you as good a rate as a bank, but it will not charge you a fee. If you get 109 *pesetas* at the hotel and 112 *pesetas* at the bank, but must pay a fee, why should you go to a bank?

But wait. Different banks charge different rates for changing money, so you can shop around for this service! The least we paid was $2; the most was $5. You can spend hours shopping for a decent rate. It's very annoying.

Since it is not safe to carry large sums of cash with you (anywhere), you are going to have to pay a lot of service charges (if you spend as much as we do, anyway) or take a beating on the exchange at your hotel. If there are several of you traveling together, pick a bank and try to exchange a larger sum of money as one transaction, and then divide it up. You don't mind paying $5 once, but once a day is quite irritating . . . and expensive.

Credit-Card Woes

As you already know, we are big believers in the American Express card, especially now that they offer Purchase Protection™. We try to travel with very little cash and to make all our purchases on our credit cards. Well, we wish you good luck if all you have is American Express. A large percentage of the stores in Spain do not take American Express but will take Visa or Master-Card. Furthermore, a lot of your shopping is going to be at markets and with street vendors, so you'll need cash. If you rely on credit cards you will be in a very sorry bargaining position if you must rely on American Express. Bring plenty of traveler's checks!

VAT / IVA

VAT means Value Added Tax, and has become a generic term for personal-use tax in Europe. In Spain you will find this tax referred to as either VAT or IVA (pronounced "Eva"), which our Spanish friend Luis tells us is jokingly said to mean *"Imposible Visitar Aquí"* (impossible to visit here). IVA was added to bills in Spain only when they joined the EEC, so some people still aren't used to it.

The good news about IVA is that the amount varies with the category of item bought, so the tax on a rental car is only 12%. (It's 28% in France!) The bad news is that it is just about impossible to get a VAT refund. Actually, it is almost impossible to even qualify for a VAT refund in Spain.

But here goes: You may receive a refund of 12% of the purchase price of any qualifying item if you buy any one single item that costs more than 47,000 *pesetas*—or about $450. This is per item, not a cumulative amount.

If you are still standing after the shock of that number, it gets better. The only places that admit to refunds are the two major department stores, which even publish brochures (in English) on how to get your VAT refund that you may pick up, free, at the information counter on the first floor. We got one Loewe store to admit to the policy, but other Loewe stores in the countryside did not know what we were talking about when we asked about VAT refunds.

Don't give up in despair, however; in Portugal it's very easy to get the VAT refund. Portugal has been organized by a company that is taking over the tax-back schemes as a business venture in many European countries—you know them by the logo they provide: It is always in the country's national colors and always encircles the words "Tax Free." So in Portugal you've got your basic green and then red border to the black words "Tax Free." When you make a purchase totaling over 10,000 *escudos* (about $75), you get a return of 17% issued in the form of a voucher check, which you can redeem at the airport. Not everyone will give it to you, true, but many stores and artisans, identified by the "Tax Free" sticker in their window, will give it. Many will even go out of their way to give you the full refund or a part of the refund.

Besides the tax-free system, some individual stores will make their own arrangements for the refund. Our refund from Casa Quintão in Lisbon (carpet heaven) came in U.S. dollars, within two weeks of the purchase of the carpet!

Portugal's tax-free system does have a few quirks to it, however. The system gives you a 17% refund redeemable at the airport after you clear Customs and show that you are taking your packages out of the country. Now, the bad news: You will move into the transit area for your refund, and you will be reimbursed in local currency only! Sure, there are several shopping pavilions right there that will take your money, but you are stuck having to spend the money . . . and the duty-free is extraordinarily overpriced. We bought a lot of Lancôme Niosôme wrinkle crème. If you had bought a carpet, you could find yourself with a refund of several hundred dollars and would have few choices of what to do with it. (Now you know why we bought wrinkle crème.)

It is virtually impossible to get your refund on your credit card.

Department Store Discounts

While the VAT refund in Spain does make you want to grit your teeth, there is one happy twist in the tale. The two major department stores, ECI and GP, each have their own immediate VAT refunds for all tourists. You get a 10% discount (not the full 12%, but who cares?) on any items bought in the store that are not from leased departments. The luggage we bought in Barcelona came from a leased department, so no deal; the shoes, the handbags, and the shawl we bought in Madrid were discounted on the spot.

The first time you buy anything in one of the stores, ask for your discount card. At GP, a saleswoman with a clipboard came up to us and wrote down information from our passports. She then issued each of us a small paper version of a credit card in navy and white. Each time we made a purchase thereafter, we showed this card and received a discount of 10% from the retail price. Sale items also were discounted!

If you think that department stores in Spain aren't quite what you wanted, we can give you 10% more reasons why you should reconsider.

Last Words: Crime

There are no international cities that are safe anymore, so to single out Spain for its crime is a tad ridiculous. However, we will mention that Sevilla has a terrible reputation for car break-ins and purse-snatching, and that no city is totally safe for women walking alone after dark. (This includes Lisbon.) In summer, it will not become dark until after the stores close, anyway, but in winter, coordinate your shopping sprees accordingly . . . or travel with a big, mean man.

We both wear money belts to carry most of our cash and our passports. We've forgotten our things (passports, plane tickets, the works) in hotel safety-deposit boxes, so we don't use them anymore, but most hotels do offer these boxes free of charge to their guests. For good reason.

If you're in Morocco, do not go into the souks without a local guide; do not wander North Africa in the dark alone. If you use good sense wherever you travel, you should be perfectly safe.

3▾IBERIAN ABCS

Your Iberian Dictionary

Those familiar with Mexico and/or Brazil will have a head start on shopping in Spain and Portugal. Mostly, you'll be buying crafts about which you need a little bit of understanding so you can buy the best. We suggest you read our dictionary first to familiarize yourself with the menu, then study up on your field of interest.

ALPARGATAS: *Alpargatas* are canvas shoes whose soles are made of rope. They are very similar to espadrilles, the French version, and are found at markets, at fairs—especially in the south and around the Alicante—or at the Rastro in Madrid. Pay about $10 for a pair, maybe less. Big American feet need not apply.

ALPUJARRAS: Las Alpujarras is a region of Spain between the Sierra Nevada and Málaga that is so well known for its rugs that a rug in the style has come to be known as an *alpujarra*. These are throw rugs, in varying sizes, made with a cotton string warp and a rag weft. The resulting carpets, in solids or multishades, have a very folksy feel to them and work well with American country-style homes. If the rags were frayed or feathered (purposefully) before they were woven, the carpet has a fuzzy aspect to it. Carpets are sold in southern regions of Spain and at the Rasto in Madrid. Prices are reasonable—about $50 for a 5x7-foot carpet.

ARMOR: Not love, you fool, but what St. George was probably wearing when he slew the dragon. You'll find complete sets of armor for sale in Madrid and Toledo in case your

27

baronial grand hall is missing a little something. Prices begin around $1,000 and go up depending on the amount of detail and the engraving on each piece.

ARRAIOLOS: This small village in Portugal has become so famous for its needlepoint carpets that the carpets are often referred to by its name, even when they are made elsewhere. (It is not true that the best ones must come from Arraiolos.) Highly prized in the U.S. and sold through such American dealers as Stark (979 Third Avenue, New York, NY 10022), these carpets are available in two sizes of stitching (either the large gros stitch or the smaller petit point); they are made of a cross-stitch over burlap in designs that are counted, not drawn, in. The larger-size stitch has much less value and is therefore cheaper (and very often, ugly). The smaller stitch is the only one to consider; the intricacy of the pattern and the size of the carpet determine its value.

You may buy *arraiolos* ready-made or commission your own. The largest selection of ready-made is in Lisbon, but we have several design sources in the countryside who can work directly with you. Big-time American designers and decorators often fly to Portugal just to get these rugs made for their rich American clients; embassies and consulates all over the world have them on display. Since each is handmade, every one is unique, although some popular designs are repeated. The yarn must be 100% wool in order for your carpet to wear and clean properly. (Feel the wool, and look at it in the light; acrylic yarn is cheaper but will not wear well.) There should be no gathers or puckers in the piece, and no seams! The carpets are available with or without fringe; locals prefer the fringe, Americans usually do not.

Today's designs are highly influenced by American designers and young mavens who know exactly what is hot, so you will have no trouble finding a piece to make your home look like the interiors of a home magazine. The carpet can have a border stitched around it, and may have a central design (the medallion) countered by four designs, one in each corner. Some designs are composed of squares like those of American quilts, although they should not be seamed together. One overall and intricate design has more value than small repeating designs, especially if those designs are in boxes or squares.

Black backgrounds sell particularly well to Americans, as do cabbage-rose patterns and traditional looks. Other patterns can be found, many of them Moorish and geometric in style, others quite contemporary. Perhaps the most handsome carpet we saw (of truly thousands) was one that had a border with monkeys running around it—extremely sophisticated and smart. There is something for every taste.

A few tips: If you are serious about one of these carpets, price sources in the U.S. and Brazilian-made copies of the art form. There is a dealer in New York called S. Chapell (1019 Lexington Avenue, at 73rd Street; telephone 212-744-7872) that specializes in needlepoint carpets; most of theirs are made in Brazil. Prices run about $1,384 for a 5x7-foot carpet and $2,300 for the 6x9-foot carpet. This is not the only source, and Stark, already mentioned, does a volume wholesale business to the trade in these carpets. While the style of the carpet can be that of an *arraiolos*, if it is made in China or Brazil it will be less expensive due to labor costs. Obviously, even in Portugal, these carpets are not cheap, so if you are not intent on the best quality and colors in the world, you may not need a real *arraiolos* to complete your home. Expect to pay $750–1,000 (the final price after you've gotten your tax back) for a 5x7-foot carpet in Portugal, $2,000 for a 10x12-foot carpet. Have plenty of traveler's checks with you; it's easier to bargain at small factories if you have cash.

Yes, you can carry these carpets in your

luggage. Yes, you will get a tax refund back. No, carpets do not count as handicrafts, so you must pay duty when you return to the U.S.

ARTESPAÑA: A series of government owned and operated shops created to push Spanish handicrafts, Artespaña is excellent in some cities (you want to jump for joy) and so bad in some others that you don't know why you wasted your time. The best Artespaña shops are in Madrid (there are several).

In a good store, you'll see everything from large pieces of furniture to handmade carpets and textiles to accessories that make stunning gifts. Prices can be high, but the quality is always superb. The good shops have room sets that are drop-dead chic; the bad shops are a jumble of so much merchandise that you can't tell that this stuff is really nice. The store on Calle Hermosilla in Madrid is an absolute must.

AZULEJOS: Nowhere is the confluence of cultures more obvious than in the small (usually 4x4-inch) tiles used on walls (inside and outside), floors, and fountains of the buildings—from humble homes to high churches—of Spain and Portugal. Called *azulejos* in both Spanish and Portuguese, these ceramic wonders are thought to have been created by the Persians, taught to the Moors, and brought to Iberia with the Moorish conquest in A.D. 711. The Iberian techniques were further influenced by the Age of Discovery, especially in Portugal where the Black Ships traveled regularly to the Orient and often returned with artwork and artisans. While delft and faience derive from the same roots, Iberian tilemaking has its own particular style because of the Oriental influence and because in mid-1800 Portugal, scenic tiles became the vogue.

Because of a religious prohibition against graven images, the Moors originally designed their tiles in geometric patterns (nonrepresentational art) using only four colors, red (rose), blue, green, and yellow, which were combined with white or black. Iberian tiles are primarily designed in blue and white or blue, white, and yellow, although all colors do appear.

Christian artisans, having no religious prohibition against drawing flowers, animals, or even people, began to embellish tiles with these motifs in cities where Moorish influence had waned or had been rejected. Geometrics and the Moorish influence remained within the design school and are still found in combination, both with animals and flowers and alone. Portuguese tiles may be decorated with strong, bold strokes, or with fine Persian strokes, and their designs are usually representational.

While various artisans and schools of tile-making have their own methods and styles of work, it is virtually impossible to differentiate between Portuguese and Spanish tiles unless you happen to recognize the work of a certain craftsperson or region you are familiar with. In many cases, Portuguese tiles are more elaborate than Spanish tiles; Spanish styles can be more folk-oriented.

Portugal offers the widest range of choice in tiles. For buying, you'll have plenty of opportunities in Lisbon, Porto, Sevilla, Toledo, Valencia (Manises), and Granada. While you can buy tiles in Madrid, they are more expensive there, and the selection is not the best. The best selection, the best craftsmanship, and the best prices are in Sevilla (see page 76).

Tiles can be bought individually or in scenics. Scenics are more popular in Portugal than in Spain. Scenics are most often sold framed, and they are very heavy. Expect to pay $150–250 for a scenic of six to twelve tiles. You can buy the tiles to a scenic and put it together yourself for less. Numbers are placed on the back of the tiles so that you can form the scenic yourself, following in order from left to right.

Quality of tiles varies enormously, as does price. A well-made tile should last centuries, especially once installed in a wall. It's not that easy to remove a tile from stucco, so there is only a small market in used and antique tiles. For a genuine selection of antique tiles, there is only one excellent source, Solar in Lisbon (see page 249). To have the most value, a tile should be handpainted, have some weight and thickness to it, and have bevels on the back. Tap it with your fingers and listen to its tone. You can hear imperfections in tiles and also the difference between less expensive and fine tiles. A sound tile rings like a church bell. The tilemaker will ring each tile before he fills your order, especially if you commission a handpainted scenic. If the tiles pass his ring test, they will not break in shipment.

Prices for excellent tiles vary. In Portugal, the best handpainted tiles begin at $3.50 each and escalate to $10 rather quickly. These tiles sell for $20–25 in New York. Antique tiles sell for $10 to $20 each. In Sevilla, you can get the best tiles for as little as $1.25 each! There are more expensive tiles, but the prices here—and the styles—are better than in Portugal. Don't forget that you can buy excellent tiles for about a dime each in Mexico City.

As you travel throughout Portugal and are wooed and wowed by the tiles on every home, no matter how poor, you realize that not everyone has $3.50 for a single tile. The compromise is commercial tiles (sold in bathroom supply and contracting stores), which are not handpainted but are nonetheless often gorgeous. You have to go out of your way to find these tiles, since tourists don't often hang out at contractors' offices, but you can find them if you try. Our best sources for these inexpensive tiles has been Portugal, where they are used far more often than in Spain. We're talking 25¢ a tile now.

Please remember that tiles were originally used as ballast for sailing ships, and they weigh a ton. You cannot carry more than about fifty in your luggage. Shipping is so expensive that it eats up the savings. If you do ship, plan to buy 10% more than you need, to allow for breakage. You may not have any breakage, especially with good tiles, but better safe than sorry, as Mother used to say.

We suggest you buy the small-sized (2 inches square) handpainted tiles, which cost about a dollar each (sometimes less), and carry them with you in your luggage. Once home, go to a tile store or a bathroom store and fill in the additional tiles you need. Both terracotta and plain white bathroom tiles are inexpensive—usually about 25¢ each—and you don't have to worry about shipping. Installation expenses may also increase the cost of a tiled floor. If you're a do-it-yourselfer pick up *Tiling Floors,* booklet #44 from Creative Homeowner Press, 24 Park Way, P.O. Box 527, Upper Saddle River, NJ 07458. To be honest, we just threw our tiles onto tabletops with Super Glue, and never even grouted them—they look great!

Please be advised that while you can certainly buy ceramic tiles in Barcelona and Madrid, these cities are not really known for ceramics, and you may have more fun in other towns. If you like to go to factory outlets or fairs that sell all kinds of ceramics, you'll do better in Valencia and Manises (Manises is the ceramics-making suburb of Valencia), Sevilla, or Toledo. Sevilla is the best source for individual tiles, and you can go to the factory that makes the tiles for the city of Sevilla. They are just black letters on white tiles, but they have some charm and are authentic. Toledo sells a lot of wares from the not-that-faraway city of Talavera de la Reina, one of the oldest ceramics cities in Spain. (From which the Mexican-style Talavera tiles are derived.)

Talavera ceramics are best known for their durability. A plate may cost $30, but you can hit it with a hammer and cause no damage. Talavera is usually made in two qualities, so less expensive doesn't mean you found a great bargain, it means lesser quality.

CRISTÓBAL BALENCIAGA: Balenciaga, the master of couture, was a Spanish dress designer who became a French couturier. A master of architecture and drape, Balenciaga sold his clothes in Madrid until the end of World War II (a dress cost $250 then), and then moved to Paris, never to look back.

BARCELOS: Barcelos is a city in northern Portugal famous for its rooster, which derives from a myth about the village and village justice. The rooster is drawn or thrown in a style you will see all over Portugal. Once someone points it out to you, you'll know it forever. Most roosters printed on T-shirts, tea towels, aprons, and other souvenir items from Portugal feature the Barcelos rooster. You can buy a Barcelos rooster at Marshall's in the U.S. for $7.95.

BOTIJO: This is a traditional Spanish folk form, a ceramic bottle designed to keep water or wine cold, although there are some made for hot-water bottles. The jug has two spouts at the top, one open, the other shaped and almost closed. Air goes into the big hole, and pressure forces liquid up out of the small hole. You drink from the small hole by pouring the liquid into your mouth—your lips never touch the jug. *Botijos* come in various sizes, from one-person to group-sized jugs. Antique jugs, often in the shapes of animals or people, are available in the $100 range. Newly made ceramic *botijos* cost between $10 and $25 depending on quality and where you buy it. (We paid $16 for one in a fancy store, then saw a similar one for $11 at the Rastro.)

BUEN RETIRO: The royal ceramics factory at Buen Retiro was created in 1760 at the behest of Charles III. Today you can still buy porcelain animals signed *"Buen Retiro."* The style is easily recognizable by its elaborate matte colors, intricacy of design, and intended realism. The style is much like that of Boehm, as is the most popular form—birds. Sold all over Spain.

CANASTA: Not the card game, but the basket; *canasta* is Spanish for basket. Baskets in the northern regions of Spain are especially interesting for collectors. In southern Spain, we found what we've been searching for for two years now: panniers—baskets for the sides of a donkey! They're called *aguaderas* there, and are made to carry large jugs of water into the fields. The best baskets are found in the southern coastal cities and around Alicante, where palm and palmetto are, naturally enough, used. You'll find a huge wicker market with some rather good baskets in Madrid, alongside the Rastro. Northern areas like Galicia and the Basque country have more original baskets in strange, wonderful shapes.

CASTANETS: If you are looking for high-quality castanets, there is a simple law of the jungle: Ask. Most stores sell touristy castanets of low quality and put the good ones away for those in the know. For those not in the know, you can buy castanets made of wood, shell, and even coconut shell (handpainted, to boot) in any TT in Spain for a few dollars. Good castanets are well carved of fine wood, preferably ebony, and cost several hundred dollars. They are passed down in a family. Sevilla is the best source.

CAVA: If it bubbles and you drink it you may call it champagne, but in Spain, champagne is called *cava*. Besides, the French are very persnickety, and technically, no one can call their bubbly "Champagne" unless it has been grown in the province of Champagne, France. There are several Spanish sparkling-wine makers—we buy Frexinet (say "Fresh-net") because they advertise a lot in the U.S. and it's inexpensive. You can buy a bottle of *cava* for about $4 in Spain; a three-pack of little splits costs $3 and makes a nice gift to bring home.

CERAMICS: It's no secret that we love ceramics, and no trip to Iberia is worthwhile if we haven't brought along the bubble wrap, the tape, and an extra tote bag so we can load up. For the most part, the ceramics in Portugal are more expensive than in Spain, and more finely crafted. One of the most interesting things we observed about the ceramics business in Portugal is that it is extremely well organized for export. American designers and importers can come to Portugal, work with a few factories, design exactly what they want, have it shipped to the U.S., and sell it for a great price. Possibly less than what you will pay in Portugal. The amount of Portuguese wares in the U.S. is large, and is a dramatic contrast to what is available in Portugal!

If you happen to live near Marshall's, an American discounter, check out their selection of Portuguese ceramics. It is often better, and cheaper, than what you'll find in Portugal. Many patterns of the dishes sold at Tiffany & Co. are made in Portugal (at Vista Alegre), but these patterns are not sold in Portugal. You'll find many fabulous pieces to buy in Portugal, and prices can be very reasonable, but know what's available in the U.S. before you go to the trouble of worrying about the trouble of getting these heavy items home.

COBI: If you are as dumb as we are, you'll spend a lot of time shopping in Spain and noticing what appear to be really bad copies of Garfield the cat. We were just about convinced that copyright violation problems had created the distortions. However, you can learn from our mistakes right here and now: That ain't Garfield, folks, it's COBI, a little tiger cat character who is the mascot of the 1992 Olympics. You'll see him on all sorts of merchandise. Our favorite COBI item is the poster you can have imprinted with the name of your choice; there's a big COBI on top and the announcement that So-and-So (you supply the name) is appearing at the Olympics. At $6 this might be one of the best souvenirs in Spain.

CORK: Cork is one of Portugal's leading exports, and can often be found in souvenir form in any TT. In fact, you can buy postcards made of cork. About the best souvenirs we can think of are the multitude of items (jars, napkin holders, desk blotters) that are crafted from cork at Sant'Anna in Lisbon.

FANS (ABANICOS): The fan was an important part of European costume for men and women for several centuries, and has pervaded Spain's costume and culture. Fans are thought to have been introduced to Europe in the early 16th century by the Black Ships, which brought them back from the Orient.

Fans are still easily found in antique as well as in new-and-touristy forms. There is no one city famous for its fanmaking, since the different parts of a fan are made in different villages and then assembled. There are also dozens of different mediums that can be used in the making of the two parts of a fan (sticks and mount). For instance, the sticks alone can be made of such diverse materials as wood, bone, tortoiseshell, leather, mother-of-pearl, plastic, and then some. To have real value, sticks must be handcarved. In 1859 machinery that automatically carved the sticks became available; machine-made sticks are considered inferior. The mount should be silk or silk that is inset with lace (although it can be paper or leaf), and should be handpainted; the more elaborate the painting, the more valuable the fan. Certain fan painters became so famous in the 17th century that even today fan painting is done "in the style of," and is recognized by locals and experts.

Should you be shopping for the man who has everything, you'll be relieved to know it is just beginning to be chic (again) for men to carry fans—small, 5-inch fans—which they place in the breast pocket of a jacket or sportcoat.

GAZPACHO SETS: Should you wander into a ceramics store (or flea market) in Spain and see what looks like a large salad bowl with six smaller, matching bowls, and ask how much the cute little salad set is, we'd like you to know now that you will soon be blushing. Forget the *ensalada*. That set is for *gazpacho*. And the answer is $30–$50.

GLASS: It's *vidrio*, and comes in many regional styles—we're particularly impressed with what you get from Mallorca or Catalonia with animals on top. Check out blue and pale turquoise.

JUDERÍA: The Jewish ghetto in a Spanish city is called the *Judería*, and while it no longer houses the Jewish population (Jews were expelled from Spain during the Inquisition), it almost always houses the cutest shops in town, or the antiques neighborhood. The best shopping part of Sevilla, Córdoba, or Barcelona is the Judería.

LLADRÓ: The most famous name in Spain, to Americans anyway, has got to be Lladró. Lladró figurines and collectibles are made in Valencia, many of them in limited numbers so that their value can increase. Collectors of Lladró are an active group, and may join the Collectors Society in Spain or in the U.S. (It happens to be considerably cheaper to join in the U.S.; write Lladró Collectors Society, P.O. Box 1122, 43 West 57th Street, New York NY 10101-1122; call toll-free, 800-345-5433 ext. 1212, or, in Illinois, 800-972-5855 ext. 1212.) As members of the Collectors Society, you will have the opportunity to buy pieces that do not come on the regular retail market, and to join regular tours of Spain, which include a private tour of the factory outside Valencia. The factory is not normally open to guests; if you are not on a Lladró tour you must write ahead for permission to visit. If you are a member of the Collectors Society (but not on a Lladró tour), you must call ahead for an appointment, but will be granted permission to visit.

If we do nothing else for you, we would like to clear up the confusion about the difference between Lladró and Nao, which unfortunately are confused by salespeople all over Spain. Anytime we hear a salesperson tell a tourist that Nao is the seconds line, we want to correct them. So here goes:

Nao is not the seconds line. If you want Lladró seconds, or Nao seconds for that matter, you can buy them. Just go to the company-owned factory outlet store across the street from the factory (see page 59).

Nao is the line of figurines on which the Lladró craftspeople train. These are very similar to Lladró figurines, but they do not have the same intricacy or depth of definition in the faces. As a result, Nao retails for 50% to 70% less than Lladró. However, it is also collectible.

Because Nao is made by Lladró, some sales-clerks in tourist shops will tell you they are the same thing. Reputable shops sell the two lines from two different areas, or at least two different shelves.

We have read that there is some market in fake Lladró. We never, in over ten trips, saw any fake Lladró. However, just to make sure, always check the stamped logo on the bottom of your piece.

You should not have any trouble with packing your figurines, as each one is sold with the box it was shipped in—complete with shredded straw to protect it. The boxes become bulky, so bring an extra suitcase (hardsided) if you plan to stock up. Know your prices in the U.S. before you go crazy buying in Spain; also be aware of the fact that stock varies from dealer to dealer (worldwide), and you may never see the same selection twice.

LOEWE: Say "Lo-Eh-Vey" in the Spanish manner and say *"si"* to an opportunity to buy a $400 handbag.

If there is any quality product in Spain that you should drool over, it is the selection and quality of handbags, clothes, and leathergoods made by Loewe. Loewe is owned by the Moët-Hennessy people. We think they're the champagne of leathergoods, and we toast them.

We also did a lot of careful comparison shopping and found prices in New York were either dollar for dollar equal to those in Madrid, or were, at most, only about 5% higher. For a handbag that costs over $450 (as most Loewe handbags do) you may get your IVA refund and therefore a small break. If you are looking in the $350 range, you'll find small selection and no price break. If you live in or near a big American city that sells Loewe, wait for the summer or winter sales.

But wait; we're not finished. It gets better. If, when you pronounce Loewe correctly you also whisper "Enrique," you get a better prize. You get to leave the regular famous Loewe boutique and find a smaller store that sells $200 handbags that look just as good as the $400 handbags. Then you have discovered Enrique Loewe.

We're not privy to the family infighting, but Enrique Loewe is the original founder of this leathergoods company that goes back to the mid-1800s. Each generation has a son named Enrique in his honor. Someplace along the line in recent history there was a squabble between the current reigning Loewe brothers and Enrique Loewe Knappe; the elder brother left the family firm to start a business on his own.

Enrique does not have a series of expensive boutiques, as does his family, but you can find his work in the duty-free shop in Madrid, in a store or two in Barcelona, and here and there if you look and ask. The Enrique Loewe line has its own logo with his (Enrique Loewe Knappe—Knappe is his mother's maiden name) initials. Handbags begin at $125, but can go to $400 or even $500. There are also accessories after the $200 point. We are forced to admit that our $200 Enrique handbag turned colors and faded within three months; no one in Spain would repair it or refund our money.

MADEIRA: Madeira is the largest of four islands situated in the Atlantic Ocean, 400 miles to the west of Morocco. It was discovered by the Portuguese in the 1400s, and has remained a colony ever since. The popularity of Madeira wine began in the late 1600s when an embargo was placed, by the British, on wines coming out of non-British ports. Because Madeira was considered to be part of Africa, it was not affected. Sailors transporting the wines to England realized that they were not harmed by long, hot sea voyages. On the contrary, the longer they stayed in the casks, the better they got. During the 18th century, grape brandy was added to the wine to stabilize it further. The demand became so great that it became impractical to age all of the needed wine on long sea voyages. Instead, the wine was stored in hot stores called *estufas* for at least six months. The cheaper Madeiras were stored in glass vats, the better vintages in wooden casks. In 1850 and 1873 two forms of disease hit the vines and all but wiped them out. Rather than replacing the original vines, the farmers brought in cheaper European-American hybrids. Today, the majority of Madeira is used for cooking wine. However bleak this sounds, Madeira is making a comeback. New regulations demand that 85% of the wine in a bottle be of the type of grape named. Therefore, varietal grape blends are no longer accepted. The four grape varieties traditionally used are malmsey, which produces the richest dark brown wine, very sweet and velvety; *bual,* a lighter Madeira, much less sweet than malmsey, yet still considered appropriate as a dessert wine; *verdelho,* an even drier wine than bual, good either before or after meals; and *sercial,* the driest of the madeiras, with a light, sweet taste like that of a Riesling.

MANTILLA: A mantilla is a lace shawl worn from combs in the hair and seen commonly in Spanish national costumes or wedding headpieces, or as worn by Catholics who still like to keep their heads covered in Church. The quality of the mantilla is dependent on the quality of the lace—machine-made lace is not very valuable. Size also is a factor. Mantillas come in black or white and sometimes ecru, and begin at $25 for the touristy ones.

MANTÓN: The *mantón* is often worn with the mantilla and is an embroidered shawl, usually covered with trellises of flowers and edged with fringe. The most valuable ones are made of pure silk and are hand-embroidered. Most often they come in contrasting colors, but white embroidery on white silk is available. With some luck, and a lot of money, you can buy an antique *mantón*. . . . They cost about $2,000.

The most difficult part of buying a new *mantón* is knowing what you are getting. Know your fabrics and look at a lot of shawls at one time, and ask the salespeople to put the handmade and the machine-made next to each other, the polyester and the silk next to each other. It's only when you compare that the differences become obvious.

Mantones come in several sizes and are sold all over Spain. We happen to prefer the antique ones, but a new shawl will be old one day, and these can be passed on. We think the best maker is in Sevilla, but there are good shawls sold everywhere.

MYRUGIA: Joya, Maja, Alada, Si Un Jour, Maderas de Oriente, 1916. . . . Does any of this smell familiar? Myrugia is a Spanish fragrance house that is internationally famous, although they no longer have very good U.S. distribution. Their Myrugia soap is best known in the U.S. because of the famous red and black box with the dancing lady in the froufrou dress. The complete line is sold in the Spanish duty-frees, although we were forced to buy retail when they sold out of Joya. Don't forget that Joya is pronounced "Hoy-ya."

NAO: See Lladró, page 38.

NATIVITY SCENES: Known internationally as a crèche, a nativity scene is also called a *belén*. For the best regional work, check out fairs from December 8 through 21 in Valencia, Madrid, Palma, and Barcelona.

PEARLS: The pearls you want to buy in Spain are not those little "Rice Krispies" ones, nor the perfectly round 7-mm cultured ones either. They are the mega pearls that you wonder how anyone could afford. In Spain it's not hard. They are called Majorica pearls, and have nothing to do with the island of Majorca, even though the names seem to go together. Majorica pearls are the invention of modern science and man's ingenuity, and also have little to do with an oyster. They are considered to be "simulated" pearls, as opposed to "artificial" or "cultured." These pearls are so well engineered that they come with a ten-year guarantee promising that the pearls were made in Manacor, Baleares, and that if there is any deterioration due to manufacturing errors they will be replaced. You can't ask for better than that. Majorica pearls come made up as necklaces, as earrings, and set in fine pieces of jewelry. Cultured pearls of the same size (10 mm and up) would cost thousands of dollars, whereas these cost hundreds. Expect a Barbara Bush–style choker of two or three strands of graduated pearls to cost $150–$250.

PICKMAN: Pickman is a Spanish pottery made in an English form. It has an English name because an Englishman founded the pottery. Thus Pickman is English pottery with transfers, scenics printed in one of several colors, including black on white. It is very formal, very nice, and very moderately priced. Shipping could be very pricey, however. Pickman is sold in almost every TT in Spain, as well as in all the department stores, and is equally popular with locals and tourists. You'll get the best price if you buy a complete set; shop around, as prices even within the same city can vary substantially.

Pickman is made outside Sevilla. No factory outlet, although there is a company-owned store in Sevilla.

POMEGRANATE: This fruit is the symbol of the city of Granada, which means "pomegranate" in Arabic. Every piece of pottery made in the city has a pomegranate motif somewhere in the design.

PORT: Port is essentially a mixture of red wine and brandy. The production of port has become a well-honed, well-regulated process. Every vineyard (some 85,000 of them) receives a classification from the Casa de Douro based on its soil, altitude, grape varieties, fertility, cultivation standards, age of the vines, and inclination. The vineyard is then given a quota for port production based on its classification. The A classification vineyard gets the highest quota. Usually less than half the crop is used to produce port, with the rest remaining wine.

It is helpful to know the classifications of port before you buy. You will see bottles labeled "Vintage," "Late-bottled vintage," "Tawny," "Ruby," and "White." These labels describe the quality and flavor of the port, and the process by which it was aged.

Once the newly made port reaches the lodge it is judged and placed, depending on its possibilities for growth, into large barrels or pipes, where it will remain for anywhere from two to fifty years. It takes at least two years to remove the sediment through a gentle rocking process. Many of the wines will be blended to control consistency.

Vintage: Every few years there will be a spectacular harvest that needs no blending. This port is bottled after two years and labeled with the shipper's name and the date. It is aged in the bottle and must be decanted before drinking. Vintage port is not sold before it is ten years old and should not be drunk for twenty years. It is considered best after sixty years, and should be consumed within twenty-four hours after decanting. Five percent of a vintage year's production is bottled, with the rest being kept for a "mother wine" that will be added to younger or mediocre harvests to even their flavor. Some of the oldest "mother wines" date back to the early 1800s.

Tawny: The next best thing to vintage, tawny ports have been aged for many years in wood barrels until the deep red color of the wine has faded to a tawny hue. Especially good tawny ports cost as much as vintage ports, because many people prefer their mellowness to the full-bodied flavor of vintage. The best tawnies can be kept up to forty years in the barrel before being bottled. Old tawnies will have their age on the label, with twenty years being a good median. Tawnies with no age on the label are probably blendings of red and white ports, which are usually inexpensive but disappointing. Some houses mark their tawnies with labels like "superior" or "personal reserve" to distinguish them from each other. The difference usually has to do with the aging and blending process.

Late-bottled vintage: This port is similar to vintage, but bottled only when mature (anywhere from four to eight years). By this time the crust has left the port and it is ready to drink. Late-bottled vintage is a yuppie port, for those who can't wait. The taste is slightly lighter than vintage. The label will have "L.B.V." and a date.

Quinta: Single *quinta* wines are vintage wines that are not of the same quality as the classic vintage wines, but still are considered to be excellent. They mature sooner than the classic vintage wines, although the process is similar. Because they are matured in the bottle, they will need to be decanted before drinking. Some of the labels to look for are: Graham's Quinta dos Malvedos, Croft's Quinta de Roeda, Calem's Quinta da Foz, and Taylor's Quinta de Vargellas.

Ruby: This port is aged in wood for a brief period of time (usually three years). It has a darker color and heavier flavor than tawny.

White: Because white port is the production of white grapes, it is often drier than the red ports, and makes a good aperitif. However, it is still heavier than sherry.

POSTELES: You'll recognize them as posters of bullfighters, and you can get them printed with whatever name you want! But this is a very competitive business, and you should know a few facts:

Try not to pay more than 500 *pesetas* (per poster), which is the high price that is charged in Madrid, for this service. If that guy in front of the Prado—who has this business sewn up in Madrid—tells you 1,000 *pesetas,* laugh in his face. Or show him this book. His name is Mark, and don't you let him try to get you. COBIs may cost 600.

Barcelona has the most shops selling the posters (all in a row, one after the next, on Las Ramblas, right near the Ramada Renaissance Hotel), and the best prices, 200–250 *pesetas,* although many charge 300 *pesetas*. The closer we get to 1992, the higher the prices could go. Madrid has the worst choice—there's just that one guy in front of the Prado, or a few guys (two or three) at the Rastro on Sunday. Sevilla has several (prices range from 450 to 600 *pesetas* here); Córdoba few (maybe none), and Granada few.

How long you wait for the poster to be made is negotiable. We only met one poster-maker who was actually setting his own type. You should be able to wait or to come back in an hour. In season and in high traffic areas, you may be asked to come back at 6 P.M.

There are about eight different poster possibilities—five different bullfight choices, two flamenco dancers (female), and one group picture of the Real Madrid team, available only in Madrid. If you have several made, make sure the right name gets on the right poster.

If the names don't fit the 17-letter requirements, change them around and make them sound Spanish.

PUIG: An old and refined Spanish name in design, now most famous for the fragrances: Verte, Azur, Zambra, Estivalia, Tess, and bathline Moana. Sold at the duty-free and in all department stores.

REXAPFEL: A sensational Spanish liqueur made from apples; we've tried several brands, and in our opinion this is the only one worth drinking. We were served this in a restaurant and have never gotten over it. This is a great under-$10 gift; buy at the grocery in department stores; it is not sold at the Madrid duty-free store.

SHERRY: The British didn't stop with port wine; they also got into the sherry business. For some reason, they could not pronounce Jerez, the city in Spain where this wine comes from, and bastardized the name into "sherry." A sherry winery is called a *bodega;* you may visit any of several *bodegas* in Jerez for the traditional tour, tasting, and trip to the factory store, but you must reserve twenty-four hours in advance. The better ones are booked way ahead in season, and are often taken by tour groups. (The best are Gonzalez Byass and Humbert & Williams, but there are many others. Pedro Domecq, a popular sherry, has no tour.)

There are three types of sherries:

Fino: Light, pale, crisp, dry; 17% to 18% alcohol.

Manzanilla: Very pale and very dry; 15.5% to 16% alcohol.

Amontillado: Gold- to amber-colored, big bouquet, nutty flavor; 17% to 20% alcohol.

SUBASTAS DE ARTE: *Subasta* is one of our favorite words in Spanish. It means auction. *Subastas de arte* are art and decorative arts auctions. Auctions are extremely popular in Spain, and are a hobby for much of the middle and upper middle class. Stores that appear to be antiques stores are quite often showrooms for auctions; the numbers posted are not prices but lot numbers.

LA TOJA: No, this is not Michael Jackson's younger sister. It is a Spanish pharmaceutical company that makes soap and bath products. Their most famous soap is called Magno—it is a black glycerine soap in an oval bar that has been made for hundreds of years. A great gift item; sold in the duty-free, but you can do better in ECI or even Simago. It sells in the U.S. for $2.50 a bar; you buy it in Spain for about 67¢.

TURRONES: A *turrón* is a candy bar made in loaf form. You can buy a *turrón* as a candy bar in the duty-free, in the grocery, and at a tobacco stand, or you can go into any of Spain's fine candy shops and have a sliver of the mother loaf cut for you. Certain *turrones* are seasonal and go with holidays or temperature (chocolate melts in summer and is therefore hard to find in the big loaf form). Dr. Debbie raves about the *turrón de coco* (coconut). Some *turrones* are named by flavor (*coco*); others are named by style. Several producers make the same kind, but in their own fashion.

WROUGHT IRON: Wrought iron is more popular in Spain than in Portugal, but you will find it in both countries. Originally, back in the 15th and 16th centuries, the iron was formed and then painted or gilded. Now it comes in pure black and can be found in fireplace accessories, lamps, and some folk-art pieces. Door handles, old and new, are a true find. They weigh a ton but are worth transporting for just the right door.

Moroccan ABCs

There are many things we love about Morocco—Royal Air Maroc; Mamounia, the fanciest hotel across the street from a souk we've ever stayed in in our lives; and especially the markets because the fun of various Moroccan cities is going to the markets and sniffing out a culture so different from anything you've seen in Europe that you'll never get over it.

Morocco is so incredibly close to the Iberian peninsula, and its design influence is so strong, that we highly recommend a trip south of the border—we hope you will take more than a day trip to Tangiers, and maybe a month in Marrakech, where Yves Saint Laurent will invite you to tea.

Tangiers isn't the best shopping city, but if it was good enough for Matisse, it's good enough for us. You can get there in an hour from Gibraltar! Otherwise, consider the four Imperial Cities (Marrakech, Fez, Rabat, and Casa) with their wonderful souks, where you can bargain like mad and come away with anything from fake Chanel T-shirts to crafts galore. Someday we'll write a whole book on Morocco; right now we'll just point you to the best buys:

BRASS: One of the better-known gift items to take home, hammered brass—in the form of pots, jars, plates, and tables—is found in all the souks. The bigger souks will have one area devoted solely to brass shops, and you can pick and choose your crafts. Large hammered plates make great wall hangings and serving trays, and last for a lifetime. Other brass items commonly found in the souks include candlesticks, sugar boxes, incense burners, lanterns, and door knockers.

CARPETS: Moroccan carpets are varied and wonderful and the most popular item that tourists take home. They come with thick piles and thin, in a Berber weave or a loose weave, in many colors or few. They have seven colors and three borders of different widths around a rectangular field of solid bright or pastel color decorated with a design. The better ones are double-knotted. In the summer, the rugs are turned upside down and the needlepoint side is walked on. This is a natural cleaning and aging process.

Fez carpets are more Persian in feeling than other Moroccan varieties. Old Berber carpets tell a story. New Berber carpets are beige and brown, with long, thick pile. Kilim carpets are woven and embroidered with a wooden needle. They are flat and have a beginning side with no fringe and an ending side with fringe. You will see many mistakes due to the long and tedious handwork that goes into each one. Often more than one person will work on each carpet.

Old Arabic carpets are between forty and eighty years old, and have a patina that comes with age. These are the most expensive and most negotiable.

The quality of the carpet has a lot to do with the number of knots per square inch or centimeter. The higher the number of knots, the more expensive the carpet. The average carpet has fifteen knots per square centimeter. Rabat carpets start at twenty-five. The seal will tell you how many knots per square centimeter your carpet has. Before you start to negotiate for carpets, check the cooperative store in town for a base price. Under no circumstances should you pay more than what you find there. Check for color on both the front and back. It should be even and rich on both sides.

CERAMICS: Moroccan ceramics and earthenware pottery are in great supply in all price ranges. Simple pottery is glazed and decorated in geometric shapes that are colorful and fanciful. Some are decorated with black designs, and look quite chic. Safi is the headquarters of the ceramics trade, where a special school has been set up to produce a variation of the Spanish metallic pottery from Málaga. Some ceramicware is covered in leather and decorated with gold. Fez is known for its blue and white pottery.

CHERTLA: Gold bracelets, called *chertla,* are one of the popular items of jewelry that can be bought in Morocco. It is fun to wear many of them together, so bargain for a combined rate. While you are at it, check out the belts, rings, and chains. Goldsmiths are usually found in their own section of the souk, and pride themselves on the delicacy of their work. You will rarely find a "simple" bracelet or ring. Most are intricately engraved with patterns and symbols. Ask to see the gold mark and verify whether it is gold-filled, 14K, 18K, or some other combination of metals.

KAFTANS: The kaftan has become a popular style of dress in all parts of the world, but the most incredible ones are still found in Morocco. Kaftans are long and loose-fitting garments, somewhat like a djellaba, but without the hood and worn exclusively by ladies. Most often they will be belted with elaborate gold-embroidered or woven belts, and worn with *baboush,* which are pointy-toed shoes that are themselves highly embroidered and decorated. Kaftans usually have long sleeves and a round or V neck.

In the fancy hotels you will see custom kaftan shops, with styles ranging from very modern silks to the traditional brocades. In the souks you will find the traditional kaftans, all brightly colored and decorated with gold thread and hand embroidery. Prices can vary from $20 to

$2,000, depending upon the quality and age of the garment. Wedding kaftans and antique wedding kaftans are the most elaborate and expensive. They are worth looking at because of the quality of the workmanship, but only worth investing in if you are a collector of antique textiles.

LEATHER: One of the best buys in Morocco is leather products. Each area has its individual look. In Fez leather bags and belts are decorated with gold leaf. In the Tetuán area, they are decorated with fringe. Handbags are often made of sheepskin that has been colored and embossed, embroidered, or studded. Look for great Cartier leather attaché and accessory copies as well.

MARQUETRY: Inlaid woodwork is a specialty of the area around Marrakech and Fez. You can buy small boxes or large pieces of furniture made from cedar or olive wood inlaid with ebony, lemonwood, or cedar. Large trays are sometimes inlaid with many different types of wood, giving them an especially rich look. Mother-of-pearl is also combined with wood and inlaid in geometric patterns.

SPICES: One of Morocco's best buys. Look for *lahchgoub*, cumin, *mahya*, thyme, saffron, 45 Variety, and Evil Eye spells. The souk will have a special section devoted to spices, which is easy enough to find if you follow your nose. One of our favorite buys in the spice market is an assortment of natural cosmetics. You can buy rouge made from berries and eyeliner made from bark. The shopkeeper is usually only too happy to give you a free makeup job as well.

TEXTILES: Handmade brocades are a real find in Morocco. The fabrics are handloomed and designed in the shops and marketplaces. You can special-order a design or fabric if you have the time, or order it and have it sent if you have the patience to wait. Or you can buy one of the ready-made ones and take the fabric home and have a wonderful dress made. Fez has the factory shop, with many of the fabrics being copies of fine European brocades at half the price.

WROUGHT IRON: A wide variety of small objects can be found in the souks. Look for plate rests, candle holders, and other knick-knacks. The wrought iron that you buy in Morocco is of very heavy and durable quality. The techniques used have been handed down from generation to generation, and as a result are often finer than what you will find in the U.S. The only drawback to buying large pieces is getting them home. Most small shops have no shipping capability, and then you are stuck trying to get a shipper or carrying the piece as excess baggage. Both options are expensive and time-consuming.

4▾ HEARTLAND OF SPAIN

Welcome to the Countryside

I t's very nice to visit the capital and the business hubs of a country, but we're firm believers that you never get to know a people, or a country, until you've gone out of the big cities and into the countryside, to the soul of the state. This is particularly easy for American tourists who can buy a domestic plane ticket to every city in Spain that's good for unlimited flights (but no backtracking) in a sixty-day period. And it only costs $199! With a deal like this, you can start in Madrid and circle your way through southern Spain in a route something like this: Barcelona, Valencia, Sevilla, Córdoba, Granada, Málaga, and then back to Madrid or on to the north of Spain! This route, which we took to try it out, allows for ground transportation from Sevilla to Málaga and gives you a solid dose of Spain in a ten-day period. You'll be back for more a year later.

Tour de Force

B ecause this is a lot of ground to cover, and everyone wants to see all these cities, you can book a tour that takes in our route or makes its own way across the southern coast or through Andalucía. These tours are often by bus, or plane and bus, and give you a tremendous amount of value considering just how much ground there is to cover. We also will advise you, right up front, that these cities are for viewing and enjoying, and the small amount of time your tour director gives you for shopping is probably going to be enough. Each city in our countryside tour has worthwhile shopping, but you can pick and choose according to your interests and spend more time in the Alcázar. Rightfully so.

Credit-Card Blues

We feel the need to warn you that credit cards are generally welcomed at big-name designer shops, department stores, and major TTs, but that a large number of stores, especially smaller ones and ceramics factories, do not take credit cards ... or have a peculiar aversion to American Express. Make sure you have a bankcard and lots of traveler's checks or cash. Street markets are often going to have the best deals in town; there, cash is imperative.

Welcome to Valencia

If you play word association with most Americans, you say "Valencia" and they say "Oranges." Play this game with us, and we have a very different answer.

Valencia?

Lladró!

We're going to be brutally honest with you. When we come to Valencia, it's only for a day or two and it's for a ceramics (and pottery) run. We don't particularly care about the

Emporio Armani shop (Plaza del Patriarca 5). We're not that interested in Las Fallas, the March 19 celebration of St. Joseph's Day with giant papier-mâché heads worn by local participants in wildly creative festivities. We do care about the central market. We care about the Lladró factory outlet. We care about the city of Manises, right next to the Valencia airport, which has been the center of the ceramics business in this part of Spain for centuries. We may have a warped view of Valencia; but we think it's the best view.

Getting There

You can connect to Valencia from the domestic part of the Madrid airport and arrive in the modern airport of Valencia just an hour later. You're a little closer to Barcelona. Either way, flying is the best bet—especially with your Iberia Visit Spain airpass. Two tips about the Valencia airport: We got the best rate of exchange and paid the least commission on changing money at the bank in the Valencia airport; and the airport gift shop that sells Lladró is nice—but prices are high.

Getting Around

You'll need taxis to get most everywhere, especially if your hotel is in the new part of town or outside of town—as many are. You can take a bus from Valencia to Manises or to Tavernes Blanques (right to the Lladró factory), but if you're only in town for a day, you'll want to make the most of your time and will be happier with cabs.

Booking Valencia / 1

The Secretaría General de Turismo publishes a lovely full-color booklet on Valencia (free) that you can get from the Spanish Tourist Bureau in the U.S. It gives you an introduction to the city and the province. All inclusive guidebooks to Spain have some information on Valencia. Unfortunately, Passport does not have a city guide to this city.

Booking Valencia / 2

MELÍA VALENCIA: Valencia has long been a one-hotel city. Although there are other hotels in town, the Melía is the only four-star, and has business and American tourist travel pretty much sewn up. Formerly known as the Rey Don Jaime, the hotel has concierge floors for businesspeople and shuttle-bus service to conventions. Breakfast is included with the room rate. The location is not first-rate (you'll have to taxi everywhere), but the hotel is. Call (800) 33-MELIA.

MELÍA VALENCIA, Avenida Baleares 2

The Lay of the Land

Despite whatever you remember from the movie *El Cid*, Valencia is not sitting on the Mediterranean Sea. Yes, there's water out there, but not immediately. Valencia is built along the River Turia. The coast is a few miles away.

The old city is located in a central area near the river. The city has spread onto both sides of the river, and you can walk or drive across the river, as you probably will several times during your stay.

Old Valencia is based around the cathedral, with shopping—a few streets away—centered around the old market building and the Plaza del Mercado. Street signs are often in both Spanish and Catalán, so you might get a little confused. We give the street names in Spanish.

Gran Vía edges the old city and represents the main drag of the newer city. This is where you'll find a lot of fast-food eateries, from Vip's to Kentucky Fried Chicken, some cinemas, a few stores, and a lovely residential stretch.

Outside of town, there are the suburbs of Manises and Tavernes Blanques (where Lladró is located). You can get to either in a $4–$5 taxi ride.

The ECI Report

The **ECI PINTOR SOROLLA** is on the edge of downtown, at Avenida Menéndez Pidal 15, next to a park that has a hippie market called **EL PARTERRE**. You can shop both at the same time, although the hippie market does not have anything you need, unless you are out of roach clips. This ECI is in the usual style: jam-packed merchandise on several floors, including basement levels and a supermarket. They do not close during lunch. The souvenir shop is one of the best in any ECI; the china department has a selection of Lladró and Pickman as well as an inexpensive china brand called Vajilla, a transfer pattern like Pickman that we happen to love. A dinner plate costs $5. Upstairs is the **CASA FALLER,** where you can buy colonial costumes or regional dress. There is another ECI in the 'burbs.

Finds

LLADRÓ FACTORY OUTLET: So we walked into the Lladró factory outlet, and there were these four big American businessmen at the cash register. They were from Pittsburgh, they were in town on business, and they had promised their wives that they would make this stop. Their wives must have placed some hefty orders, since each man was buying six blue boxes.

And so it is at the Lladró factory store. People do not buy one item. They take advantage of the incredible savings, and they buy as much as they can carry. (The store will not ship.)

Those items that end up in the factory store have minimal damages—perhaps you can see a brush stroke in a skirt—and seem quite perfect to the average eye. Real glaring mistakes are destroyed in the factory. The items sold here just aren't as perfectly perfect as Sr. Lladró wants them to be. So you can get a crack at them at 35% to 40% below Spanish retail. Your average figurine, which costs about $175 in the store in Spain, costs $95 at the outlet.

They also sell Nao. And since Nao is much

cheaper, by the time you get to the outlet prices, you're talking $25 for a lamp! Be still, my heart!

The store is not easy to find, so have your taxi take you directly to the door, and get his card, as you will have to call for a pickup. Lladró is located in what one might presume was the lobby of an apartment building. No sign, no neon, *nada*. But everybody in Valencia knows this place, so you will not have any trouble with a taxi.

You walk into the shop and are met with a small grocery store of choices—there are shelves against the walls, tables come halfway out across the floor, and there are two salons in the back, one for Nao and one for España, another house line for pottery and planters. Like all suppliers of Lladró, this shop has a simple rule: What you see is what you get.

These works are signed, but they have dots on them that indicate they are seconds, so they will not have the same value as firsts, which are collector's items. There are usually some two dozen of a certain popular figurine, with a much smaller number of pieces of the more elaborately made items. There are also spoons, small boxes, flowers, and other Lladró collectibles. And there are some items from the leathergoods line—the selection depends on availability and what is left over from the recently passed season.

The store is open nonstop from 9 A.M. to 7 P.M. Monday through Friday and 9 A.M. to 1 P.M. on Saturdays. If you love this stuff, you might want to start here first thing in the morning, so you have plenty of time. Or you may want to come during lunchtime, when most other stores are closed. Each item you buy will be packed in its own Lladró box, which is stuffed with shredded straw so your items is protected and you don't have to worry about breakage, even if you place the box in your luggage. There is a machine at the cash register that compresses boxes and strings them together with shipping bands for those who buy, say, six items. Some English spoken. All credit cards.

Oh yes, there's one more thing. If you want to be totally prepared for your Lladró shopping venture, you might want to give a call to Edwardo Galleries in New York (800-872-0270), because this small shop at 501 Fifth Avenue discounts Lladró and ships all over the world. You don't get the same bargains that you will at the factory outlet, but after the factory outlet, Edwardo's prices may be better than other regular prices in Spain! Before you go to the factory, know the regular retail price in the U.S., the Edwardo price, and the regular Spanish retail price, and then shop with ease at the factory.

LLADRÓ FACTORY OUTLET, Calle 1 de Mayo 32, Tavernes Blanques

▼

MERCADO CENTRAL: The Central Market in Valencia is one of the most famous in Spain, and is a must-see even for the non-shopper. Almost 10,000 square feet large, its real beauty is the glass ceiling decorated with stained-glass pictures of—you guessed it—oranges. There are over 1,000 stalls here—everything including skinned rabbits hanging by their little feet. The produce is so breathtakingly beautiful that you have to stare at the acres of strawberries, oranges, tangerines, and clementines. If you aren't a fan of the realities of market life, stay to the front where the produce is. Outside, on the street portion of the market, there is a stand selling fresh orange juice and ice cream, and then a row of dealers who sell leather *botijos*.

MERCADO CENTRAL, Plaza del Mercado

▼

PLAZA REDONDA: Just a block or so from the Central Market, through the old streets of Valencia and right off the Plaza de la Lope de Vega, you'll find a secluded little plaza that houses a circle of shops that sell ceramics. Some of these are simply TTs; others offer all that you want from local ceramics shops. (But no Lladró.) There are also some other vendors selling trimmings, work clothes, umbrellas, and pets. Real people shop here and it is authentic and charming.

The stores begin to open at 10 A.M., but it's a lazy beginning; everything will be open by 11 A.M. Check out **CHEZ RAMÓN** (No. 2), a TT with lots of local ceramics; **COLLA MONLLEO** (No. 12), an excellent ceramics shop that's only a bit touristy—don't miss the small back room; and **LA CASA DE LOS BOTIJOS,** a very small shop offering a nice selection of everything from bullfighter tiles to faience.

PLAZA REDONDA, off Plaza de la Lope de Vega

▼

CERÁMICAS VILAR: If the Plaza Redonda should be too crass for your tastes; if you're the type who needs to travel right to the source; if you want the best visual stimulation the city has to offer—then you have no choice but to grab a cab and head for Cerámicas Vilar, on the edge of Manises.

Cerámicas Vilar is in a fabulous tiled house, the likes of which you will see only a few times in your life. Inside there are three connecting salons stocked with scenic panels, numbers, decorated tiles, a few plates, and some dish sets. Anyone who loves tiles should make a pilgrimage here. A large tile filled with a floral pattern costs $7.50. Visit Vilar and then go on to Leopoldo Moro, in the center of Manises proper, and you will have seen the top of the line.

CERÁMICAS VILAR, Calle Valencia 34, Manises

CALATRAVA: If country faience is your taste, this is perhaps the best shop in Manises for plates and little giftables. This entire street, for one long block, is a ceramics city, so you should go into every shop that interests you. This particular shop isn't crammed to the gills with merchandise, but what's here is quite nice.

CALATRAVA, Calle Maestro Guillem 28, Manises

▼

EL ARCS: Parallel to Calle Maestro Guillem is yet another street filled with ceramics shops; be sure you hit this one too. El Arcs is a large shop that has a selection of items representative of the different kinds of work from the area. There is a good bit of faience, and the store is large and well lit, so you can browse and really learn while you shop. This is probably your best opportunity to see a lot of different styles under one roof.

EL ARCS, Avenida Blasco Ibáñez 6, Manises

▼

LEOPOLDO MORO: This is a factory showroom for tiles and bathroom fixtures, and is the best place in Valencia for American decorators and designers who are used to working with showrooms. They are extremely professional here, and work with your measurements and needs. The public can buy tiles, planters, scenics, and mirrors. They will also do custom designs. Many of the designs are reproductions of French and antique styles.

LEOPOLDO MORO, Avenida Blasco Ibáñez 14, Manises

Welcome to Sevilla

Sevilla just may be everyone's favorite city in Spain. We think it is the very definition of charm. And it has the best ceramics shopping in southern Spain.

While Sevilla is a large city, one that grows larger every day as it prepares to host the 1992 World's Fair, its center can be walked and shopped in an enjoyable day. Across the river—also an enjoyable walk—is Triana. Some of the best ceramics shops in Spain (no, in the world) are in Triana. Shopping Sevilla is an intimate affair, and an affair to remember because of the storybook architecture, the flowering orange trees, and the scads of boutiques selling antiques, souvenirs, crafts, and ceramics.

Shopping Sevilla

The best buys of Sevilla are found in ceramics, dresses in the layered and flounced Sevillana style (which are called *vestida sevillana,* or Sevillana dresses—but we call them froufrous because of their many flounces), souvenirs including wonderfully tacky items with La Macarena (one of the city's most famous virgins), fans, antiques, and some shoes and leathergoods. For fashion items, you're going to want to forget Sevilla, but shoe freaks please note: There is a branch of **LOEWE** and also of a terrific shoe store—**YANKO**, and there are a handful of other stores that will fill your needs. You won't be bowled over by high fashion in Sevilla, but you can find it. Better you should buy a froufrou.

Getting There

You can fly directly to Sevilla's modern airport, or you may take the *talgo* train from Madrid (Madrid-Toledo-Córdoba-Sevilla). Some people drive from the Algarve of Portugal—Sevilla is about an hour and a half from the coastal border.

Getting Around

We can't imagine that anyone would want to drive in Sevilla's already congested streets. It's not possible to park; your car is at risk if it is unguarded. (We suffered a break-in.) You can really walk just about everywhere, or take a city bus. And don't forget the paddleboats on the Guadalquivir.

Booking Sevilla / I

The book that taught us the most about Sevilla is called *Seville: Everything Under the Sun*, published by Passport. There is a local booklet called *El Giraldillo*, which is published monthly and given away free at hotels. It lists cultural events and restaurants, not shops, and is in Spanish. But there are ads that have illustrations, so you can make guesses.

Booking Sevilla/2

Hotels in Sevilla are all in downtown locations and are ranked according to price, with inexpensive rooms costing less than $100 per night, moderate rooms from $100–$150 per night, and expensive rooms costing over $150 per night.

MELÍA SEVILLA: The Melía Sevilla is a brand-new, modern luxury hotel with a pink and red lobby that is built along the lines of a Memphis Milano showroom. It is gorgeous! This is a large four-star hotel with a concierge floor, business amenities, and a good location, considering that very few hotels are in the heart of Sevilla. The Melía stands at the edge of town but is within walking distance of town and of Triana. Moderate. Call (800) 33-MELIA.

MELÍA SEVILLA, Doctor Pedro de Castro 1

▼

HOTEL ALFONSO XIII: Book for '92 right now, or you'll never get into this chicer-than-thou CIGA hotel located just a block from the Alcázar in the heart of town. Built for a world's fair in 1929, this is the most splendid hotel in town. If you can't afford to stay here, stop in for tea or drinks. The interior courtyard with mosaic tiles is a work of art. Some shops in the lobby. Expensive. Local phone: 222-850.

HOTEL ALFONSO XIII, San Fernando 2

▼

HOTEL TRYP COLÓN: On the other side of downtown, at the edge of the shopping district, this once grand five-star hotel has just been renovated by the Tryp chain, and is somewhat restored to its former glory. It's located near the train station and the bullfight ring. Prices are based on four different seasons, so a double room can range from just under $150 to $350. Expensive. Local phone: 222-900.

HOTEL TRYP COLÓN, Canalejas 1

The Lay of the Land

Sevilla is built on the banks of the Guadalquivir River. The heart of the city is around the cathedral and the Giralda, a tower that adjoins it—both are at the edge of the Alcázar. The cute stores are in the pedestrian-only neighborhood that served as the Jewish ghetto (Judería) centuries ago and is now called the Barrio de Santa Cruz, or just plain Santa Cruz. This should be your first stop.

Triana is located across the bridge from Sevilla, and was once the heart of the ceramics industry. When our friend Luis was growing up in Sevilla after the Civil War, locals never even went to Triana—unless they worked there. Now it's considered an extension of the city, and is very built up, with its own branch stores, its own fast-food restaurants, its own ambience. Now everyone goes to Triana.

In downtown Sevilla, as you move from the old part of the city next to the Giralda to the newer part, you encounter the pedestrian shopping street Calle Sierpes. This primary shopping street winds along for a few blocks until it dead-ends. You're then just a short walk away from **EL CORTE INGLÉS** at the Plaza del Duque and from another main shopping area. It's an easy walk from the Giralda to ECI, and one you will enjoy. There are ice cream vendors on Calle Sierpes who will turn your stroll into a party.

Sevilla

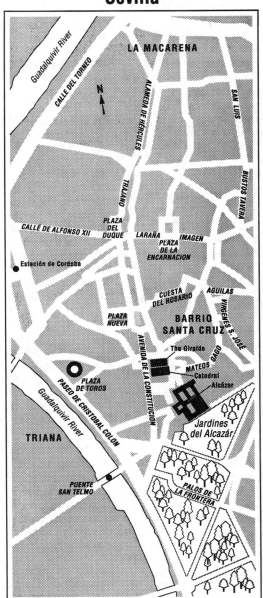

Snack and Shop

EL GIRALDILLO: This is the most obvious restaurant in town, and we apologize for being such suckers, but we like it here. Directly across from the Giralda, this tavern offers regional specialties and indoor and outdoor dining. Lunch for two is about $40. They start serving at noon, which is early by Spanish standards but welcome to American stomachs.

EL GIRALDILLO, Plaza Virgen de los Reyes 2

▼

FIGÓN DEL CABILDO: The perfect place for a big lunch after shopping and sightseeing. Located off a little square (where the stamp market is held) and about a block from the Giralda, this regional restaurant is known to locals as one of the best in town. Closed Sunday afternoon. Expensive.

FIGÓN DEL CABILDO, Plaza del Cabildo

Pack and Shop

I f you're planning on buying ceramics, you should bring your bubble wrap and an extra hard-sided suitcase. Or a lot of dirty laundry. This is where you'll be loading up, and it does not pay to ship ceramics.

Crime Report

As we mentioned, we did have a little crime problem on our first trip to Sevilla. It was, luckily, our only crime problem in Spain. We mention this because every guidebook you read warns you about the crime in Sevilla, and every American tourist we met on a tour group wanted to know about crime in Sevilla, or already had a tale to tell. Luis, who sometimes lives in Sevilla and who grew up there, says it's very simple: Don't go out alone after dark; don't go wandering in the Judería (even in small groups) in the dark.

We carry little cash, and we use a money belt to carry funds, passport, and two credit cards. Use common sense and watch your valuables, as always.

The ECI Report

The downtown ECI is located on the far side of the old part of town, at the Plaza del Duque. This is downtown, within easy walking distance. While this ECI is no different from most, it does have a fabulous supermarket in the basement, and if you are tired of paying $50 for lunch every day, you'll do what we do and get a picnic at the supermarket.

Sunday Shopping

T he official stores are all closed; but wait, are those TTs we see glistening in the sunshine? Oh yes! The TTs surrounding the Giralda are open on Sundays! Furthermore, there are several flea markets, so you can have a rather busy day of it. Sunday in Sevilla is a day to remember.

Flea Markets

ALAMEDA DE HÉRCULES: Located in a long rectangular square not far from ECI, this weekly flea market is in an area that is not supposed to be too safe (according to our hotel concierge). The only problem we found is that it's boring. If you are not used to typical Spanish flea markets, you too might find it very boring. It's not visually stimulating; a bunch of average-looking people sit next to blankets loaded with oranges or garlics. Very little of what's sold here is pretty to look at or enticing to the tourist. But when you hit a good bargain, you'll know it. We found a ceramics stand where the faience was incredibly inexpensive and turned out to be 25% less expensive even than at the factories in Triana. And we found a guy who was selling "antique" plates from the back of his car. Even if these were imitations (which they probably were), they were a steal at $30 each. The real thing sells for $200 each! If you're in town, it doesn't hurt to visit. Don't expect much and then you won't be disappointed. But if you find those $30 plates again, buy us a few. Sunday, after 10 A.M.

ALAMEDA DE HÉRCULES, Alameda de Hércules

EL JUEVES: This market is named after the day of the week on which it is held—Thursday. We think it is the city's best flea market for antiques and junk. The crowd really gets going after 10 A.M., and it closes around 3 P.M. Bargain like mad, and if you can speak Spanish, do, because tourists are definitely at a disadvantage.

EL JUEVES, Calle Feria

▼

PLAZA DE LA ALFALFA: This picturesque pet market is just off the Calle Sierpes, right downtown and not far from other Sunday goings-on. Very European. We want to buy all the animals and free them. Sunday morning until 1 P.M.

PLAZA DE LA ALFALFA, Plaza de la Alfalfa

▼

PLAZA DEL DUQUE: A cheap hippie market held during the week directly in front of ECI, where you are a captive audience and must walk through the tie-dye and the bad leather. Try not to look.

PLAZA DEL DUQUE, Plaza del Duque

▼

PLAZA DEL CABILDO: This is a little hard to find but is worth it, if only to see the architecture of the half-moon building over the plaza. In the circle, stamp and coin dealers set up their tables. Some rocks, minerals, and gemstones also sold. Sunday 9 A.M.–1 P.M.

PLAZA DEL CABILDO, Plaza del Cabildo

▼

Finds

GALERÍAS SEVILLANAS: This store stands in a category by itself because it sells *vestidas sevillanas* and all the regional costumes needed for men, women, children, and gauchos. Women wear these dresses for *ferria* (the bullfight), which in Sevilla is held for several days shortly after Easter. So this shop is not just for tourists. A good dress costs well over $400, and then must be completed with the right shawl, shoes, bangles, and hair accessories (usually a comb with mantilla). This is not an inexpensive proposition. Most dresses are patterned with polka dots, but there are some solids with contrasting trim and some florals available.

This delicious shop is right off the main drag (Calle Sierpes) and behind a wedding-gown shop, and even if you're not in the market for a dress you should stop in to admire the tiers of skirts fluttering off hangers. Don't miss it. If you are standing on Calle Sierpes and walking toward ECI, turn right on Calle Cerrajería, then left into the first alley. You will end up right in front of the shop.

GALERÍAS SEVILLANAS, Sagasta 16 and Mondardes 7

▼

ENRIQUE MORENO: If you don't want a *sevillana* dress, perhaps you want a mask hand-crafted from leather and molded to the contours of your face, created by an artist and guaranteed to take your breath away? In Barrio de Santa Cruz.

ENRIQUE MORENO, Pasaje de Andreu 1

▼

FELICIANO FORONDA: The city's most famous maker of shawls and mantillas is located not far from the Giralda on a teeny-tiny side street that is difficult to find unless you ask directions. Press on. This entire neighborhood is beautiful to look at, and the shop has incredible wares. Even if you don't want to go to the shop, find the street to imagine yourself back in time a few centuries.

Feliciano Foronda is more like a shipping office with a small showroom than a traditional shop. Linens are sold, as well as shawls and mantillas. The shawls come in silk or polyester, embroidered by hand or by machine and in various sizes. Prices begin at $125 but escalate as you get into serious stuff. This is the most famous maker in town, a true insider source. It helps if you speak Spanish, but it's not essential. Unfortunately, there are no antique shawls.

FELICIANO FORONDA, Alverez Quintero 52

▼

CASA RUBIO: At first glance you might write this off as a TT, but actually this is the most famous resource in town for fans. The really good stuff is put away, or up high in display cases. The store sells souvenirs, as well as umbrellas and castanets, but they are famous for their fans, which come in hundreds of variations in quality and type. See page 37 for more on how to buy a fan. While you're here, don't forget to buy the fan stand to display your fan. If you express an interest (and speak Spanish!), you'll get a free lecture on all aspects of the history and practice of fanmaking—as well as a few lessons in opening and closing a fan with the proper flair.

CASA RUBIO, Sierpes 56

▼

BOLSOS CASAL: This small leathergoods shop on the main shopping street has handbags that look like famous-maker bags but that cost $75–$125. Chanel-style bags begin at $75, Loewe-inspired bags at $100. Bags are grouped by color; the salesladies will bring them down for you.

BOLSOS CASAL, Sierpes 73

TTs

ABELARDO LINARES: Linares is both an adequate TT and a good antiques store. As silly as the combination is, it works and can probably satisfy every type of shopper. There are tiles in the far back of the store, antiques and paintings to the right. Then there are all the usual souvenir items, including plates with embroidered images of La Macarena on them (the plates do not cry real tears, however). This could be the only store you need in Sevilla. Open Sunday.

ABELARDO LINARES, Mateos Gago 4

DIAZ: This is one of our favorite marketing stories. The family that owns this shop owns two others that sell pretty much the same thing, but they have named the other shops with the same letters in a different order—hence ZADI and DIZA. All sell souvenirs, Lladró, and Nao.

DIAZ, Sierpes 71
ZADI, Sierpes 48
DIZA, Tetuán 5

▼

ARTESANÍA SANTA TERESA: No question about it, this is a TT. But they sell Pickman china; they have a shawl catalogue, tiles, flamenco costumes for all ages, Joan Miró T-shirts, religious postcards, bullfight postcards, Picasso sweatshirts, fans, and most other kinds of souvenirs you can imagine. It lacks charm, but not stock.

ARTESANÍA SANTA TERESA, Santa Teresa 1

▼

LOS VENERABLES: A TT that is mostly dedicated to ceramics is our kind of TT. This one is small and crowded and hard to move around in for fear you will break something. There are ceramics everywhere. The prices for plates—we hang ours on the kitchen wall—are good. They ship. Pricewise, you might do better in Triana, but there's a lot of charm to this little shop and since it's right in the Judería (Barrio Santa Cruz), it's convenient to a lot of other shops. Little gift items available for less than $5.

LOS VENERABLES, Gloria 1

▼

ARTE SEVILLANO: This is one of our favorite TTs because it is rather upscale. They stock a large selection of Nao and Lladró figurines. Pickman is sold by the set; without shipping the prices stand around $320 for a 42-piece set, $100 for a 15-piece tea set, but they will ship at extra cost. There are also guidebooks and pearls.

ARTE SEVILLANO, Plaza Doña Elvira

Ceramics

CERÁMICA SANTA ANA: Every city in Spain has one or two shops where you can tell, just from looking at the outside, that there are going to be national treasures. The surest sign is if the shop is covered with *azulejos*. The outside of Santa Ana reminds us of a very similar shop in Lisbon, also clad in tiles covered with figures. This store even has ceramic finials on top. If you've got it, flaunt it. Santa Ana has two showrooms that form an L off the lobby area, where you pay. Go back into the front room, slightly to your left as you enter, and find all the tile numbers and letters of the alphabet you need as well as everyday floor tiles and household needs. Go to the showroom to the right and you'll find the plates, the planters, the scenics, the bells, the dishes, the goods. Prices are so moderate that you think they are a steal—as it turns out, prices here happen to be high, but you have to be a local to know that. To an American, $4 for a handpainted 8-inch planter is a bargain!

Because of the proximity of several other tile and ceramics shops, you should scope out Santa Ana, do the rest of the looking in Triana, and then maybe return. We're talking about four shops in a one-block area, so spend some time and see it all. Santa Ana is probably the best resource for dishes and plates, although it's not the best for all individual tiles. But the prices on the letters are the cheapest in town, since Santa Ana happens to supply to the city— all street signs in Sevilla are made from these same tiles. Santa Ana does a huge tourist and international business and will ship to the U.S. They also carry some Pickman china. Closed for lunch from 1:30 until 4:30 P.M.

CERÁMICA SANTA ANA, San Jorge 31, Triana

▼

CERÁMICA RUÍZ: Because this shop is across the street from Santa Ana, you have to go inside. Besides, it's a very nice shop. This is the only shop where we saw white majolica in Spain. The house specialty is finely painted faience with skinny little brush strokes. Jars for flour, etc., cost $50 each and are made in an antique style—they're real finds, if you can get them home. The prices seem a bit high to us, but the style is refreshingly different from everyone else's.

CERÁMICA RUÍZ, San Jorge 27, Triana

▼

CERÁMICA SANTA ISABEL: Planters and pottery (even potting soil) are the house specialty, but there are lots of little items that make great gifts, and quite a number of tiles. The shop is not pretentious and has a nice country feel to it ... kind of like a pottery general store. An item we bought elsewhere for $4 cost $3.50 here. The tiles with letters of the alphabet are more expensive than at Santa Ana; there's some stock in Pickman china. You can get a 3-inch La Macarena for your door for $2. Picture frames (ceramic) begin at $3. The courtyard is where the tiles are sold, and it's fun to poke around as you work the area.

CERÁMICA SANTA ISABEL, Antillano Campos 9

▼

CERÁMICA MONTALVÁN: If we had to name the single best tile store in the world, this would be it. Gorgeous tiles begin at $1 each. Intricate multicolored tiles are no more than $2.50 each. But it's not simply that the prices are better than most; it's also that there are better designs, and wider selection. Walk in and step down to a musty chamber of tiles that feel very authentic. Believe it or not, there's more. Turn left, follow the hallway, and you are in a showroom full of ceramics. You will just lose your mind. But before you buy it all up, remember: They don't ship.

CERÁMICA MONTALVÁN, Alfarería 21–13, Triana

CERÁMICA SEVILLA: Some tour buses bring groups here and claim it is a factory, but we know better. But it is a nice shop; in fact, it's one of the nicest in Sevilla and is located in the picturebook Barrio Santa Cruz. About half of the work is in the Moorish style with gold rims; the other half is faience.

CERÁMICA SEVILLA, Gloria 5

▼

CERÁMICA SANTA CRUZ: Another shop that specializes in the Moorish ceramics. You can watch them paint the designs in the back. Located a block from the Giralda in the strip of shops and TTs that line the way. Very impressive.

CERÁMICA SANTA CRUZ, Mateos Gago 10

▼

EL AZULEJO: Next door to the TTs and some other ceramic shops, El Azulejo is a class act, with expensive and beautifully made tiles and ceramics. They have a distinctive house style. The designs are smaller, more compactly placed, more Persian than everyone else's. There's nothing touristy about this store or its wares.

EL AZULEJO, Mateos Gago 10

▼

LA ALACENA: Sevilla's very own Pickman china (see page 43) was originally made on La Cartuja, but was removed to a site outside of town where the factory still works. (They claim not to have a factory outlet.) There is a fancy factory store right downtown, about a block down the street from ECI and the Plaza del Duque. The store will not ship, but they do have a beautiful display of all the Pickman pieces, which are English-style transfer-printed porcelains. Blue on white is the most popular choice, but several colors are available. This is one of the best finds in all of Spain.

LA ALACENA, Alfonso XII 25

Antiques

ANTONIO LINARES MUÑOZ: This shop's yet another offering from the Linares family. But let's face it: These guys have a certain style to them. At first glance, the shop in the Barrio Santa Cruz looks like a TT. But go inside, poke around, explore some of the alcoves, and it's possible to discover fun stuff. Some is worthwhile. There are tiles and religious antiques, some antique shawls (about $2,000 each—this is the going price), and then the usual postcards, wooden carvings of Don Quixote, and black velvet miniature bulls.

ANTONIO LINARES MUÑOZ, Rodrigo Caro 11, Plaza de la Alianza

▼

PEDRO LUIS MONTELONGO: This small, serious shop in the Barrio Santa Cruz sells large, serious paintings and some important furniture; a few religious items. Everything is top quality.

PEDRO LUIS MONTELONGO, Santa Teresa 17, Plaza de Santa Cruz

▼

MANUEL ESPINOSA DE LOS MONTEROS: This simply fabulous shop in the Barrio Santa Cruz should be one of your first stops. You may buy nothing, but the atmosphere is better than theater. Things hang from walls and ceiling to create a cave of treasures where a little of everything is sold, from matadors' costumes to old keys.

MANUEL ESPINOSA DE LOS MONTEROS, Rodrigo Caro 16

▼

ALTAMIRA: Antique shawls here start at $1,000. Ignore the ratty furs and concentrate on the old clothes, costumes, and shawls. One of the few sources for fine, antique shawls in Barrio Santa Cruz.

ALTAMIRA, Rodrigo Caro 7

Welcome to Córdoba

Córdoba is not particularly known as a shopping city. Everyone comes to view the Mezquita, one of the most breathtaking pieces of architecture ever built. If you still want to shop, you'll find that, conveniently, the Mezquita is surrounded by TTs.

So welcome to Córdoba, where your tour director will not let you linger long, but where you'll see funky charm; where an ancient Judería is also laden with shops—as in Sevilla—but has turned ugly, crass, and commercial. Welcome to Córdoba, where you might not want to buy anything, or where you may be so taken with the low-key atmosphere of this small town that you buy up the place. Welcome to the kind of place you have to see once in order to understand it.

Getting There

Córdoba, in Andalucía, is about an hour- or an hour-and-a-half train ride from Sevilla—depending on which train you take! The *talgo* is more expensive, but gets you there faster. Many people like to rent a car in Sevilla and drive through the province, taking in Córdoba and Granada and ending up in Málaga, where they can connect to a flight to the States.

We must add that one of the reasons people get cars is the fact that train connections out of Córdoba are just about impossible. It is worth thinking about visiting Córdoba on a day trip from Sevilla, or rearranging your schedule if you do not want to drive. You cannot easily get to Granada by train from Córdoba, and God help you if you don't speak Spanish when you start dealing with the officials at the Córdoba RENFE station.

To get the record straight, it *is* possible to get from Córdoba to Granada. It just isn't easy, since there is no direct train. You switch trains and lay over in Boabadilla: it takes four to six hours—or more—before you see Granada. You'll be ready to hang yourself from the Alhambra by the time you get there.

So when you think about getting to Córdoba, you'd better think about getting *from* Córdoba, as well. Consider the Sevilla-Córdoba-Toledo run, which is very convenient (and a very nice train) and will give you much pleasure. The Sevilla-Córdoba-Granada trip can be done delightfully with the Andalusian Express; otherwise, plan to drive or go with a tour.

Getting Around

The old part of Córdoba is the interesting part, and this is all easily walkable. You'll need to call a taxi if you venture farther.

Booking Córdoba / 1

Passport Books does publish a Córdoba edition—they call this city the "dazzling jewel of Moorish Spain." However, note that this edition does not have a shopping section in it.

Booking Córdoba / 2

HOTELES ADARVE: If you stay at the Adarve, you might actually love Córdoba and want to stay forever. This hotel is very Moorish and modern at the same time, is located directly across the street from the Mezquita, and is really the only place in town that a snob wants to stay. Four stars. Expensive. Local phone: 48.13.37.

HOTELES ADARVE, Magistral Gonzalez Frances 15

▼

HOTEL MAIMONIDES: Owned by the same people who own the Adarve, and also across the street from the Mezquita (but on a different side of the square from the Adarve), this hotel is a three-star with a lot of funky charm and a great location. Moderate. Local phone: 47-15-00.

HOTEL MAIMONIDES, Torrijos 4

▼

EL OASIS: The only thing wrong with El Oasis is its location. You must taxi everywhere. Even to catch the city bus, you must walk three long blocks. Like a real oasis, it is in the middle of nowhere. But it's inexpensive! Lots of tour groups come here; the hotel is always mobbed. Very clean; one of the best bargains in Spain, with rooms at about $50 a night. Local phone: 29-13-50.

EL OASIS, Avenida Cádiz 78

▼

MELÍA CÓRDOBA: In the center of a park-like area at the center of the newer part of town, without being in downtown, this Melía hotel may be the most attractive new structure in Córdoba. You're still not within walking distance of the old part of town, but you are in very, very pleasant surroundings in this giant, modern hotel. You're also close to many car rental agencies, if you're tired of taking the train. Call (800) 33-MELIA.

MELÍA CÓRDOBA, Jardines de la Victoria

The Lay of the Land

T he old city is built up against the Guadalquivir River, which was once navigable to Sevilla. There is an Alcázar to one side, but the central part of the old city—

and any trip to Córdoba—is the walled block that encloses the Mezquita and its small orange grove. Inside the Mezquita is a cathedral. You may enter the walls for free, but there is a charge to enter the Mezquita. The gates close during lunch from 1:30 to 4 P.M.

Directly behind this walled beauty lies the Judería, the old Jewish ghetto, which is where the touristy stores are. And they are very touristy. You may walk right through the Judería up the hill and into the center of modern downtown Córdoba, but you still won't find any great shops. (There is a **SIMAGO,** the Spanish version of K mart.) As we said, Córdoba just isn't a great shopping city.

Snack and Shop

EL CABALLO ROJO: Right on the main square across from the Mezquita and in between the TTs, El Caballo Rojo is one of the most famous restaurants in town and is the nice lunch you deserve, especially if you've just driven in from Sevilla and had to make your way over the mountains. The regional cooking here is a real treat. If you eat early (they open for lunch at 1 P.M.) you will not need a reservation; if you plan to eat at 3 P.M. call 47-53-75 to reserve.

EL CABALLO ROJO, Cardenal Herrero 28

▼

EL CHURRASCO: A block from the Mezquita, in the Judería, this fine restaurant specializes in regional foods and grilled meats. You eat in a tented courtyard. Closed on Thursday and during the month of August.

EL CHURRASCO, Romero 16

Finds

STREET VENDOR: The best part about Córdoba is the weird, wonderful musical sound you hear piped to you from a street vendor as you enter the main gate to get to the Mezquita. This young man is playing an *asubio,* a nose instrument something like a recorder that makes an eerie Moorish sound that would please a snake. They cost about $5 each; your kids will love them.

STREET VENDOR, main gate to Mezquita

▼

LIBRERÍA SEFARAD: A tiny shop selling books on medieval Judaism, Bibles, what they call "Jewish pottery" (pottery with Hebrew lettering, Passover plates), and tapes of Sephardic music.

LIBRERÍA SEFARAD, Romero 14

▼

ARTY: A small ceramics shop selling Granada *fajaluaza* ceramics (see page 92). This unique shop is one of the nicest in town, because you don't see these wares elsewhere in Córdoba— although you will see tons of the stuff in Granada. One of the nicest shops in town.

ARTY, Tomas Conude 12

TTs

Most of the TTs are so similar to each other that there's no reason to praise one at the expense of another. They all sell about the same stuff at the same prices. Two we like because they are bigger and well lit are **LA MAZQUITA,** Cardenal Herrero 22, and **LA TORRE,** Cardenal Herrero 16. We also like **ANTONIO ADARVE GONZALEZ,** Torrijos 8, because it is the biggest and fanciest TT in town—it's almost like a department store. This giant shop has a special room for Lladró figurines; it has a case of antique Judaica; it has its own restaurant. There are signs in English ("We pack and ship") and lots of different types of souvenirs and regional crafts items. The bathrooms are clean and well-marked.

Welcome to Granada

I t's easy to understand why the Moors held on to Granada for so long—who would ever want to leave? While once again it is the old city that is the most charming, the newer part of the city isn't bad either, and the suburbs are just as nice. You just may want to retire to Granada.

The tourist part of Granada is more built up than anywhere else in Spain. But this is the real thing, and man, oh, man, they just don't build 'em like this anymore.

Shopping Granada

T he shopping in Granada is far better than in Córdoba. For ceramics, yes, it's great; for fashions and shoes, not so hot. There are a tremendous number of TTs, but many of these are actually fun . . . and not too offensive. We found no shoes, handbags, linens, or *sevillana* dresses worthy of mention.

There are some antiques and reproduction antiques that are worth a look.

Getting There

We drove to Granada from Córdoba on our trips there—we just couldn't figure out any other way to get there easily. The drive is very nice, but difficult if you aren't a mountain goat. If you do not like driving curvy roads, you'd better think this one through. You can take the train from Sevilla to Granada easily if you bypass Córdoba. It's worth considering.

Getting Around

You can walk just about everywhere in Granada, if you are big on walking. We do warn you that the Alhambra is practically straight up, and a cab might be better, especially on the way up. You can walk around and explore and then walk down. You can take the number 2 bus from the Puerta Real to the Alhambra, but you need to know exactly where you are going. We did this and spent three hours lost while we wandered every hillside but the right one. The actual entrance to the Alhambra, which is at the Recinto de Alhambra, is not easy to find from the bus stop (at the Washington Irving Hotel), so don't stumble around.

Booking Granada / 1

P assport publishes one of their handy city guides for Granada. The local freebie handout is called *Guía* (which means Guide); it's in Spanish.

Booking Granada / 2

HOTEL VICTORIA: This is the only hotel for the true shopper and for the person who likes to get everywhere and see everything, because it is truly in the center of town and within walking distance of everything. Ask for a back room away from the main street if you are sensitive to street noise. This turn-of-the-century three-star hotel has tiles everywhere and funky yet grand Victorian furnishings that combine to make it absolutely charming. Inexpensive to moderate. Local phone: 25-77-00.

HOTEL VICTORIA, Puerta Real 3

▼

PARADOR NACIONAL DE SAN FRANCISCO: It's pretty hard to get reservations at this famous *parador*, partly because everyone knows that it is one of the best hotels in the world in terms of romance, glamour, and location. Built into a former convent, the Parador is right inside the Alhambra, and could not be more exciting. It only has thirty-two rooms; you must book months in advance. Local phone: 221-493.

PARADOR NACIONAL DE SAN FRANCISCO, Alhambra

The Lay of the Land

The Alhambra sits on top of a hill. There are a few other hotels and some TTs up there with it (besides the Parador), but that's it for this hill. On a hill directly across from it is the old city, called Albaicín, which has some shops but is mostly occupied by homes with gorgeous views. To one side of Albaicín are the caves where the Gypsies live and where you do not want to visit. (It's considered dangerous.)

At the base of these two hills the city begins at the Plaza Nueva and stretches along one of the main drags—Calle de los Reyes Católicos—until it ends at the Puerta Real. Running perpendicular to Reyes Católicos is the Gran Vía de Colón, which is like the downtown street in any American city—where the locals shop. Calle de los Reyes Católicos is more fun than Gran Vía, and is the natural walking path from the Alhambra into town.

At the Puerta Real, surrounding the cathedral, is a warren of little streets—most of them for pedestrians only—which make up the cute shopping area of town. Here you'll find the branch stores of Spanish chains (**CORTEFIEL**) and international chains (**BENETTON**). There's a nice European flavor to these streets, and there are some TTs to browse. The best shopping is at the base of the Alhambra.

The ECI Report

There is an ECI outside of town, but tourists who want another big department store should turn to the local Galerías Preciados (GP), which is conveniently located at the Puerta Real. This is a nicer than usual GP, complete with a handsome supermarket in the basement. Do not buy ceramics here (prices are very high); the shops surrounding the Plaza Nueva have better prices and better selection. But then, GP does not close for lunch.

Snack and Shop

LOS LEONES: We eat here at least once a day when we are in Granada, sometimes more often! Right at the Puerta Real, a half block from the Hotel Victoria, this local tavern has regional charm and low to moderate prices. Too many tourists, of course.

LOS LEONES, Av. José Antonio 10, Puerta Real

Finds

ROSSELLI: Worth checking out for classic men's and women's shoes in the low- to mid-price range. Although the goods look expensive from the window, you'll be surprised at how affordable they really are. Prices can begin at $45 when there's a sale. They also have fashionable handbags.

ROSSELLI, Puerta Real 2A

▼

CERÁMICA FAJALUAZA: Ask a taxi to take you to the Bib Fajaluaza (*Bab* is Moroccan for gate; *bib* is the Spanish form of the same word), which is a small tiled gate at the top of the Albaicín hill. It is also called the Puerta Fajaluaza. Next door to the gate, and sharing the same wall as the gate, is a pottery factory! They do not speak English, and they do not get many tourists. But it's worth it for you to visit if you love pottery. They have big, dramatic pieces, as well as tiles and small items. In business since 1910, the factory makes your basic Granada-style pottery, which can always be recognized by the painted pomegranate in the design. (*Granada* means pomegranate.) Most of the wares are painted with blue on off-white, although the traditional *fajaluaza* style (blue and green together) is also made. If you are looking for one giant urn, or bowl, or plate—something that says SPAIN in a country rustic way—this is your source. Cash only. The street is Carretera de Murcia, and you want to be right there at the gate, which is a tourist attraction. A taxi driver will know. Tell him to wait, because the only other way down is by foot or by mule.

CERÁMICA FAJALUAZA, Carretera de Murcia 42

▼

ALCAICERÍA: This is not a specific store but an alley lined with shops in stalls—all of which are TTs. We read a guidebook that called this a Moroccan bazaar; if you are harboring a similar illusion, we'd like to dissuade you right now. This is a cute little alley next to the church, manufactured just for tourists. If you are on the pedestrian street Zacatín, you'll see an arch that says ALCAICERÍA on it; just walk in there. Of all the stores in here, there's only one that we can get really serious about, **BERNARTE,** at number 10, because they sell antique shawls as well as souvenirs and giftables.

ALCAICERÍA, Puerta Real, off Zacatín

▼

RUIZ LINARES: Here they are again, those merchandising Linareses. The familiar setup is a bit different this time. There are three different shops. Two of them are at the Alhambra (one in the parking lot; one inside the gates), and one is on the walking street Zacatín. The Zacatín shop is rather fancy. The other two shops are like all other Linares stores: half TT and half serious antiques shops. They always have the good stuff; you just have to look around for it some. They also sell some Lladró.

RUIZ LINARES
  Alhambra 64
  Zacatín 21A
HIJOS DE RUIZ LINARES, Puerta del Vino 2, Recinto de la Alhambra

▼

ARTESANÍA BARROSO: This is not for the ordinary shopper. While the store does have a few ceramics pieces, what it really sells are mirrors and frames—the kind you see in museums: big, carved, gold, elaborate. The prices are a small fraction of U.S. costs for such items. But just try packing them. And you'll have to—no shipping here.

ARTESANÍA BARROSO, Elvira 5, Plaza Nueva

▼

CORTTY: This is the local mall and *hypermarché,* on the edge of town and not really for tourists. But if you want to see how the real people live, or you need a great grocery store, here you go.

CORTTY, Mendez Nunez

Ceramics

CERÁMICA PUERTAS: This is a TT at the Plaza Santa Ana, which is at the base of the Alhambra and the top of the Plaza Nueva, so you can't miss it. It's one of several TTs, but at this one the owner gave us lessons in potterymaking and how fine ceramics should ring. You may think this stuff is a dime a dozen, but in reality you should either be buying up at the Fajaluaza factory or from one of these shops on the Plaza Santa Ana. You won't find better selection or prices.

CERÁMICA PUERTAS, Plaza Santa Ana 2

▼

MALDONADO: This ceramic shop has a wide range of many different styles of work, some from other regions. It's nice to get a look here and at some of the shops next door before you decide.

MALDONADO, Plaza Santa Ana 1–3

▼

AL-YARRAR: If you happen to be walking down the hill (or up the hill) through Albaicín, you'll have fun looking in at this *fábrica* (factory). You can see the ovens from the patio. Don't miss the view across to the Alhambra. The shop is in the front room of a little villa in the hillside. The work is very Moorish in feel and quite different from the everyday stuff.

AL-YARRAR, Calle Bañuelo 5, Albaicín

5 ▼ SHOPPING MADRID

Welcome to Madrid

They really were dancing in the streets in Madrid. We saw it with our own eyes. They were drunk, we're certain of it, but they were dancing—and having a ball. And watching them, there on the curbs of the little streets below the Plaza Mayor, we thought that everything we had heard about the New Spain must be true, and we thought that Madrid was the best place in the world to be.

Almost every time we are in Madrid, we think it is one of the best places to be. Dr. Debbie wants to move here. We're certain to come to visit her frequently. Our Spanish isn't as good as hers, but we're catching on fast: Madrid is the place to be these days. *Sí, sí;* we're ready.

Visitors from all over the world are flocking to Madrid, and Americans are only a small part of the crowd. Some come because they heard it was inexpensive. (They heard wrong.) Some come because the hype in the international travel press is so intense that they just have to be where the in crowd is. Some come for the shopping: Finding antiques in Spain—and even in Madrid—is being considered as a new Olympic sport. (Be careful, a lot of furniture and decorative arts that are for sale cannot be exported.)

But most tourists come because they know one of the great truths of the decade: Madrid is Europe's last great old city.

When we wander around Madrid these days we do so with worries that what we have now will change—that the globalization of the world and the unification of Europe will mean the addition of more bland American-style malls, where shops and people try to look alike, more sophistication and less charm. Today Madrid has a fabulous, sublime blend of Old World charm and New World chutzpah—we just hope that it lasts!

So welcome to Madrid, where you can buy shoes and then more shoes and then a few handbags; where you can see the best of European fashions and sample the bright new Spanish designers; where the locals look to traditional British good-sense looks as their uniforms but still wear polka-dot *sevillana* dresses when they dance.

Getting There

Getting to Madrid is extremely easy. Almost every international carrier flies here—because when you're hot, you're hot—and every carrier wants to go where the crowd is going. Don't overlook the Madrid Amigo program (page 11), in which you get a free stopover in Madrid if you are traveling elsewhere.

You may also connect to Madrid via train from all over Europe; there is a daily train to and from Paris.

Getting Around

Madrid is a pretty big city, but it has a rather good Metro system. Metro cars are clean and bright, and although the stations themselves will win no awards for design, they aren't as dirty and depressing as other subway stations. You may buy a ticket to ride as needed (about 60¢ per journey) or get a ten-ride pass, which you insert in the box and retrieve. Each use is electronically tallied and totaled so that the ticket is rejected after the tenth use. You may pass the ticket back and forth to family members in order to share. We noticed we weren't the only ones doing this.

There are city buses, but you must take some time to learn the routes, since a bus map is not easy to come by. (You can buy one at a newsstand, however.) There are big central multistop areas (like the one at Plaza Puerta de Sol) where the various stops are plainly marked. Stand in line accordingly; buses usually come every ten minutes. You'll need exact change (slightly under 100 *pesetas*.) If your hotel is on the Paseo de la Castellana, you'll have fun riding the bus and enjoying the sprawl of Madrid's wide boulevards from a window seat.

If you're not adventurous enough to try the bus, there's always a taxi. Taxis are basically cheap, although every now and then someone will try to cheat you. Don't be afraid to argue. For some reason we cannot figure out, the taxi fare from Barajas (the international airport) into Madrid is one price and the fare from Madrid to Barajas is usually half that! There is a *tarifa* (about $1.00 more) for taxi fare at night.

While you may want to rent a car to drive around Spain, you certainly don't want to drive in Madrid. You probably don't even want to drive to Toledo or even to the outskirts of Madrid (take the train).

About Addresses

n some cases, a few stores will have the same address—this is because they are storefronts located in the same giant building, a building that may even take up a whole block.

Madrid

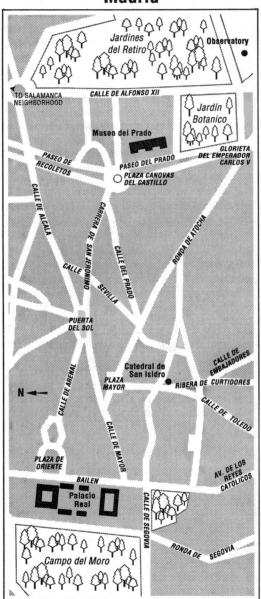

Watch for addresses with the abbreviation "esq." in them; this stands for *esquina,* which means corner. The address is where the two streets meet.

Also watch for zip codes on business cards as a tipoff to location. Buy a big, good city map (we use the Almax edition; $5 at Bob's, see page 104) that is marked with postal codes. You'll soon see how the shopping areas break down and how to combine your own tours to get around town efficiently. The big letters in soft gray type are the zip codes; the code for the Salamanca shopping area is 1, so look for that one in order to orient yourself.

While many streets in Madrid are called either *Calle* (street) or *Avenida* (avenue), it is very unusual for either of these two words to be listed in an address. Addresses for locations in Madrid merely state the name of the street itself and then the number on the street. For example: Goya 72. Such an address would not usually be written as Calle de Goya 72, and certainly never 72 Goya Street.

Finally, if a store is inside a mall or a building, it is so indicated with an additional address written with the word *local* ("Mercado de Puerto de Toledo, local 12"). All shops in the Puerto de Toledo have the location number in their ads or on their cards.

Booking Madrid/I

The Ayuntamiento de Madrid publishes a series of guides to the city that are free and fabulous. And they are being translated into English, to make them even better. There is a pamphlet called *Madrid Ciudad, Viva de Compras* (Life of Shopping) that breaks the city down into neighborhoods and lists shops in many categories. They don't editorialize about the merits of the shops, but the book is lovely to look at and handy to use; it's also purse-size. It would probably take two months of shopping six days a week to see every store in it. Ask for this freebie when you stop by the city tourist office, or at the Plaza Mayor.

Madrid Concept is very different, but also nice; it's a glossy magazine ($4.50) similar to *Vogue* (available on newsstands), with advertising and information about food, restaurants, events, and fashion. It's very upscale and includes editorial ratings, so that even if you can't read Spanish, you can get a sense of the shop by studying the numbers in their listings.

It's handy to have a map, not only of the city, but of the Metro. ECI provides the whole thing, for free, at their stores, and you can probably get one from your hotel's concierge desk. Tourist offices will also hand out this map, as well as their map. The tourist office map (Plano Monumental) is a better map, but we find the ECI map is more handy. Don't leave home without it.

Booking Madrid/2

We have personally tested our Madrid hotels, which were chosen for the right combination of luxury and convenience to shopping and: business. Hotels are rated as expensive: over $150 a night; moderate: $101–$149 a night; and inexpensive: $100 a night and less. Breakfast may or may not be included in your room rate (always ask the hotel or your travel agent). IVA taxes are usually added to the price of the room when you check out, but are sometimes included in the price quoted you, especially on tours and package groups. Ask, as your hotel room may be 12% more than you thought it would be.

VILLA MAGNA HOTEL: If you want a five-star deluxe hotel that is not only luxurious but also located right smack in the most perfect shopping area in town, you want the Villa Magna, which is a Leading Hotel of the World and has its back door leading directly into a local department store. Located in the middle of the Castellana, in the heart of the Salamanca shopping district, the only thing wrong with this hotel is that it's not particularly convenient to a Metro stop. Taxi everywhere with ease, or walk. It's close to the Prado, but you might be too tired to prowl after arriving. Expensive. Local phone: 261-4900.

VILLA MAGNA HOTEL, Paseo de la Castellana 22 (Metro: Serrano)

▼

MIGUEL ÁNGEL: This is another modern and swank five-star hotel on the top edge of the Salamanca shopping neighborhood and more convenient to the new and growing business section of Madrid and the Zona Norte. It's also located only a block from a Metro stop (Rubén Dario). The hotel faces on the Castellana, but its address is that of the side street on the corner. Expensive. Local phone: 442-8199.

MIGUEL ÁNGEL, Miguel Ángel 28–31 (Metro: Rubén Dario)

▼

HOTELES MELÍA: There are two Melía hotels in Madrid, at different ends of town. The Melía Madrid is on Calle de la Princesa right off the Gran Vía and in the heart of the downtown business area. The Melía Castilla is in the Zona Norte, the northern part of town up the Paseo de la Castellana and not far from the convention center. The Melía Castilla has a casino and a big-time nightclub show that is extremely popular with tours. Melía clients are usually businesspeople or Europeans who know the chain; Melía is still making its name in the U.S. Both Madrid hotels are five-star properties that are expensive but not as high as the Ritz. For U.S. reservations call (800) 33-MELIA.

MELÍA MADRID, Princesa 27 (Metro: Argüelles; local phone: 241-82-00)
MELÍA CASTILLA, Capitán Haya 43 (Metro: Castilla; local phone: 270-84-00)

Snack and Shop

LHARDY: Lhardy is a mere block (OK, a long block, maybe two blocks) from the Prado, right at the edge of the Puerta del Sol, so it's on your way to everything. Even if you aren't a major shopper, you'll find yourself headed this way. Lhardy was established in 1839 and it is basically a restaurant and take-out deli, although they hardly ever use the word *deli* in Spain. You'll know it from its storefront, which has remained unchanged since opening; inside you can buy carry-out foods and make a picnic, which, considering the price of eating out in Madrid, is an excellent idea. In the back, where it's so dark you didn't know there was anything, is the entrance to the restaurant. Lunch is served after 1 P.M. Prices are moderate to expensive. You probably don't need a reservation for an early lunch, but you will for a late (Spanish-style) lunch or for dinner; call 521-3385. The Metro station is Sol; this is the downtown area called Centro.

LHARDY, Carrera de San Jerónimo 8 (Metro: Sol)

PALACIO DEL JAMÓN: If you want junk food American-style, there is a McDonald's in the Puerta del Sol area. We prefer the local version of fast food—this is a place for inexpensive meals that usually include the famous local Serrano ham. You may eat at the counter downstairs, or at a table upstairs where there is waiter service. You can get a plate of sliced ham and cheese for about $8, which happens to be a steal in Madrid. A good location in Centro, one block from ECI and two blocks from Plaza Mayor. They also serve the traditional Spanish breakfast of *churros* and hot chocolate. You can walk the three blocks to the Prado from here or explore Centro easily. Clean bathrooms, downstairs.

PALACIO DEL JAMÓN, Arenal 6 (Metro: Sol)

▼

POSADA DE LA VILLA: This is a taverna in the heart of the old city that dates back to 1642; it looks to us like it has not changed a bit. Its wooden double doors, stucco walls, and plank tables would pretty much fit the bill as a movie set. They serve basic regional fare and grilled meats for both lunch and dinner. The prices are moderate. The perfect Sunday lunch after the Rastro (walking distance); make reservations if you don't go at 1 P.M. Unfortunately, all the tourists in the world know about this place, so there can be a crowd. Local phone: 266-1860.

POSADA DE LA VILLA, Cava Baja 9 (Metro: La Latina)

Sunday Shopping

Sunday shopping is still developing in Madrid. There has always been the Rastro, of course, and there are a few bookstores that are opening up for browsing after brunch—which is becoming the thing to do. **BOB'S** and **VIP'S,** actually owned by the same company, are two cafeteria–cum–one-stop shops that are open on Sunday and late at night, and they're currently where everyone ends up to hang out. Find one or the other (sometimes both) in every major neighborhood. Count on these stores for inexpensive meals, soft drinks, snack supplies, books, records, tapes, videos, and some gift items. There's always a big selection of magazines from around the world and all the maps and tourist guides you'll need. There are also some items for kids. It's kind of a fancy European 7-Eleven.

Best Buys of Madrid

The shopping in Madrid is the best there is in Spain, and is equal to the shopping in any major European capital. You've got your choice of several shopping neighborhoods (see page 108) where all you have to do is walk the streets to experience adventure and good buys. You've got big department stores; the funky old part of town; the "real people" streets full of local stores; and the big-name designer district. It's all here.

There's only one trick. The European designer clothes are not particularly cheaper in Madrid than they are at home—so you'd better know your stuff. Within the same store you can find one item that's less expensive than in the U.S. and another that's equal in price. Go figure.

The best buys in Madrid, as you were expecting, are in shoes and leathergoods. This city is also great for antiques shops (and junk stores) and for gourmet-food stores. Ceramics buffs can find what they want but won't feel fulfilled—but then, Toledo is just a day trip away.

Loading Up on Lladró

While the department stores do sell Lladró, it is the TTs that have a bigger selection and that may negotiate on prices. Some stores sell both Nao and Lladró in the same space; some separate the two. In a few cases, a less than scrupulous retailer will have a sign that says "Lladró" but the merchandise displayed will be Nao—he may tell you they are the same thing, which is technically correct, but . . . (See page 38.)

A few figurines are sold on the airplanes; there is not a big selection of Lladró at the airport or at the duty-free. Most hotel gift shops also sell Lladró. It is possible at some of these shops (or at your hotel) to get a free brochure from Lladró that is like a catalogue, with color pictures of many models. This is not like the book that retailers have that shows the whole line, but it does show pictures of the more popular items so you can pick what you want and then hunt it down. It took us visits to over two dozen shops to find the particular model that we wanted, since stock varies from shop to shop. Unless you hit a sale or promotion or buy a lot and get someone to offer you a special price, prices will be the same throughout town.

OBJETOS DE ARTE TOLEDANO: This store is also listed on page 107 as a TT. It is right across from the Prado and offers a wide selection of Nao figurines. Next door to this store is a shop marked "Lladró" that sells only Lladró. There is a large selection of all sizes and shapes and price ranges. Sometimes the Lladró part of the store is dark and locked; ask the sales help at the TT part of the store to open up for you. Lladró leathergoods are also sold.

OBJETOS DE ARTE TOLEDANO, Paseo del Prado 10 (Metro: Sevilla)

▼

LASARTE: This shop just sells porcelains and fine glass, much of it from France and Italy. There is a lot of Lladró in the window, and the downstairs salon is almost all Lladró. The salesclerks speak English and will calculate prices in both currencies for you. They're helpful without being too pushy. They'll also ship to the U.S.

LASARTE, Gran Vía 44 (Metro: Gran Vía)

▼

REGALOS AR: This very crowded china shop has some Lladró as well as many other brands from around the world. There's so much crammed in here that it's hard to concentrate, but you might find a style you've been looking for.

REGALOS AR, Gran Vía 46 (Metro: Gran Vía)

Madrid's TTs

Tourist traps in Madrid are a little different from those in other areas of Spain, and aren't nearly as much fun. There is only one excellent all-purpose TT: Objetos de Arte Toledano. Other than that, you'll find Madrid's TTs break down into two basic categories: North African TTs, which sell a little of everything that the souks have to offer—at prices much higher than those found in Morocco—and hodgepodge TTs, most of which are crammed around the Plaza Mayor at the far end, which are tiny and poor and don't have the room or the stock to impress themselves, let alone visiting Americans who have seen it all.

Just about any TT (except the one near the Prado) will make up *posteles* for you—the bull-fight and flamenco posters we love to buy as gifts. Quality, price, and selection vary from store to store, so shop around a bit before you commit.

Street vendors do a pretty good business in souvenirs, especially posters. The atmosphere around the street vendors adds to the pleasure of your purchase. You may enjoy your souvenir all the more if you bought it at 10 P.M. while the press of the crowd was at its height and throngs around you were dancing on the curb. Seek out the tiny streets behind the Plaza Mayor—for the street vendors and the party.

OBJETOS DE ARTE TOLEDANO: For reasons we cannot fathom, Madrid does not have a lot of TTs. Perhaps it is because this one is so good that no others could compete. The store owns a Lladró gallery (next door at No. 12), and sells Nao inside its big salon. Upstairs there's a wide selection of regional pottery, with dishes from just about everywhere. There's even some armor upstairs. The main salon, in back on the street level, is crammed with souvenirs. Against the back wall is the T-shirt bar, with a little of everything, including Barcelona '92 shirts for the Olympics. This store really has everything, and prices are pretty good, even on the Lladró. Directly across from the Prado. They accept all credit cards.

OBJETOS DE ARTE TOLEDANO, Paseo del Prado 10 (Metro: Sevilla)

▼

EL ESCUDO DE TOLEDO: Almost next door to Objetos de Arte Toledano, this is not a great TT and may not interest you at all. But they do have the best tourist swords in Spain.

EL ESCUDO DE TOLEDO, Plaza de Cánovas 4 (Metro: Sevilla)

Madrid's Shopping Neighborhoods

Madrid is a sprawling city, but the shopping neighborhoods are easy to get to by public transportation (take the Metro). The European-flavored streets provide the perfect ambience for strolling. While there is a Benetton on every corner—just like at home—there are also a lot of stores and boutiques that are not international chains or big names and that offer a breath of fresh shopping air.

Spanish neighborhoods are called *barrios*. This word does not mean ghetto or Spanish Harlem, as some jaded travelers may think. It is particularly important to remember when talking about Barrio de Salamanca, since there is a city of Salamanca, not too far from Madrid.

Barrio de Salamanca

The fanciest neighborhood in Madrid, the one that most reminds us of Paris, is Barrio de Salamanca, where you'll find all the big-name designer shops, a branch of each Spanish department store, and all the expensive, high-quality merchandise you've ever wanted to see. This neighborhood is too large to handle with ease, so study a map to come up with a plan of attack to see everything you want to—or plan to have two days to conquer it. Yes, you can go out, wander the main drag (Calle Serrano), and weave in and out of the streets that cross it (Hermosilla and Ayala are our favorites), but there're miles of stylish shopping in this area before the neighborhood veers off to become the Alcalá neighborhood (where you'll find mostly furniture, important antiques, and interior design showrooms) and the Goya neighborhood (where locals shop). Natives lump these three areas generally into Salamanca. Add to that the fact that Calle Claudio Coello runs parallel to Calle Serrano and is jammed with even more stores, and you begin to see the problem—you can't walk up and down Serrano and Coello at the same time!

Since this is the part of Madrid you'll be shopping the most, we have done a few things to help you out:

▼ There's a Salamanca tour on page 173 that will conveniently get you through the best of it.

▼ There's a list of the Continental Big-Name designers with their shop addresses on page 128—we have not described these shops in this list. If you don't already know what's in a Louis Vuitton shop already, you won't be reading the list to begin with.

▼ There's a section with a lot of listings in the Salamanca area for the person who wants a lot of detail (see page 123) and the complete rundown of the local talent.

Salamanca Neighborhood

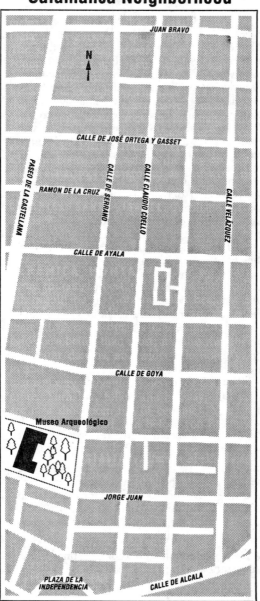

▼ For the person who just wants to wander, we suggest you study the map and know which are the main streets to hit. Don't miss Serrano, which everyone knows is the main drag, or our favorite street, Claudio Coello (parallel to Serrano), for fun, funky stuff. Velázquez has some don't-miss stores, so don't overlook this street (parallel to Serrano, higher up than Coello). The side streets all offer something: Ayala, Ortega y Gasset, and Hermosilla have the bigger names in designer boutiques.

If you are only planning to shop in Madrid for one day or part of one day, and you are into fancy shopping styles, head straight to Barrio de Salamanca for cosmopolitan chic. It's very hard to pinpoint what we consider the highlights of the neighborhood, since we like just about everything here. What follows is a list of the stores we always visit:

ARTESPAÑA: Although there are a few branches of Artespaña in Madrid (including one across the street from the Palace Hotel), the very best one is on Hermosilla. Artespaña, as you may already know, is a home-furnishings business set up to represent various craftspeople from different regions in Spain. It is the shopper's only opportunity to buy from a range of regions in one fell swoop and to get quality merchandise at the same time. The Hermosilla shop looks more like a showroom in Los Angeles than a government-sponsored handicrafts store: It's large and spacious, and various room sets are set up so you can imagine them reassembled in your home. There're also gift items and small decorative art objects that will fit into your suitcase. Prices are top-of-the-line, but the selection and quality are superior.

ARTESPAÑA, Hermosilla 14 (Metro: Serrano)

▼

B. D. MADRID: There is a B. D. in Barcelona, but if you're not planning on visiting Barcelona, by all means stop by. B. D. is certainly famous enough (*The New York Times* has written them up). This furniture resource for the Spanish version of Memphis Milano makes reproductions of famous pieces of furniture (some by Gaudí) and markets itself mostly through designers. It does, however, have showrooms open to the public. There are two levels of expensive furniture to gawk at.

B. D. MADRID, Villanueva 5 (Metro: Serrano)

▼

SYBILLA: We've discussed Sybilla at length in our section on Spanish designers (see page 125), and since she is Spain's most exciting designer, we remind you that her shop is in Barrio de Salamanca, and, although it is hard to find, it should not be missed. (It's off that alley to your right if Serrano is to your back.) Definitely worth the hunt.

SYBILLA, Jorge Juan 12 (Metro: Serrano)

▼

ZARA: Zara is one of Spain's top chain stores for hot fashions at low prices; there is a Zara shop just about everywhere you look—anywhere in Spain and in no time throughout Europe and the U.S. (The New York store is across the street from Bloomingdale's.) Each branch of the store has slightly different architecture; we recommend this—our favorite branch—because it's cleaner, neater, and easier to shop than the one at Sol, which is five stories of narrow space. The store sells the look of the moment at really low prices; lots of it is forgettable, but a fair percentage of it is fabulous. Wool skirts at $44 cannot be ignored.

ZARA, Velázquez 45 (Metro: Serrano)

Almirante

You know that we're brutally honest. Well, we're about to tell you about Almirante. We like Almirante; we think you'll like Almirante. But it is a neighborhood that is still growing and changing and taking shape. Don't expect too much and you'll have a great time. If you think you're going to be knocked out, you will only be disappointed.

The younger Spanish designers have found a home on Almirante, across the busy Plaza de Colón from the Salamanca designer district, and not too far north from the Prado (an easy walk). Here, as they say, anything goes. Shops are experimental, fun, strange, wonderful, and anything but boring. Because this area is changing so rapidly, we won't guarantee that any of today's stores will still be there when you drop in, but there's no question that the city has designated this as the hot new neighborhood for fun and fashion.

Although there are many small streets in this little neighborhood area, the main action is on Almirante. This too could change. We suggest that you start at the bottom, near Paseo de Recoletos, and walk up the street until it dead-ends into Calle Barquillo and changes its name. Along the way you will find some of our fascinating finds:

PEDRO MORAGO: One of the up-and-coming Spanish fashion stars, Pedro Morago has shops here and in Barcelona. His look is spare, Japanese, flowing, and European chic. The shop is all marble and glass, with the clothing (men only) displayed like pieces of art.

PEDRO MORAGO, Almirante 20 (Metro: Colón)

▼

LA TIERRA: Although La Tierra is a decorator shop, it fits in perfectly with the ambience of the other designer boutiques on Almirante. The store specializes in earthenware urns, Roman and Greek busts, ceramic pitchers and plates, antique fabrics, and wall tiles. It is a potpourri of unusual items. You are overwhelmed by the sheer number of urns and their interesting forms and sizes. At some point, you can focus on everything else. We know exactly where to put everything in this store; we just don't have the deed to the museum yet.

LA TIERRA, Almirante 28 (Metro: Colón)

▼

JESUS DEL POZO: After Pozo did a collection of crystal-pleated clothes, not unlike the styles designed by America's Mary McFadden, he became known locally as the wrinkle man. He continues to design in stressed and wrinkled silks that are fluid, easy to wear and move in, and look divine on many figure types.

JESUS DEL POZO, Almirante 28 (Metro: Colón)

▼

ARARAT: One of the Ararat shops is located in a building at Almirante 11. The old interior of the town house has been whitewashed and decorated in marble, with wall sconces and Roman statues artfully placed in hallways and stairs. The clothing here is mostly imports from Marithe & François Girbaud, Gaultier, and other European designers. There is children's clothing as well, although the emphasis is on the early-twenties crowd. The larger Ararat shop across the street at No. 10 is just plain fun. The clothing is creative, artistic, and sometimes outrageous. You can walk out of here wearing leather trimmed in fringe or sequins.

We feel too old to even walk in, much less wear the clothes.

A R A R A T, Almirante 10 and 11 (Metro: Colón)

▼

FRANCISCO VALENTE: The most couture version of men's fashions in the neighborhood is at the very end of the street, where Francisco Valente takes himself very seriously. His shop is drop-dead spectacular in its simplicity of design. The blond-wood-and-black-metal interior provides a serene background for his beautifully tailored, simple designs in silks and wools. Women's clothing is on the main floor, men's downstairs.

FRANCISCO VALENTE, Almirante 1 (Metro: Colón)

▼

FRANCIS MONTESINOS: Around the corner from Almirante is the shop of a graphics designer, Francis Montesinos. Montesinos's art is on the walls and on the T-shirts he designs and sells. If you are looking for a Barcelona '92 shirt that is not the usual tourist fare, try here.

FRANCIS MONTESINOS, Argensola 8 (Metro: Colón)

Sol

We're going to be a little daring here and call Sol—the area around the Plaza del Sol—a neighborhood unto itself. Sol is the gateway to Old Madrid (page 118), it's true, but Sol has its own soul. The hustling and bustling central square, where taxis waltz and buses two-step and hordes of passersby keep on passing by, is very different in feel from Old Madrid. As a major retail center of the city, it has plenty of new stores, chain stores, old stores, and tricks of its own. Leading away from the plaza, in the opposite direction from the Plaza Mayor and away from Old Madrid, you have a pedestrian street, Calle Preciados, that leads to the Gran Vía. This is a major shopping street for chain stores, and is also home to a branch of ECI and a branch of GP, one block away.

GIL, SUCESOR DE ANTOLIN QUEVEDO: Do you love the name or what? This happens to be a common practice, and you will see it in many shop names. Now then: a few secrets about Gil. The old guy gave up trying to sell the good stuff and has a rather average to not-so-great TT, selling mostly shawls and mantillas. Check out the challis shawls and ethnic, regional garb. If it doesn't cost several hundred dollars, you've got the tourist wares. Do your best to ignore the furs.

GIL, SUCESOR DE ANTOLIN QUEVEDO, Carrera de San Jerónimo 2 (Metro: Sol)

▼

MATY: Maty is the leading chachacha shop in Madrid, where you buy *sevillana* dresses for *ferria* and dress-up (or for Halloween, if you are a tourist). The store has a double storefront but only one door, so you first walk into the dance and exercise portion, which is not terribly exciting. You must go through the open wall at the back counter to pass into the visual treat that is Maty. The dresses practically dance off the racks, their gigantic circular skirts and petticoats pushing against each other and competing to get your attention. Polka dots are the most popular, but there are solids (with contrasting trims) and some florals. There are also some children's costumes here, especially in winter when it is popular for locals to dress up for Carnival. Tourist stores sell a small selection of these things, but Maty is an acknowledged specialist and probably has the best selection in town. Prices are competitive to low, especially when compared to prices in Sevilla. You can get a grown-up *sevillana* dress beginning at $200; really good ones cost about $400. And that's without all the accessories—which Maty also sells.

Now for the bad news: At Maty we were once incorrectly informed that what we knew was a polyester shawl was made of 100% silk.

Credit cards accepted at this shop right behind ECI. There are branch stores for locals at Hileras 7 and Maestro Victoria 2.

MATY, Plaza del Comandante las Morenas 5 (Metro: Sol)

▼

CORTEFIEL: This is a Spanish chain selling moderately priced fashion to working men and women—stores are often divided into one for men and one for women; they may adjoin or be near to each other. In some cases the merchandise is together in the same store. Cortefiel's men's shop is on the plaza; the women's store is on Calle Preciados. Men may find mass-produced YSL here that's made in Spain, but we don't think this is what you came to Spain to see.

CORTEFIEL
Plaza del Sol 3 (men's) (Metro: Sol)
Preciados 13 (women's) (Metro: Callao)

▼

ZARA: Zara is one of the most popular chain stores in Spain, selling hip fashion looks for teens and young women at very low prices. The quality of some of the clothing would not be acceptable to an American teen, but a lot of this stuff is for one-season wearing anyway.

There's also some men's clothing; don't forget to go upstairs for the rest of the selection. They do not close for siesta!

ZARA, Preciados 20 (Metro: Callao)

▼

CASA DE DIEGO: Whatever it takes to make a good fan must also be required in a good umbrella, because all over Spain the old fan shops also sell umbrellas—and sometimes only these two items are stocked. Casa de Diego is such a store. The good stuff is put away. Ask to see it.

CASA DE DIEGO, Plaza del Sol 12 (Metro: Sol)

▼

UNIÓN MUSICAL ESPAÑOLA: So maybe you aren't looking for a piano while you're in town. We still insist you poke your head in here and gawk. This is what retailing used to be all about. Who knows what this store used to be—quite possibly a private home. The architectural details are so breathtaking (is that an organ set into the wall?) and the woodwork so special that we want to share it with you.

UNIÓN MUSICAL ESPAÑOLA, Carrera de San Jerónimo 26 (Metro: Sol)

Old Madrid

OK, so we know all about the death of Franco and the birth of the new Madrid. We hope you see dancing in the streets, too. But we also hope you see the Old Madrid and shop the old parts of the city, which are more special than a dream. Old Madrid alone is worth the price of your ticket to Spain; everything else is just a bonus.

Locals may call it Centro, or downtown, but it is more than that—the area stretching around the Puerta del Sol and the Plaza Mayor is a maze of little streets and old stores that look as though they haven't changed in a hundred years. We're all for the new Madrid and the unification of Europe and modern man, but this is the soul of Spain, and this is why you come to Madrid.

Come here to wander. Yes, some addresses will be helpful, and we'll give you listings in other parts of this book. But for now, just put on those Reeboks, tuck the map away, and get yourself lost and found as you discover your own special finds. Start at the Sol Metro, explore the Plaza del Sol (and the statue of the bear, which is very famous), and then work your way back into the Plaza Mayor, through the Plaza Mayor and all the way south to the Rastro, if you want. Back here you'll find a ton of tavernas for *tapas* and dinner; you'll see the throngs at night, both tourists and locals; and you'll find street vendors and artists.

Every time we venture into the heart of the Old Madrid, we get lost. We'd like to give you a path to follow, but frankly—we can't. We rarely go the same way. We do have one must-see, however: Calle Cava Baja. Go ahead, cheat, find it on your map and use it as a guiding beacon.

Gran Vía

The Gran Vía is the main street of the newer Madrid, although you don't hear much about it because it's not going anywhere. . . . It ain't the New Madrid and it ain't the Old Madrid. It's middle earth.

Jutting off from the Castellana at an angle, the Gran Vía is slowly turning seedy. It reminds us of the downtown area of an American city that has lost its population to the suburbs. Ah, the glory that is gone.

Yet there, among the discarded McDonald's wrappers and the blinking neon, are some of Madrid's best addresses, like **LOEWE** and **FABERGÉ**. There are also scads of TTs here, some of them good for Lladró collectors. (See page 105.)

Although the area is less than scenic, and there is better shopping elsewhere, don't simply ignore it. One handy thing to remember is that many airlines have their offices on the Gran Vía. There is also a palatial McDonald's here. . . . Really, it looks like a palace, with marble floors and crystal chandeliers.

Princesa

The area we call Princesa, because it is around the main shopping area on the Calle de la Princesa, is also called Universidad by some people, mostly those who are students attending the university in this part of town. Because of the number of young people around here, there's a lot of life to the shopping district (especially on Saturdays), and stores specialize in young, kicky clothes or jeans. Calle de la Princesa is actually an extension of the Gran Vía, and you can walk the length of it if you want, although traffic can jam up and it can be congested and busy in the center. Use the Metro for quick and easy access.

Zona Norte

The Zona Norte is the part of Madrid where the newer development is going on, and where the yuppies live. It's actually anything north of the Nuevos Ministerios Metro station, huddled around the convention center. Tourists who are staying in one of the convention hotels explore this area automatically, but many do not venture forth.

We're suckers for "real people" neighborhoods, especially when they are upscale enough for us to imagine living in them. The shopping neighborhood on the Calle Orense, around the convention center and all the way to the ECI at Nuevos Ministerios, is only a few blocks deep and is comfortable and attractive; it gives you a much better feel for the real Madrid than the upscale Barrio de Salamanca, where everything costs more. On the Calle Orense itself there are branches of some famous stores such as **RODIER DE ESPAÑA** and **LURUEÑA.** There's a rather boring *multicentro,* several fast-food eateries, and a wonderful, modern supermarket called **EXPRESSO** (No. 25) with automated doors. There is also the pathway to the Moda Shopping center, an indoor mall we describe on page 133. You can also cross the plaza from Moda Shopping and go into the giant ECI, so big it is divided into restaurant, supermarket, home departments, and car park.

The Zona Norte area actually stretches up to the Plaza Castilla, but there isn't that much shopping at the top end, except for the Tetuán flea market on weekends.

Puerta de Toledo

We call this a neighborhood; others may call it a happening. Locals say this is part of Centro. While the city gate called the Puerta de Toledo has been here for some time now, what we really love about Puerta de Toledo is the relatively new shopping center (called the Mercado del Puerta de Toledo) that opened in 1989 right over the Puerta de Toledo Metro station. This is an American-style mall of the nouveau neo-Deco style, with layers of floors, cutouts, ramps, circles of shops, and all sorts of architectural contortions that make it a little inconvenient to shop but a pleasure to view. What's most exciting about the space is the mix of stores: There's not one Benetton here, and we don't expect The Gap to open. There are a few branch stores of Madrid big names like **SESEÑA,** there are a lot of teeny designer shops, and then there are tons of very fancy hoity-toity antiques stores. There are a couple of cafés as well. If you're only in Madrid for a day, this is a good place to check out for one-stop shopping.

Note: The space stays open during siesta hours, while 97% of the stores are closed. Hours: Tuesday through Saturday, 11:30 A.M.–8 P.M.; Sunday and holidays, 11:30 A.M.–3 P.M. Closed Monday. These are the building hours, not the store hours! Most stores are closed during siesta! If you are pushed, however, this is a good time to tour and see what it's like. Otherwise, this might be the only shopping experience you'll need in Madrid. Don't miss:

SESEÑA: You should actually visit the original Seseña, which is a wonderful old-fashioned store (Cruz 23). Although the shop is not large, it is bigger than this atelier in the mall. This is the store that has been making traditional Spanish capes for a hundred years. The king and queen wear them; so does everyone else. Capes come in solids, in two tones, with contrasting trim and with velvet lining. They will bring out the Napoleon in you.

SESEÑA, Mercado del Puerta de Toledo (Metro: Puerto de Toledo)

▼

SARA NAVARRO: Shoes of suede and leather and some clothes. It looks to us like this store is hoping to give both Loewe and Maud Frizon a run for their money. Young, important, expensive.

SARA NAVARRO, Mercado del Puerta de Toledo (Metro: Puerto de Toledo)

▼

CRISTINA DE J'OSH: Fabulous, formal, expensive, extravagant white linens and Victorian underclothes collections. Also antique dolls of the same period.

CRISTINA DE J'OSH, Mercado del Puerta de Toledo (Metro: Puerto de Toledo)

▼

ARCADIA: This is one of the few stores that stays open during siesta, and it has very nice things representing a cross section of Spanish artisans.

ARCADIA, Mercado del Puerta de Toledo (Metro: Puerto de Toledo)

Spanish Big Names

ADOLFO DOMINGUEZ: International fashion finally has another Adolfo. The American Adolfo is Cuban; this Adolfo is from Madrid, but now has shops in every major Spanish city and in London, and will probably expand to all over the world. He became hot in the American market when someone realized he was responsible for Don Johnson's wardrobe in the heyday of *Miami Vice*. Dominguez designs a men's and a women's line. Sometimes they are shown together in the same shop; sometimes there are different stores for each sex. The clothes are usually made of natural fibers and are architectural without being constricting. Prices range from moderate ($100) to more pricey ($600 for a suit) but not that expensive when compared to Armani.

ADOLFO DOMINGUEZ
Serrano 98–96 (Metro: Serrano)
Ayala 24 (Metro: Serrano)

▼

ALFREDO CARAL: Alfredo Caral is attempting to challenge Valentino. His shop, located on Serrano, just below Goya, is rich in detail while giving the impression of stylish simplicity. Caral's clothing is very similar to Valentino's. Suits are tailored to perfection and designed in rich fabrics that hang softly on the body. There are tucks and inside buttons on all of the suits. Details that you would not normally see even on a well-tailored piece of clothing are present in Caral's. It is the extras that make the difference. Caral carries a complete line of handbags, sweaters, and shirts, and jewelry as well. We think that his clothing is a good investment. Major credit cards accepted.

ALFREDO CARAL, Serrano 34 (Metro: Serrano)

▼

ALVAREZ GÓMEZ: Alvarez Gómez has such a strong reputation among locals for his old-fashioned perfumes that you tend to think the stores will be the Spanish version of Caswell-Massey. Instead they look like pharmacy-style perfume shops and sell all the top brands from the big names of Europe. You have to look carefully, or ask, for the part of the store devoted to the one-hundred-year-old fragrances the firm still makes and packages and sells for less than $10 per spray bottle. We bought the bestseller, "Aqua de Colonia Concentrada," which actually says what it is without naming the product—perhaps it has no name. It has a yellow label and a yellow plastic top and smells very green and fresh and citrusy—it is used by men and by women—and makes a great gift to take home because of the fame of the local maker.

There are three branch stores; each is in a convenient shopping neighborhood.

ALVAREZ GÓMEZ
Sevilla 2 (Metro: Sevilla)
Serrano 14 (Metro: Serrano)
Paseo de la Castellana 111 (Metro: Nuevos Ministerios)

FRANCIS MONTESINOS: A way-out and exciting young designer from Valencia who displays a wide variety of tricks, all designed to impress those who need to be wearing the latest looks and most inventive notions.

FRANCIS MONTESINOS, Argensola 8 (Metro: Colón)

▼

TERESA RAMALLAL: Elegant fashion in a Japanese-influenced vein. It reminds us of Gaultier, only more wearable. One of Spain's most talked-about avant-garde designers, she's known for her mix of simple, natural fibers with metallic fabrics and shoes.

TERESA RAMALLAL, Almirante 5 (Metro: Colón)

▼

LOEWE: Loewe, Loewe, Loewe, that's all you ever hear in Spain. See page 39 for the details. They publish their own house brochure, with a foldout map of each city in Spain where they have a shop (marked on the map) and all the information about getting your VAT refund. The brochure is in English and Japanese. The Gran Vía shop does not close for lunch.

LOEWE
Gran Vía 8 (Metro: Callao)
Palace Hotel, Plaza de la Cortés 7 (Metro: Sevilla)
Serrano 26 (Metro: Serrano)
Serrano 34 (Metro: Serrano)

SYBILLA: If you are in the fashion business, or are one of those women who dresses on the cutting edge, you have already heard of Sybilla, who seems to be the hottest news in Madrid since Lanvin took on Castillo. Currently sold in the U.S. in Bergdorf's, Bloomie's, Barneys, Charivari, and a handful of specialty stores in other cities outside New York, Sybilla is considered the girl wonder of Spanish design. She began her fashion life in the cutting room at YSL in Paris, and now makes her own inventive clothes known for their lavish quality.

There are a few more concrete details you should know about Sybilla before you head off for the must-see shop: Even though your teacher taught you that two *l*s equal a *y* sound in Spanish, in this particular case the name Sybilla is based on the original Greek name, and therefore the *l*s are sounded. If you go around saying, in perfect Spanish, "Where is Sibiya's shop?" you will have a hard time finding it.

And it's not easy finding it in the first place, because, despite its address, the store is not on Jorge Juan at number 12 as you might think. It is down a little unmarked alley! It's very safe, very cute little alley, more like a courtyard, but you won't see a storefront on Calle Jorge Juan that says "Sybilla" on it.

Once you find it, Sybilla is the place to go. The store feels like a Santa Fe retreat; the clothes, bags, gloves, and goodies are gorgeous. Prices are not nearly as high as the Ungaro and YSL crowd. You can buy something fabulous in the $200–$500 range.

SYBILLA, Jorge Juan 12 (Metro: Serrano)

▼

MANUEL PIÑA: One of the first Spanish designers to get international recognition, Piña was poised on the brink of fame long before Sybilla came along. The balding man with the sometimes beard and the big grin has often used regional Spanish dress for his inspiration, although there is nothing folksy about his high-fashion looks.

MANUEL PIÑA, Valenzuela 9 (Metro: Serrano)

ROBERTO VERINNO: Although Roberto Verinno's ads in *Vogue* show rather exotic runway clothes, the ones on display in his boutiques in ECI stores all over Spain are very average working-woman clothes, with the emphasis on a solid suit. These clothes are so American they may not seem different enough to a tourist.

ROBERTO VERINNO, El Corte Inglés department stores

▼

AGATHA RUIZ DE LA PRADA: A woman with a sense of humor who is not afraid of color and bold design, Ruiz makes shoes and fun clothes that are sold in SoHo in New York or in her own shop in the Puerta de Toledo. The shoe line is made (and sold) by Camper, a shoe chain with stores everywhere.

AGATHA RUIZ DE LA PRADA, Mercado del Puerta de Toledo (Metro: Puerta de Toledo)

▼

ELENA BENARROCH: A fur designer who is making it big in the U.S., Elena has her own shop on Madison Avenue in New York, where she does the young furry look—not that different from Fendi, with a more upscale edge.

ELENA BENARROCH, Monte Esquinza 18–24 (Metro: Colón)

▼

SARA NAVARRO: Most famous for couture and high-fashion leathergoods, Sara Navarro has shops in Madrid and in Barcelona. The Barcelona store is stunning, but in Madrid there are two conveniently located shops: in the Mercado and right on Goya, where you'll find a very classy operation selling shoes, hand-bags, and leather clothes that compete in quality and price with Loewe. We're talking $100 for a wallet, $550 for a leather skirt.

SARA NAVARRO
   Goya 75 (Metro: Goya)
   Mercado del Puerta de Toledo (Metro: Puerta de Toledo)

▼

JESUS DEL POZO: It is very hard to describe the kind of look Del Pozo promotes. We call it Memphis Milano for the lady. We mean clothing that is carefully structured to look unstructured. Sort of a Spanish Issey Miyake look. Del Pozo carries a mix-and-match variety of tops and skirts as well as pulled-together ensembles that swing and flow. Some people look great in this style; others look silly. If you are lucky enough to look good, you will make a haul.

JESUS DEL POZO, Almirante 28 (Metro: Colón)

▼

MASSIMO DUTTI: Dutti is in a category somewhat different from others. He owns a chain of men's stores all over Spain, and we mean all over. He carries everything from blue jeans to British chic, and is such a big name to local men that he has to be included in any list of influential fashion makers.

MASSIMO DUTTI, Velázquez 46 (Metro: Serrano)

Continental Big Names

EMPORIO ARMANI, Claudio Coello 77
GIORGIO ARMANI, José Ortega y Gasset 15

BENETTON
   Puerta del Sol 12
   Velázquez 21
CACHAREL
   Serrano 78
   Claudio Coello 68
ISABEL CANOVAS, Hermosilla 29
CARTIER, Serrano 57
CÉLINE, Castelló 74
ROBERT CLERGIE, Almirante 6
COURRÈGES, José Ortega y Gasset 17
DESCAMPS, Serrano 57
DUNHILL, José Ortega y Gasset 17
ESCADA, José Ortega y Gasset 21
FENDI, Serrano 84
GIANFRANCO FERRÉ, Serrano 29
FOGAL, Serrano 57
GUCCI, Don Ramon de la Cruz 2–4
HERMÈS, José Ortega y Gasset 26
CHARLES JOURDAN
   Serrano 6
   Gran Vía 1
KENZO, José Ortega y Gasset 11
ALAIN MANOUKIAN
   Claudio Coello 85
   José Ortega y Gasset 19
PRADA, Goya 4
SOULEIADO, Columela 1
TRUSSARDI, Velázquez 58
EL VAQUERO, Lascasca 47
GIANNI VERSACE, José Ortega y Gasset 10
LOUIS VUITTON, José Ortega y Gasset 17
YSL RIVE GAUCHE, Ayala 4

Department Stores

There're only two things you need to be able to say when it comes to Madrid's department stores: "ECI" and "GP."
   ECI means El Corte Inglés, and GP

means Galerías Preciados. These are Spain's two leading and competing department stores. While they might not give Harrods, Macy's, or Bloomie's a run for their money, we will nonetheless tell you to take a run at them, for several reasons.

In order to get the tourist business, both department stores have in-store discount policies (see page 25), which allow you to get, on many (but not all) purchases, an immediate 10% discount, right there at the cash register. This discount represents the IVA refund, but you don't have to go through Customs to get it or do any messy (or time-consuming) paperwork.

Now then, about the stores. We find ECI a little more upscale than GP, but the GP in Barrio de Salamanca—conveniently adjoining the Villa Magna hotel at the back end—has been the source of many a splendid buy. Never turn down the chance to shop a GP just because we told you ECI was splashier.

Both stores have souvenir departments; both usually have a supermarket—in the basement or upstairs. They have restaurants, and they have clean bathrooms. They are also crammed with merchandise. If you like street shopping and funky shopping, you'll find the prices in the department stores are high. (But then, you will be getting a 10% discount.) Certainly you shouldn't buy ceramics here. Shoes and handbags are a good buy—if they're on sale and you include the discount. While both stores have large handbag departments, you may not find a lot of stunning bags in the under-$100 range. We must confess that we saw the best vinyl Kelley-style handbag we've ever seen in our entire lives as shoppers for $39, and that we did score on several handbags (about $125 each after the discount) in the GP on Calle Serrano. Dr. Debbie was buying shoes at $25 a pair at a shoe sale. The shawl we were undecided about at $100 looked a little better to us at $90.

Mostly, you should use the department stores to research basic prices and see what's available. Come back for serious shopping after you've looked around and know that the 10% discount makes it worthwhile.

GALERÍAS PRECIADOS
Plaza de Callao 1 (Metro: Callao)
Serrano 47 (Metro: Serrano)
Goya 87 (Metro: Goya)

EL CORTE INGLÉS
Preciados 1 and 2 (Metro: Sol)
Paseo de la Castellana/Raimundo Fernandez
    Villaverde 79 (Metro: Nuevos Ministerios)
Goya 76 (Metro: Goya)
Princesa 42 (Metro: Argüelles)

▼

CELSO GARCÍA: It would be unfair to the city of Madrid to say that GP and ECI are its only department stores—they are simply the best. The Salamanca district also houses a third possibility, Celso García, which does not compete with the other two in any way. We would tell you that this store is not as good as K mart and shrug our shoulders, except that one time we found fabulous knit skirts and sweaters of very high quality at moderate prices. The fashions here are banal at best, but if you need high-quality basics, sort of along the line of those provided by Marks & Spencer, then you just might want to take a peek. There is a freestanding men's store and a family department store a few yards away.

CELSO GARCÍA, Serrano 50 (Metro: Serrano)
CELSO GARCÍA HOMBRE, Serrano 60 (Metro: Serrano)

Malls and Shopping Centers

Madrid has two types of malls: the big, enclosed American-style malls, which are found in suburbs, not in Centro (downtown); and what are called *multicentros,* indoor minimalls, often a few levels with many small shops that approximate a mall but are usually dark and crowded and don't have that big, airy feeling we Americans associate with a mall. We've never met a *multicentro* we adored, and frankly, having taken the time to explore these thoroughly, we can tell you that if you don't want to bother, it's OK with us. We know what it's like: You stand there on the sidewalk trying to decide if you want to go in, if the rewards will be worth it. After doing all the legwork for you, our opinion is simple: malls: *sí; multicentros: no.*

MADRID 2: This is the big American-style mall at the north end of the city, just about at the end of the Metro line. It is the pride of Madrid and all of Europe, as it is the single largest shopping mall currently existing on the continent. (Watch for this record to be broken, of course.) As wonderful as this 300-store mall is, you really need to ask yourself the bigger question: Did I come all the way to Spain to visit an American-style shopping mall? If the answer is yes, you probably won't be disappointed—there are branches of all the big chain stores and department stores, supermarkets, and big-name boutiques. There are amusements for kids; there's even a bowling alley. And, of course, you'll get the sociologist's view of the real Madrid—or at least, the real, rich, yuppie Madrid.

It'll take you forty or fifty minutes to get

here on public transportation, but because the mall is open on Sunday afternoons, you just might want to visit when other shopping opportunities are slow. Not all of the stores are open on Sunday, unless it is before Christmas. *Please note:* The name of the mall can be confusing, because while Madrid 2 is correct, it is also called by another name, La Vaguada—which is the name of the neighborhood it's located in.

Hours are 10 A.M. to 10 P.M. during the week; noon to 8 P.M. on Sunday. Most people come by car (free parking); if you come by Metro you get off at Barrio del Pilar on the number 9 line (check your map) and then take the bus to the mall. If you are staying in the Castellana part of Madrid, or are exploring northern Madrid, you are not too far from the mall already.

MADRID 2, Barrio del Pilar (Metro: Barrio del Pilar)

▼

MODA SHOPPING: This mall is also called by another name, AZCA Shopping, because it is located next to the convention center that bears the same initials. This is in northern Madrid and is particularly convenient to several big hotels—it's not as far out as the Madrid 2 mall.

Moda is an enclosed mall but not nearly as large as Madrid 2, nor as American—it's a fancier *multicentro* than others, very upscale, tony, and bright (most *multicentros* lack good light). There are only 100 shops; a few are branches of some International Big names (**ALAIN MANOUKIAN, BENETTON, SISLEY, DESCAMPS, PRENATAL, RAGAZZERIA, STEFANEL**), some local well-knowns (**ROBERT MAX, BOCH, BRETÓN**), and some very nice, upscale shops. Try **ACME** for sweaters from the Zara style but more designery. There is a bookstore (**LIBRAS DE ARTE**) that sells art and architecture books and is outstanding—books are offered in several languages.

Moda Shopping is located right off the Calle Orense, which, where it meets the Castellana, is a big commercial area for middle- to upper-middle-class residents. Surely you should wander the area before or after your tour of the mall, then end up at the ECI on the corner of the Castellana. (See Neighborhoods, page 108.)

Mall hours Monday through Saturday are 8 A.M.–10 P.M., Sunday and holidays 11 A.M.–10 P.M. That's what it says on the door, anyway. We think it's unlikely that the retail shops open before 10 A.M. during the week, however.

We like this center, and we like the Orense neighborhood, but plan your visit here carefully and be prepared to spring for taxis, because the Metro line that services this area does not connect easily to other Metro lines—so know where you want to go. If you are having a mall day, you can easily go on to Madrid 2. Otherwise, be prepared to make several changes to get back into a more central location—or simply take a taxi. There are buses that go up and down the Castellana; these too can be of service—especially if your hotel is along this route.

MODA SHOPPING, AZCA CENTER, General Peron 40 (Entrance at Paseo de la Castellana and Orense. Metro: Nuevos Ministerios)

▼

MULTICENTRO PRINCESA: Directly across the street from ECI's Princesa branch store, this center has an orange and yellow target logo that might make you think you've found the local Target discount store. No such luck. This is another of Madrid's infamous *multicentros* that we are so fond of. There are tiny boutiques selling blue jeans and fashions for the young set that haunts this neighborhood. Teens might really enjoy the scene, as will college students—this is, after all, the university area. This neighborhood is so much fun that it seems a shame to go indoors. Unless you are under twenty-four, don't.

MULTICENTRO PRINCESA, Princesa 47 (Metro: Argüelles)

▼

MULTICENTRO SERRANO: Just a few jumps up the street from the Serrano branch of GP, this small center has slightly over fifty shops—most of them are small and dark but sell hot fashions that range from U.S. basketball merchandise (which is very hot all over Spain) to French blue jeans and a few designer things. There are also a few nice linen shops, and there is a café. Is it really worth your time? Maybe, if only to get an idea of what a *multicentro* is about—this is one of the nicer ones. After you see this one, you can decide for yourself about visiting others.

MULTICENTRO SERRANO, Serrano 88 (Metro: Serrano)

▼

LA GALERÍA DEL PRADO: This is Madrid's second most splashy shopping center, second to the Mercado del Puerta de Toledo. La Galería del Prado, as the name implies, is directly across the street from the Prado museum, and is itself a monument to good taste and refined glitz. It's a small mall, built into the base of the Palace Hotel, with entrances from the front or the side and two levels including a sunken atrium complete with café and still more shops. It's all rather dazzling.

All of the shops are expensive and highend; a few are branches of names you will see elsewhere in Madrid. There are thirty-eight shops, a hairdresser, and a restaurant, as well as a gourmet food store where you can get take-away (say *"para llevar"*). Among the international big names, there's an **ALAIN MANOUKIAN, THIERRY MUGLER, GOLDPFEIL, GODIVA** (yes, chocolates), and **DESCAMPS;** among local big names check out **YANKO, FARRUTX, CRISTINA DE J'OSH, ANTINOOS,** and **ROBBERT MAX.**

LA GALERÍA DEL PRADO, Plaza de Neptune (Metro: Sevilla)

Markets and Flea Markets

THE RASTRO: The Rastro is heaven for Madrid's compulsive shoppers, the place to go when you are looking for excitement. You can go there looking for a bargain but may not find one; but you'll always find a good time. You can't be in Madrid without a trip to the Rastro; we've outlined it all for you on page 167. While tourists have come to believe that the Rastro is open only on Sundays, we encourage you to stop by just about any day of the week except maybe Mondays. The complexion of the area is different during the week, but the antiques stores are open, and there can be a good bit of street action. Saturdays are a busy day too. We've been there on several different weekdays and seen various shopping scenarios, none of which particularly match up. On one weekday visit there were vans and trucks you could rent like taxis to schlepp your furniture purchases for you; the same day a few months later—no such trucks. Another weekday we saw tables piled high with junk; the same day a few months later—no tables. Regardless of all this extra dressing, this is still an area for antiques shops. You can enjoy this area any time of the week, any day of the year. Bring cash, but stash it carefully.

THE RASTRO, Ribera de Curtidores (Metro: La Latina)

SANTA ANA MERCADO: We wish we could rave about this hippie fair and tell you that your Saturday afternoon will be enriched if you stop by. We were appalled by the quality of the handicrafts: very tie-dye city. The local crafts fair held at our high school has better stuff! The area is cute and supposedly some of these vendors also sell at the Rastro on Sunday, but we were not impressed. There are several cute tavernas around the plaza, so you can have *tapas* and enjoy the neighborhood; you are downtown, in Centro. Everyone sets up at about 5 P.M. and stays until after dark.

SANTA ANA MERCADO, Plaza de Santa Ana (Metro: Sol)

▼

CUESTA DE MOYANO: There's a bit of sidewalk-cum-alley near the Prado and Calle Claudio de Moyano that is sort of a standing book fair. They close for lunch. This is very picturesque and very fun to browse, but be warned—few books are in English. If you luck into picture books, you can make a score if you are willing to cut them up and frame the pictures.

CUESTA DE MOYANO, Claudio de Moyano, at the Atocha Circle near the Prado (Metro: Sol)

▼

CENTRO COMERCIAL LA PAZ: This is not a *multicentro* or a shopping center, but it is so wonderful, so delicious, and so delightful that we want to make sure you stop by. La Paz is the original neighborhood market for the tony Barrio de Salamanca district. This is where the butcher, the baker, and the candlestick maker hang out. But because this is Madrid's fanciest neighborhood, they are very fancy tradespeople. The covered market itself is set back off the street; the entry is a gallery of shops selling either specialty items (chocolate) or prepared foodstuffs. Inside there are a few dry-goods dealers (and even a videotape rental office), but here you'll find the cheese man, the fishmonger, the veggies, the eggs, the gorgeous colors, and the bright array of plenty. There are some eighty-five vendors here; surely enough for you to choose what you need for a proper picnic. Bring the kids; bring a tote bag. This is Europe and Madrid at its finest.

CENTRO COMERCIAL LA PAZ, Claudio Coello 48 (Metro: Serrano)

Finds

CASA BONET, S.A.: The oldest established linen shop in Madrid is Casa Bonet. We discovered it five years ago when a friend of ours asked us to pick up some extra place mats for her. At the time we thought that she was crazy to expect to match something that she had purchased two years earlier. So off we went. The shop is located in the residential part of the Barrio de Salamanca district. It is rather unimposing from the outside, and very simple inside. It isn't until you start to go through the drawers of place mats and look at the tablecloths that you realize that you have stumbled into one of Madrid's best finds. Casa Bonet carries classically patterned linens. If you buy a pattern and realize later that you need more, ask Ms. Pilar, the manager, to send them to you. The quality of the workmanship is in every way special. We bought blue and white place mats on our first visit and, just to make sure the service was still tops, went back to buy another six this time. Sure enough, Ms. Pilar produced the exact same linens from her drawer. The price had gone up about 20%.

Other napkins that we wanted she was out of, but was willing to special-order for no extra charge. Casa Bonet has branch stores in Palma de Mallorca and Marbella. No credit cards are accepted here, but you can pay with a personal check if you do not have cash or traveler's checks.

CASA BONET, S.A., Núnez de Balboa 76 (Metro: Serrano)

▼

LIBRERIA RELIGIOSA HERNANDEZ: This is one of many shops selling religious items for the devout. There are many small, connecting salons, each filled with merchandise that ranges from the touching to the tacky. There are all kinds of religious souvenirs and postcards here. In fact, we spent a lot of time in search of the perfect religious postcard, and we think this store has about the best Madrid can offer. There are fancy 3-D and embroidered varieties, but we like the old-fashioned baroque ones. They are pricey—almost $1 each.

LIBRERIA RELIGIOSA HERNANDEZ, Paz 4 (Metro: Sol)

Shoes and Leathergoods

O f course you came to Spain to buy shoes and leathergoods. And yes, you'll do so. But first we want to teach you the lay of the land. That means that cheap and wonderful handbags do not grow on trees. The cheap handbags in Spain are cheap, and it shows. They're not even always that inexpensive. Even many of the expensive handbags are cheap looking, but don't despair. Because Madrid has such big department stores, you'll have plenty of opportunity to see all the possibilities; try the fancy boutiques and the wholesale shoe street (see page 148). We were searching for a handbag that looked like it cost $350 but actually cost $150, and had a lot of trouble—but we did ultimately succeed. (We found three great bags at the GP on Calle Serrano.) Also remember that you have one last shot at the airport, where you can get some name-brand goods at the duty-free. However, we bought our Enrique Loewe bag here, and they would not take it back, repair it, or exchange it.

GRANADA: We are not talking about the city, but about quality leather and suede. We found this shop one day while we were lost in the Plaza Mayor district. The windows looked pretty, so we walked in. One hour later, checkbooks much lighter, we left with arms full. The quality of the leather far surpasses anything we have seen, except in Loewe. We can't say that it is much less expensive than Loewe, unfortunately, but it is somewhat less. What impressed us most was the casual elegance of the clothing, wallets, and bags. Granada has just introduced a new leather line in conjunction with Carrera y Carrera goldsmiths that is quite unusual. Carrera y Carrera (see page 153), the famous jeweler, handtools the fittings for the wallets and purses in 18K gold, and Granada designs the leather products to go with them. It is a Spanish version of the Judith Leiber touch. The price on these items, versus the same pieces in plain leather, is about double, but you really are buying a piece of jewelry, not just a wallet. This new leather line has an innovative finish that allows it to be washed with a soft cloth and mild suds. All major credit cards accepted.

GRANADA, Vergara 12 (Metro: Ópera)

LEPANTO: We have never in our lives seen a leather supermarket, but that is the best way we have of describing the Lepanto experience. Our friends who told us about the store mentioned that it was popular with Japanese tourists. They did not tell us that the store has become so popular with the Japanese that they have printed a special map for them in Japanese, hired Japanese-speaking staff, and carry petite sizes to fit the Japanese body. That does not mean that they are not just as happy to have anyone else shop there. On the contrary, the store is so service-oriented that they serve you, or your husband who wishes to wait while you shop, coffee or soda. The shop is extremely large. It carries racks and racks of jackets, and coats, and handbags from its own collection as well as bags from Céline, YSL, and Aries, which we were told is made in the Loewe factory. You will not find a more extensive collection of leather garments under one roof in Madrid. Whether you like the quality is simply a matter of choice. All major credit cards accepted. . . . We wouldn't be surprised if they took yen too!

LEPANTO, Plaza de Oriente 3 (Metro: Ópera)

▼

CARLOS ACOSTA: Here is one of our best secrets. This rather average-looking leather shop that sells shoes and handbags happens to have some of the best Kelley-type bags we've seen this side of Hermès. They will make one up for you if you want, or sell you their usual two-tone in black and brown leather. At $110, this could be the best handbag deal in all of Spain. We did see a vinyl Kelley-style bag at the GP on Calle Serrano, but this is real leather, and a real deal.

CARLOS ACOSTA, Claudio Coello 21 (Metro: Serrano)

LOEWE: We've already run on about Loewe (page 39) in order to give you some background on this famous leathergoods maker. While in Madrid you will end up visiting at least one of their shops.

The Gran Vía shop is the closest to many of the major hotels, but is by far the least well supplied. The store itself is magnificent. It is appointed in beige and cream with a black exterior, and must have been a town house or mansion before it became a store. The handbags are carefully displayed along the side shelves, but there seem to be so few of them that you almost hate to buy one and ruin the display. Upstairs there is carefully selected clothing and a back room full of luggage and accessories.

We prefer shopping at the Serrano shop, which has a much wider variety in an equally sumptuous atmosphere—although this store is modern, not Baroque. It has a few levels you can explore, so don't just sniff at the bags and then leave. Check out the whole place.

There is a teeny-tiny boutique in the Palace Hotel, which we mention for good reason: When the other stores are shut, this one may be open. They also have some Sunday hours.

All major credit cards accepted; IVA given for purchases over 47,000 *pesetas*.

LOEWE
Gran Vía 1 (Metro: Gran Vía)
Serrano 26 (Metro: Serrano)
The Palace Hotel (Metro: Sevilla)
LOEWE MAN, Serrano 34 (Metro: Serrano)

▼

MANUEL HERRERO: On the upper end of the busiest shopping street, Herrero has branches all over Madrid, as well as in New York and Puerto Rico. As a result they cater to an international design taste and offer styles that are flashier than average for Madrid. All major credit cards accepted.

MANUEL HERRERO, Serrano 76 (Metro: Serrano)

▼

GONZAPUR PELETERÍA: If you are looking for lots of choices in mixed leather, suede, and fur, or in leather and suede, visit Gonzapur. You will find racks upon racks of bomber jackets, leather jackets, coats, and fun fashions in all sizes, colors, and styles, for men and women. Prices are moderate, as leather prices in Spain go. All major credit cards accepted.

GONZAPUR PELETERÍA, Serrano 63 (Metro: Serrano)

▼

LA CASA DE LAS MALETAS: We went to both branches and each time came out raving. The main store, at Alcalá 151, caters more to the luggage trade. If you buy too many leather jackets and can't fit everything in your backpack, you can find a good selection of bags to choose from here. Both stores carry the Salvador Bachiller line of black or brown luggage and handbags with contrasting natural belting and leather trim, which we fell in love with. The prices are moderate while the styling is trendy chic. *Muy bien hecho,* as they say. One of the best stops in Madrid; don't miss it.

LA CASA DE LAS MALETAS
  Alcalá 151 (Metro: S. Bernardo)
  Claudio Coello 45 (Metro: Serrano)

▼

FARRUTX: Farrutx (say "Far-too") is one of Spain's biggest names in fashion footwear. Because they carry other brands besides their own, you may get confused. We predict the F logo will soon be as popular as Fendi's, so go with the house styles in high-tech fashion footwear. The main shop is very large and light, with the shoes displayed in minimalist surroundings as if they were pieces of art. The Farrutx private label is sold along with Stephane Kélian. Farrutx also has a branch in Galerías del Prado and has opened in Manhattan's SoHo. Check out our discount shoe pages (148–149) for possible sources for discounted Farrutx.

FARRUTX, Serrano 7 (Metro: Serrano)

▼

ZAPATERÍA HIJOS GARCIA TENORIO: This is a secret listing, known by locals who don't mind the fact that there's nothing much else interesting on this street and who are quite willing to search out this shop specially. This is the shop of a shoemaker. But what a shoemaker! Little has changed in one hundred years, except perhaps the reputation, which just gets bigger. One of our husbands had boots custom-made here. They came out crafted in the old-fashioned way, with the kind of workmanship that you have to travel to Europe to find.

ZAPATERÍA HIJOS GARCIA TENORIO, Bolsa 9 (Metro: Sol)

▼

HAREL: If we only send you to one shoe store in Spain, perhaps it should be this one—not only to buy the shoes, but to look at the shoes. These are French couture shoes that come in four different heel heights and in colors ranging from olive to aubergine to plain old black—only their plain old black is far from plain. There are two shops in Paris (one on our beloved Avenue Montaigne), and the shoes have a very French feel to their look (though not to their instep). The handbags are chicer than anything Hermès has made in years. Everything here is in that stiff Duchess of Windsor Hair Spray Perfection style that announces to the world that you have arrived.

HAREL, Hermosilla 29 (Metro: Serrano)

▼

LOS PEQUEÑOS SUIZOS: This is a small chain of shoe and leathergoods stores with branches in Madrid and around the country. It is not one of those big fancy places, but a small, sincere shop where you get very good shoes for very little money. For about $75 a pair, you can buy either men's or women's shoes—and if you hit a sale, get ready to shop. The handbags are about the best we saw in Spain in the $100–$135 price range. There are two stores in the Barrio de Salamanca.

LOS PEQUEÑOS SUIZOS
  Serrano 68 (Metro: Serrano)
  Claudio Coello 41 (Metro: Serrano)
  Alberto Aquilera 37 (Metro: San Bernardo)

▼

LURUEÑA: Lurueña is a chain of shoe stores with several branches in Spanish cities as well as offices in New York. They are a major dealer in Spanish-made shoes as well as in many brand names, some recognizable to Americans, some not. The usual shop is a fancy salon where you sit in an armchair as you view scads of shoes—most of which are in the $100-a-pair range. For the person who wants to see a lot, most of it traditional but with fashion, this is a possibility. They have a large handbag section as well.

LURUEÑA
  Serrano 54 (Metro: Serrano)
  Gran Vía 60 (Metro: Gran Vía)
  Madrid 2 ("La Vaguada" shopping center)
    (Metro: Barrio del Pilar)

CHARLES JOURDAN: A short story about our green handbag: One day last spring we walked into Charles Jourdan on Fifth Avenue in New York and asked to look at handbags. We chose a funny-shaped little blue leather bag. It cost $320. We asked to see the almost identical funny-shaped little green leather bag. It cost $140. Why the difference, we asked our saleslady. Because, she told us with a withering smile, the cheap bag was made in Spain, not France. We buy the made-in-Spain merchandise for the moderate savings. French-made Jourdan is outrageously expensive in Spain.

We rest our case. And our handbag too.

CHARLES JOURDAN
  Serrano 6 (Metro: Serrano)
  Gran Vía 1 (Metro: Gran Vía)

▼

GUTIERREZ: When you're taking your Salamanca stroll through the Goya section of the district, where the real people shop, you'll find our favorite branch of this small but excellent shoe source. There are other branches in Barrio de Salamanca and in Princesa, so fear not. This is the kind of store that simply has great traditional shoes at great prices. We found a lot of Ralph Lauren preppy looks, and a lot of low-heeled work shoes, all in the $75 price range. The lunch hour is slightly shorter here than elsewhere; the store is closed from 2 P.M. to 5 P.M.

GUTIERREZ
  Goya 85 (Metro: Goya)
  Serrano 66 (Metro: Serrano)
  Princesa 45 (Metro: Argüelles)

▼

IDEE: While in the Goya area, you can stock up on colorful and cheap high-style shoes for teens or young trendsetters. The average price of a pair of shoes here is $35, and there are ballerina-style flats in every shade of the rainbow (also $35).

IDEE, Goya 68 (Metro: Goya)

▼

YANKO: The shop on Lagasca is two stories in Milano green, with tortoiseshell trompe l'oeil walls and an entry that catwalks over the basement level. Yanko specializes in suedes, leathers . . . and high style. The clothing designs are original and well-made. The shoes and handbags are classic but interesting. There are shops in Palma, Sevilla, Barcelona, Alicante, and Valladolid as well. This is one of Spain's major high-end shoe chains, selling a certain type of chic. You're either the Yanko type or you aren't. Stop by to find out. Major credit cards accepted.

YANKO, Lagasca 52 (Metro: Serrano)

▼

BOLSOS MENA: There are four branches of Bolsos Mena in Madrid, but the one on Gran Vía is the largest. This company makes their own bags and belts and carries other lines of luggage and shoes. You can find everything from fancy alligator handbags (beginning at $1,500) to Samsonite hardsided luggage. Bolsos Mena even has its own Louis Vuitton look-alike bags, covered with the initials B. M. All major credit cards accepted.

BOLSOS MENA
   Gran Vía 43 (Metro: Callao)
   Princesa 70 (Metro: Princesa)

▼

GAITAN: This could be the best secret source we have for mixing the old Madrid and the lost way of life that went out with mass production with the modern luxe Madrid. The shoes at Gaitan are handmade and only handmade; they are custom-crafted to fit your foot. Styles are traditional, with a hint of chic, very much in the Hermès vein. Expect to pay $300 for a pair of shoes; you'll never get over this place. They do not speak English and do not particularly cater to tourists, so be patient and let your feet do the talking.

GAITAN, Jorge Juan 13 (Metro: Serrano)

▼

ORLAN: There are brightly colored bags, belts, briefcases, and wallets. They are well priced, with small purses starting at $66. Major credit cards accepted.

ORLAN, Serrano 28 (Metro: Serrano)

Discount Shoes and Leathergoods

We owe this all to Dr. Amelia, who shared her best Madrid shopping secrets with us: we never could have found this area on our own. Shoe jobbers are called *muestrarios* in Spanish—they sell leftovers. Look for the word as you roam the Calle Augusto Figueroa, which is two blocks of shoe jobbers selling discounted brands—some you've never heard of, some famous (in Spain, anyway), some internationally famous. We did buy a Sybilla handbag (just a teeny-tiny one) for $90. Just go from store to store and see what they've got. Don't expect anyone to speak English; try to know your foot size in European sizes and in Span-

ish words (or write it down); carry cash—
although several of the stores do take credit
cards. The area is not far from Sol, but use the
Metro for darting in and out—there aren't
many sights worth wandering this part of the
neighborhood for.

To find more sources for discount leathergoods, take the Metro to Chueca, exit for
Calle Augusto Figueroa, and try **PUNTA PIEL**
(No. 20) for cheap flats in the $30–$40 range.
RAFAEL & ESTELLE'S (No. 22 Calle San Barto-
lomé on the corner of Augusto Figueroa) is a
chain with about six shops for men's and wom-
en's shoes starting at $40–$50 and boots from
$70 up. **VIME** (No. 18) is one of the better
shops, with many brand names—we saw Yanko
and Nina Ricci at an average price of $40–$50.
Our vote for the best store of them all goes to
CALIGAE (No 27), which is small, high-tech,
and filled with big-name designer goods including Farrutx and Sybilla. We can't make
promises about what might be in stock when
you pounce, but they take American Express
should you hit a gold mine. While the selection is not huge and you may find the merchandise overbearingly stylish, we think you
should make this your first foot stop.

Traditional Madrid

L ong before the New Madrid and the hot
new designers, fashionable Madrid dressed
in a very British manner. As a result,
many of the best stores in Madrid are not
unlike London's better stores, and sell merchandise that is suitable for an international
preppy look. This stuff is not cheap, but it is
made well and lasts forever. It's very conservative, with a slightly tweedy British country
charm.

SANCHEZ RUBIO: Across the street from the Loewe shop on Gran Vía is an elegant, conservative shop for men's and women's fashions. The clothing looks similar to what you would expect to find in Gucci or Céline, although we think some of the outfits carry conservative to the dowdy extreme. We especially like the men's clothing, which works well in the ultra-tailored styles. But the reason we come to this store is to buy suede and leathergoods. The suede and leather jackets for men are unusually good. Gran Vía is almost impossible to cross at this store, so you have to either go to the corner and walk back to visit Loewe or take your life in your hands.

SANCHEZ RUBIO, Gran Vía 11 (Metro: Gran Vía)

▼

ROBBERT MAX: For the Madrid man who is very traditional and wants gorgeous clothes with higher-than-need-be price tags. But just take a look at the colors some of those wool melton jackets come in.

ROBBERT MAX, Moda Shopping (Metro: Nuevos Ministerios)

▼

BRETÓN: Opposite the Galerías Preciados on Serrano is the very, very, ever so very elegant men's shop Bretón. There are branch stores elsewhere, but this is the main showplace. The Bretón man has the Ralph Lauren look of casual, conservative savoir faire. The outside of the store is beautiful carved wood. Inside, it is equally manly. There is a complete selection of everything that a man could possibly need to be well groomed, from socks to luggage to butter-soft suede coats. European lines carried include Zegna, Dior, and the leather line Yanko. Major credit cards accepted.

BRETÓN: Serrano 66 (Metro: Serrano)

Young and Kicky

EKSEPTION: This store is wonderful not just for the merchandise it sells, but for its architecture and very ambience. This shop sells more than just clothes; it sells style, the unisex, young, kicky jeans, Euro-American hip fashions that can be found in any number of cities around the world. Enter this store, which feels like a theme park. Walk down a very, very long entryway, past the desks and into the body of the store. Video screens flash, music blares—it's the younger generation making itself heard.

EKSEPTION, Velázquez 28 (Metro: Serrano)

▼

GLOBE: Globe is a Spanish chain that is sort of a cross between The Gap and Benetton, with maybe a dash of Banana Republic thrown in. The clothes are inexpensive and appropriate for the casual jeans crowd. There's a branch in almost every city in Spain; this store is in the university area—of course.

GLOBE, Princesa 47 (Metro: Argüelles)

▼

TOKIO: This chain sells bodywear: dance leotards, underwear, panty hose, etc. The styles are very young and hip, and the store is very popular with the with-it crowd. You'll see quite a few of them around town.

TOKIO, Almirante 8 (Metro: Colón)

▼

DON CARLOS: If you are looking for one of Madrid's top boutiques selling European collections (Byblos, etc.) with flair and style, then you have come to the right place. This spacious shop has big, wide windows and lots of display space. It's very hot with those who can afford to dress like this. To carry off this look in Madrid, we suggest you wear very heavy red lipstick and blow smoke rings ... and maybe hitch a ride on the back of someone's motorcycle while wearing very high heels.

DON CARLOS, Serrano 92 (Metro: Serrano)

▼

CHARRO: This is one of our favorite stores in Madrid. It's very American, and we are ashamed of ourselves, but we have to give credit to whoever adopted this combination of Ralph Lauren western wear and real-life western wear and opened this store that sells what can only be described as a European version of that combination. The handtooled leather luggage would make Lauren himself envious.

CHARRO, Claudio Coello 50 (Metro: Serrano)

▼

ANTINOOS: A high-tech and drop-dead-chic men's shop at the edge of the Barrio de Salamanca that is worth going out of your way to get to—if you are a young, thin man with money to burn and the desire to look like a movie star. The look is *très* European. There is a shop on Orense (No. 12), but it isn't nearly as nice as this one; there are also men's and women's shops—two different boutiques—in the Galería del Prado.

ANTINOOS, Padilla 1 (Metro: Serrano)

Jewelry

SPLEEN: The best bet in Madrid, perhaps all of Spain, is this chain of costume jewelry shops. You'll find several in Barcelona, but since we know you want to explore the hip Almirante neighborhood, you'll be right at this branch, where you can buy inventive earrings, Chanel-style everything, summer looks in plastics and papier-mâché, and everything that will be fashionable in the next year. These designers are just enough ahead of the times to make you look like you have an inside track on the cutting edge. Prices are moderate but not cheap. Expect to pay $30–$50 for a pair of great earrings. If you miss the Madrid shop, not to worry—catch Spleen in every other city in Spain.

SPLEEN, Almirante 8 (Metro: Colón)

▼

CARRERA Y CARRERA: If you are looking for important jewelry or a big-name watch, this is the place. You can find it all here, and spend it all here, too. This is the fanciest name in jewelry to locals; their designs have been introduced to the U.S. market by Hans Stern, who often shows the line in his Fifth Avenue shop.

CARRERA Y CARRERA, Serrano 27 (Metro: Serrano)

▼

PLATAVIA: Silver lives and has been fashioned into some inventive bracelets, necklaces, earrings, and good-luck charms. This shop in the Almirante area is definitely worth checking out if you collect silver jewelry and like high-fashion pieces that really make a statement.

PLATAVIA, Argensola 2 (Metro: Colón)

▼

FABERGÉ: With the Russian double-eagle crest on the door, this shop appears to be related to the real thing. It is an old-fashioned jewelry store with an auction business, although we didn't see any jewel-encrusted Easter eggs on display. They specialize in expensive antique jewelry backed up by their good reputation.

FABERGÉ, Gran Vía 1 (Metro: Banco de España or Gran Vía)

▼

ROSSY: You might sail right by this little shop if we didn't tell you that it had some of the best costume jewelry in town. Ignore the ready-to-wear, unless you are looking for a luncheon suit with a collar of maribou feathers.

ROSSY, Serrano 44 (Metro: Serrano)

▼

DEL PINO: With big, heavy, glitzy costume jewelry the rage of Europe these days, you'll find a very timely selection at Del Pino—a small shop where every inch of space is hung with samples. All the big-name European designers are sold here. While the house specialty is the big and garish stuff that Christian Lacroix has made so chic, there are *faux* copies of important little baubles à la Bulgari, etc. Almost everything is priced over $100.

DEL PINO, Serrano 48 (Metro: Serrano)

Children

BOUTIQUE SELVOS: On the corner of Calle de Preciados and Gran Vía, at Plaza del Callao, you will see yellow awnings reminiscent of Fred Hayman's Beverly Hills. But Selvos is a much more conservative store, more on the level of Talbots than Beverly Hills glitz. We think the children's shop around the corner is more special than the main store. This is where you can find the beautiful handsmocked dresses that are so famous. The sizes go up to 14, although the baby clothing is the best. Boys are not left out. You can find sailor suits and knits that will make your boy look like a royal. All major credit cards accepted.

BOUTIQUE SELVOS, Preciados 25 (Metro: Callao)

▼

MUÑECOS SÁNCHEZ RUIZ: If you are a doll collector, or enjoy bringing home memorabilia from places where you have traveled, Sánchez Ruiz is a must. The store is vast and has Spanish dolls in every imaginable size and price range. On one of our trips, we not only bought dolls but outfitted our children in flamenco costumes for Halloween. All major credit cards accepted.

MUÑECOS SÁNCHEZ RUIZ, Gran Vía 47 (Metro: Callao)

▼

LA CIGÜEÑA DE PARIS: Here is a shop where your fantasies can run wild, along with your checkbook. The children's clothing carried at La Cigüeña runs the gamut from darling and practical to outrageously beautiful. Many French and Spanish lines are carried in sizes up to 12. Major credit cards accepted.

LA CIGÜEÑA DE PARIS, Serrano 3 (Metro: Serrano)

▼

CRECER: Even if you don't have kids, you should take a look at this store simply for the privilege of seeing retailing at its best. Clothing (with some accessories) for boys and girls is sold here—eveything for the look is included, right down to shoes and belts. The look is casually rich, with coordinated fabric, small blazers, great colors, and better-than-usual fabrics, without being too stiff or too grown-up. For sizes up to age 14.

CRECER, Hermosilla 16 (Metro: Serrano)

▼

FRIKI 12–18: A well-bought blend of designer names creates a prosperous upper-middle-class look that is hip without being too wild. Some old-fashioned party looks as well. Some good, conservative Ralph Lauren–type looks, especially in the boys' clothing.

FRIKI 12–18, Velázquez 35 (Metro: Serrano)

Ceramics

ANTIQUA CASA TALAVERA: This is the most impressive tile and Talavera shop in Madrid and is worth going out of your way for. It's downtown, although luckily the store is a few feet from the Metro exit. This small shop is decorated with tiles and is filled with ceramics in both qualities of Talavera. The very expensive plates ($30 each) are the ones made of iron; those for $15 are not of the same quality. The store tends to be a tad expensive, but if you have no other chance of going to a factory for better prices, you will not be disappointed here. The quality is sublime. They will not ship directly, but will arrange shipping for you through TWA's air courier service.

ANTIQUA CASA TALAVERA, Isabel la Católica 2 (Metro: Santo Domingo)

▼

REGALOS MOLINA: If you prefer an informal atmosphere with fun, inexpensive merchandise that's nice but can't begin to compare to the quality at Antiqua Casa Talavera, you'll enjoy this shop in the Rastro. It's almost as good as a trip to Toledo, with both types of wares being sold, as well as some lamps and lanterns at fair prices. Plates begin at $8. We bought ceramic lanterns at $12 each. The big drawback is that the shop is not open on Sunday.

REGALOS MOLINA, Ribera de Curtidores 27 (Metro: La Latina)

Foodstuffs

CASA MIRA: This is one of those old-timey Madrid shops where it appears that nothing has changed in one hundred years or more. Notice the wood panels outside, the carved columns, the Victorian interior created in 1848. This candy store sells tea cakes and sweets, but is most famous for their *turrones*. If you are bringing a gift to a Spanish hostess, there is no better resource.

CASA MIRA, Carrera de San Jerónimo 30 (Metro: Sevilla or Sol)

▼

LA VIOLETA: In case you want to eat yourself across Madrid, stopping in all the sweet shops from Casa Mira to La Pajarita, don't pass up this shop along your way. This tiny little place specializes in candied violets.

LA VIOLETA, Plaza de Canalejas 6 (Metro: Sol)

▼

LA PAJARITA: You have to buy something in here just to see the Victorian-looking pink paper that your packages are wrapped in. This shop was built in 1852, and is directly on the Plaza del Sol. The specialty of the house is caramel candy.

LA PAJARITA, Puerta del Sol 6 (Metro: Sol)

▼

CHARLOT: This is a *charcutería* where you buy prepared foods, although you can get pastries and a snack to go. The caviar happens to be much less expensive than in the U.S. This is a beautiful salon where rich people shop and where you'll swear you are in Paris. Some wines and *cavas*. If you're planning an elegant picnic, this is the place.

CHARLOT, José Ortega y Gasset 8 (Metro: Serrano)

▼

PALACIO DE LOS QUESOS: OK, this is what you do. You buy some slices of ham in the market (just around the corner); you stop here for a few slices of cheese; then you have a picnic at the Plaza Mayor. Processed cheese may legally be brought into the U.S.

PALACIO DE LOS QUESOS, Plaza Mayor 53 (Metro: Sol)

▼

CAFÉ POZO: This store—right on the Plaza Benavente—is in the heart of Old Madrid and a block from the cape store Seseña. It's a food store specializing in coffee but also selling *turrones,* hard candies, and some gourmet foods. We come for the coffee, which is sold in a red and yellow package (with black print). Coffee beans are called *mezcla;* you will be asked if you want *molinar*—this means ground beans. We buy whole beans because they stay fresher and don't make as big a mess if the package opens in your suitcase. A small bag of 250 grams of coffee makes an ideal gift and costs about $2.50.

CAFÉ POZO, Plaza Benavente (Metro: Sol)

Design and Antiques

Madrid remains the place to buy antiques and decorative arts with prices that are lower than in France and often better than the rest of Europe. Auctions are very popular, and should be considered by the serious shopper (get a translator); pieces range from Iberian country to Regency and beyond. There are also several neighborhoods where strolling will be a delight and where you can visit many shops, one after the next.

For a quick overview of what's out there, try the Puerta de Toledo mall, which is about half filled with antiques dealers (see our list of shops below), and Ribera de Curtidores, which is the street that hosts the Rastro. On weekdays it's filled with antiques shops and furniture galleries, some junky, many serious. Check out the courtyard at No. 12, which has over a dozen shops, certainly the best combination of strong shops in the Rastro area. A third possibility is Calle del Prado, a small street that is almost all antiques shops—most of them very good ones. Finally, the Salamanca district has the fanciest shops, a few antiques centers, and the heart of the hoity-toity auction and antiques business. There's just a shop or two near the Palace Hotel (and on the way to Calle del Prado) that you should also check out. As you wander, don't miss:

The following are a few antiques shops at Puerta de Toledo that we recommend ("Local" indicates shop number): **ALLOR,** Local 4113; **AROYA ANTIGÜEDADES,** Local 3124; **LUIS CODOSERO,** Local 2215-17-18; **RICARDO CONRADO,** Local 2219; **LUIS ELVIRA,** Local 2114; **LUIS MORUECO** C. de B., Local 2223; **LUIS ROMERO,** Local 2133; and **G. ZARO,** Local 2002.

ABELARDO LINARES, S.A.: One of the biggest and most respected antiques houses in Madrid is very close to the Prado museum. Linares is housed across from the Palace Hotel, in a grand Baroque mansion that is the perfect setting for the five rooms of antiques within. As you enter, you will feel that the air is noticeably cooler. This could either be because there are few windows and the lights are kept very low, or because the walls are so thick that they keep in the cool.

The main room is filled with large pieces of antique furniture and art. The back rooms are full of everything imaginable, including daggers, tapestries, silver, and tiles. There is even a special section for Majorica pearls, which are not antique at all. The staff is very protective, and follows you around, which is somewhat disconcerting if you are simply browsing. All major credit cards accepted. Shipping can be arranged.

ABELARDO LINARES, S.A., Carrera de San Jerónimo 48 (Metro: Banco de España)

▼

GALERÍAS SAN AGUSTÍN: This store is the best welcome to Spain we can think of. Not that you'll buy anything, but visit this wonderful shop next to the Prado just to soak up the atmosphere. This is a good-sized antiques shop filled with antique Talavera plates (beginning at $250 each), strewn with tables with a glossy patina or a handhewn roughness and then crammed with statues of the Lord Jesus and His friends. Even the breathing space is filled with merchandise; furniture is piled and stacked in dusty corners, and chandeliers swing, heavy with wooden candlesticks. If you decide to buy, the store will arrange shipping.

GALERÍAS SAN AGUSTÍN, San Agustín 3 (Corner of Plaza de la Cortés. Metro: Sevilla)

▼

ESTABLECIMIENTOS FLANDEZ S.L.: Religious articles and war memorabilia seem to be a strange combination, although many wars have been fought in the name of religion. We were first attracted to this shop by the display of war medals in the window. We went in and discovered a wide variety of medals, patches, military caps, flags, miniature cannons, braid, swords, statues, and even full war medallions to wear around your neck. You can also buy a crèche scene to put under your Christmas tree, or vestments for your chapel. Strange but true. Major credit cards accepted.

ESTABLECIMIENTOS FLANDEZ S.L., Mayor 11 (Metro: Sol)

LA CERÁMICA ESPAÑOLA: If you were always fascinated by your grandmother's closets and shelves, this antiques shop will make you feel right at home. It is quite large, but there is so much packed into every nook and cranny that you have to be a good sleuth to find the real treasures. If you need to add pieces to a china set, you could be successful. If you want period cut glass you will definitely be successful. If you are on the trail of Lladró, new or old, you will be in heaven. Major credit cards accepted.

LA CERÁMICA ESPAÑOLA, Genova 18 (Metro: Alonso Martines)

▼

PLATERÍA SERRANO: It is lucky that we discovered this store on a day when we had left our credit cards and money in the safety deposit box at the hotel. Serrano is silver plate paradise. We drove the owner crazy asking to see all the miniature pieces of furniture, animals, candlesticks, serving pieces, goblets, wine bottle tops, picture frames, napkin rings, small boxes, small clocks, jewelry, letter openers, dinner bells, spoons, and mirrors. Next time, we are bringing cash.

PLATERÍA SERRANO, Infantas 25 (Metro: Gran Vía)

▼

TALLERIES DE ARTE GRANADA: If you want to know what goes into the grandest of grand Spanish mansions, take a walk around this gallery of fine art and furniture. The scale of the showroom is overwhelming. The pieces of Baroque wood furniture look at home here, surrounded by fine works of art, accessories, and wall hangings. However, try to put them into a small room and you will be in trouble.

TALLERIES DE ARTE GRANADA, Serrano 56 (Metro: Serrano)

▼

A. HÍPOLA: Calle Serrano, south of Goya and close to the Biblioteca Nacional, is a good antiques area. A. Hípola is one of the many shops that you will encounter while browsing. It is hard to say that they have any one particular type of merchandise, because it comes and goes so fast. There are paintings, wood pieces, art, china, and crystal as well as tabletop items. Prices vary according to value and size.

A. HÍPOLA, Serrano 28 (Metro: Serrano)

▼

DURÁN: Durán has two immense showrooms filled with paintings, furniture, vases, silver, jewelry, and china. If you look carelessly, you'll think the numbers are price tags. They are not. They are lot numbers.

Durán is an auction house and the area that looks like an antiques showroom is just that, the viewing space for the upcoming auctions.

Some of the pieces are fit for a castle; others are scaled for a regular home. They have so much of everything that it is impossible to take it all in and make choices in just one visit. The shop at No. 12 has larger pieces, while the shop next door at No. 8 caters more to the ornamental and decorative arts. Major credit cards accepted. Shipping is possible. Although auctions are conducted in Spanish, the house will show you how to submit a written bid.

DURÁN, Serrano 12 and 8 (Metro: Serrano)

▼

CENTRO DE ARTE Y ANTIGÜEDADES:

The one-stop shopping antiques center at the corner of Calle de Recoletas and Calle Serrano is as much fun to visit because of its architecture as it is for its antiques. From the outside, the building looks like any monumental stone building. Inside, it has been gutted, the flying beams sandblasted, and the rooms replaced with glass storefronts and brick-walled spaces. Catwalks and escalators take you from floor to floor. Many shops have taken over more than one space. Despite its potential, we think the center will be transitional until major tenants settle in. On our last inspection, we were less than impressed. Still, it may be worth a look when you visit.

CENTRO DE ARTE Y ANTIGÜEDADES, Serrano
   5 (Metro: Serrano)

▼

CENTRO DE ANTICUARIOS LAGASCA:

Lagasca is one of the decorator streets in the Salamanca district. Below Goya and above Jorge Juan you will find home-accessories stores, kitchen showrooms, fabric houses, and art galleries. Centro de Anticuarios Lagasca is a minimall of mostly small antiques shops where you can comparison-shop in one building. We prefer this building to the ultramodern center on Serrano simply because it feels more authentic and the entire area is chic and glamorous.

CENTRO DE ANTICUARIOS LAGASCA, Lagasca
   36 (Metro: Serrano)

▼

MARINA F. CÓRDOVA ANTIGÜEDADES:

This is one of the tonier antiques shops in the Salamanca district. Since it is located in the heart of the designer-boutique area, we feel confident in saying that the quality sold here will pass muster with the most discriminating of tastes. We certainly would have liked to move many of the pieces home with us, but were already carrying too much pottery to attempt it. The pieces tend toward the unusual and large. We especially liked the silver-topped glass urns, and the fine marquetry table on which they sat.

MARINA F. CÓRDOVA ANTIGÜEDADES, Don Ramón de la Cruz 27 (Metro: Serrano)

▼

VILLANUEVA Y LAISECA: Of the many elegant jewelry and fine silver shops in Madrid, Villanueva y Laiseca stands out because of its simplicity. The outside of the shop is all gorgeous green marble columns and brass-fitted display windows, which would lead you to think that it is a glitzy store. Once inside, however, the atmosphere is more like a museum. You must know what you want to look at, because it is not a browsing kind of store. Their specialty is fine jewelry, china, antique war medals, and antique silver replicas. We were especially drawn to the fine craftsmanship of the carved silver animals. The shop is located at the corner of the Plaza de Canalejas, before you get to the Puerta del Sol, on Carrera de San Jerónimo. All major credit cards accepted.

VILLANUEVA Y LAISECA, Carrera de San Jerónimo 9 (Metro: Sol)

▼

NESOFSKY: For the unusual in decor visit Nesofsky, a furniture store that carries new, old, and repro furniture on a grand scale. In the displays, you will see black Roman pedestals mixed with Art Nouveau screens and chinoiserie chairs. As strange as it might sound, it works.

NESOFSKY, Serrano 59 (Metro: Serrano)

LOPEZ: Dr. Amelia sent us here, too. Lopez is a shop selling new antiques in a strip of antiques shops not far from the Prado. The house specialty is sterling silver. Everything in the shop is silver; there is no plate. Everything is a brand-new reproduction of an antiquity or a museum-quality piece. Upstairs is the heavy-duty stuff in terms of tabletop, with a few pieces of jewelry; downstairs are the medallions, baby rattles, votives, etc. Now the bad news: cash only. We bought a group of tiny votive medallions for $30–$50 each (price depends on size) that are incredible! For anyone who loves the old, the special, the gift with special meaning—this is the find of the century. Oh yes, one final explanation: The store sign says "Lo" and then has a picture of a fish. You'll get it once you know that *pez* means fish—this is a pictorial pun.

LOPEZ, Prado 3 (Metro: Sol)

▼

REAL FÁBRICA DE TAPICES: This listing isn't for everyone, but if you've been needing a tapestry for your castle—we do know how damp the walls can get—you'll want to take a taxi to the edge of Madrid to visit the royal factory, where a private firm has taken over this ancient business begun by Philip V. All the work is custom-made, and it does take a while for delivery, but this work is done the old-fashioned way. This is worth seeing just for the education.

REAL FÁBRICA DE TAPICES, Fuenterrabia 2

Antiques Stores at the Rastro

T he Rastro is the famous flea market of Madrid held on Sundays, but the neighborhood where the market is held is open during the week, and houses many of the city's antiques (and junk) dealers, as well as numerous street vendors who set up their tables on some weekdays for those who happen by. The Rastro is held on Ribera de Curtidores, although no one calls this area anything but El Rastro. To get there take the Metro to Puerta de Toledo and walk along the Ronda de Toledo until you get to the Ribera and then head up it toward the Plaza Mayor. Or get off the Metro at La Latina and walk a very short block to the top of the Ribera and begin your prowl there. We get there by walking along the Calle de Toledo until it forks (shortly after Simago) at the Plaza de la Cebada (at the La Latina Metro stop). Since the streets are closed off with barriers, since you will see the stalls beckoning you in the sunlight, it will not be hard to know how to navigate through the throngs of people. It's really quite simple. Walk a short block from Plaza de la Cebada to Plaza Cascorro, which is the top of the Rastro. Then stroll downhill toward the Ronda de Toledo.

There are stalls everywhere, most of them selling junk you don't want to buy and may not even want to look at—cheap belts, tie-dyed T-shirts, etc. But every now and then a discerning eye will find something of interest. There are a number of craftspeople, but there are not a lot of ceramics stands.

The Rastro gets going around 9:30 or 10 A.M. Around 11 the antiques dealers—located in the buildings on both sides of the street and behind the stalls on the sidewalks—begin to open. Not every store will open, but the big ones will. So the Rastro becomes fun when you combine the junkiness of the street stalls with a hunt-and-peck method in the better shops.

There are a few vendors selling bullfight posters: they will make them up while you wait. (See page 46.)

Bargaining is expected (also in the antiques stores); if you speak no Spanish, use paper and pencil. Check addition of sums; count change; count your wares; don't believe anything you are told about the provenance of what you have bought.

Friday at the Rastro

We were under the impression that the Rastro wasn't a very exciting place if you didn't hit it on a Sunday, but have learned that it's not dead during the week. Dr. Amelia tells us that different days of the week have varying degrees of action. Certainly the scene is entirely different.

When you get to the Plaza de Cascorro on Friday, there are no stalls, just herds of delivery trucks with a card in each window with the word *libre*. These are taxi trucks—after you've bought furniture in the Rastro, you rent a taxi truck to deliver it for you! Unfortunately, they did not deliver to Pittsburgh. As you walk down the hill, you'll see tables set up on the sidewalk—not stalls like on Sunday. These tables are filled with clothes: cheap work clothes and everyday clothes that locals buy. Some tables are piled with mounds of shoes; others have women's sweaters. Needless to say, there are no designer clothes.

If you're looking for something a little more civilized than the scene at the plaza, check out some of the shops:

ALMONEDA: Almoneda specializes in antique dolls, including the now hard to find old-fashioned nun dolls. Mercedes Cabeza de Vaca Avial runs the store and also uses the initials M. C. de V. on her cards; don't get confused. This shop is one of the best in the Rastro, and is in a little shopping plaza surrounded by a courtyard of enjoyable shops. Two nun dolls, by the way, cost $1,500!

ALMONEDA, Tienda 13, Ribera de Curtidores 12 (Metro: La Latina)

▼

GALERÍA DE ANTIGÜEDADES: This is one of the shopping centers of antiques stalls on the Ribera: it's fun to poke around here, but the choices are not high-end. There are stores on several levels; most take credit cards.

GALERÍA DE ANTIGÜEDADES, Ribera de Curtidores 15 (Metro: La Latina)

▼

JOSÉ MARIA DEL REY: Located in the same plaza as Almoneda, this antiques shop is extremely high-end and specializes in furniture and religious articles.

JOSÉ MARIA DEL REY, Ribera de Curtidores 12 (Metro: La Latina)

▼

FELIPE FERMIN: This dealer specializes in early-1900s–style wrought iron and has many table bases that he can take apart and tape together for you to carry on the plane with you. We thought this wasn't too bad a deal for $80! His family business was founded in 1860;

the factory is on the premises. White or black
wrought iron available.

FELIPE FERMIN, Ribera de Curtidores 18
(Metro: La Latina)

▼

GONZÁLVES: This small shop in the Rastro
is nearly movie-set perfection. This dealer sells
mostly brass and his small space is nearly taken
over by his wares. Door knockers are heavy, but
wonderful. You'll also find candlesticks, door
pulls, hinges for doors, and picture frames.

GONZÁLVES, Ribera de Curtidores 12 (Metro:
La Latina)

Madrid on a Schedule

Tour 1: Art, Antiques, Markets, and Old Madrid Tour

1. Try to do this tour on a Sunday, when the
   Rastro, Madrid's flea market, is in full swing.
   Start your tour at the Prado museum. When
   your eyes tire of fabulous Goyas and Velázquez masterpieces, head for the Prado gift
   shop, which is good for postcards or posters of art from the museum's permanent
   collection. As you leave the Prado museum, cross half of Paseo del Prado, to the
   center grassy square. Here you will find
   vendors selling all kinds of souvenir items
   from blankets spread on the grass. We especially like the fellow who sells bullfight
   posters that you can have stamped with
   your name or the name of a friend. The
   price of these posters should not be more

than $5, even though the stand owner will quote you $10. You must bargain hard before getting him down this low. If you don't have time to wait for the posters, you can hold off until Barcelona, where they are actually cheaper. If you are not going to Barcelona, the Moscow Rule of Shopping applies (If you see it, and like it, buy it).

2. Farther across the square, on the other side of Paseo del Prado, at No. 10, is our favorite store for souvenirs: Objetos de Arte Toledano. We bought our Barcelona '92 T-shirts here, and never saw the same ones in Barcelona. The selection of Lladró, silver, swords, brass, and dolls is superb, and the prices are fair enough.

3. Upon leaving Objetos de Arte Toledano enter the Galería del Prado, next door, then circle around the Plaza Canovas del Castillo and up Carrera de San Jerónimo. This will bring you face-to-face with one of the oldest antiques areas of Madrid. Abelardo Linares is on the corner of Carrera de San Jerónimo and Prado. If you are looking for authentic old Spanish furniture and collectibles, this is a fine place to start ... But not on Sunday.

4. Take a left on Prado and wander in and out of the little shops that look like they have been selling antiques for centuries. Each one houses a different type of antique collectible.

5. Continue to walk on Prado until you get to Plaza de Santa Ana, where you should pay attention to the old tavernas that line the square. On Friday and Saturday there is a hippie flea market in this square that is very reminiscent of the '60s.

6. Now, with your back to Prado, turn right and head in the direction of Puerta del Sol on Carreras. When you reach Plaza del Sol

you will be in front of one of the better El Corte Inglés department stores. If you are looking for good souvenirs and didn't buy any before, stop here.

7. All around the El Corte Inglés are many of Madrid's most famous shops. To the right on Puerta del Sol is Casa de Diego (No. 12), famous for its fans. Seseña, the only shop—as far as we're concerned—for Spanish capes, is down the street at Cruz 23. Lhardy (Carrera de San Jerónimo 8) is the perfect place to pick up a snack or to stop for lunch; they open at 1 P.M.

8. If this is Sunday you will want to visit the Rastro. If it is not a Sunday, however, many of the shops will still be open on the main street where the market is held. To get there, take the red line on the Metro at Puerta del Sol to Ópera, then transfer to the green line and exit at La Latina. You will come out at the Rastro, Madrid's infamous flea market. Follow the crowds to the main street, Ribera de Curtidores. In the middle of the street, you will find stalls selling every imaginable form of junk. On the sides of the street are the more established antiques stores. If you are there during the week, they will all be open. On Sunday only a select few care to deal with the crush of people. The majority of items being sold at the market are not of interest to the average tourist. Some of the crafts pieces are nice, but don't expect to come away with loads of ceramic goodies. However, it's hard not to buy just one or two trinkets to take home. If you like Talavera pottery you might get lucky. Above all, don't forget to bargain for everything. Some of our favorite shops on the street include Almoneda (No. 12) for dolls, Galería de Antigüedades (No. 15) for a variety of small specialty shops, and Gonzálves (No. 12)

for incredible door knockers, door pulls, and hinges in brass.

9. By the time you reach the end of Ribera de Curtidores as it intersects Ronda de Toledo, you will probably be "shopped out." If you are, hail a taxi and put your feet up for a deserved rest.

10. If not, head right to the Puerta de Toledo and one of Madrid's most exciting shopping plazas, named after its location. If you are doing this tour on a Sunday, note that the building closes at 3 P.M. Any other day, the stores and the building stay open until 8 P.M., with the exception of Monday, when everything is closed tight. (See page 121.)

Tour 2: Madrid, Classy and Classic

1. The two areas of Madrid that we like the best are the Barrio de Salamanca and the central city. Combine the two for an enlightening contrast in culture, art, and ambience that is the essence of Madrid. Start this tour at the Villa Magna Hotel, where you can get a wonderful and filling breakfast to fortify yourself for the shopping day ahead.

2. Exit the back of the hotel, past the airline desks, and enter the back of one of Madrid's Galerías Preciados. This particular store is geared to local shopping, but is a good source for local trinkets. As you exit the front of the store, you will be on the main shopping street of the Salamanca area, Serrano. Take a left and walk up as far as José Ortega y Gasset. Along the way you will find a variety of shoe and leather shops that are interesting. Take a right on José Ortega y Gasset and explore designer boutiques like Gianni Versace (No. 10), Kenzo (No. 11), Louis Vuitton (No. 17), and

Courrèges (No. 17). Although we don't think the prices offer any big breaks, the architecture of some of the shops is worth the stop.

3. At this point you can choose to return to Serrano and continue walking toward the Serrano Metro at Goya, or start weaving through the side streets, moving from Serrano to Claudio Coello, which parallels Serrano, and back along the streets that intersect them. Shops you definitely want to hit on your walk include: Isabel Canovas (Hermosilla 29) for incredible art jewelry, La Casa de Las Maletas (Claudio Coello 45) for leather bags and cases, Yanko (Lagasca 52) for wild architecture and leather, Harel (Hermosilla 29) for the best in handbags and shoes, Rossy (Serrano 44) for great *faux* jewelry, and Casa Bonet (Núnez de Balboa 76) for the finest linens Spain has to offer. See pages 109–111 for more listings. Every time you stroll through this area, you will find a new "find."

4. Eventually you will reach Goya and the Metro stop. From here we suggest you explore farther down Serrano to find the antiques section of the street. Two big antiques and auction houses are located on the left: A. Hípola (No. 28) and Durán (No. 12). Farther down Serrano is the antiques showroom Centro de Arte y Antigüedades (No. 5).

5. The area to the left, as you are walking away from the Serrano Metro, is the design section of Madrid. Shop after shop is filled with fabrics and furniture, some of which are uniquely Spanish. Explore the streets called Jorge Juan, Claudio Coello, and Núnez de Balboa below Goya for some special treats.

6. At this point, hop into a taxi and ask the driver to take you to the corner of Almirante

and Paseo de Recoletos. If you are a marathon walker, you can easily walk there from the Serrano area. However, we like to conserve our energy for pacing in the stores rather than walking between areas, whenever possible. Almirante has become home to the experimental young and hip designers who are appearing more and more in international fashion magazines. This area is no longer considered part of Salamanca, and therefore the rents are lower and designers on the cutting edge of fashion can afford to set up shop.

7. Walk along Almirante, crossing back and forth as you go to find one shop more interesting than the next. Be sure to visit our favorites, Pedro Morago (No. 20), La Tierra (No. 28), and Francisco Valente (No. 1). When you get to the end of Almirante, turn right onto Barquillo and then right again onto Argensola.

8. When you dead-end into Génova, peek into the china shop at the corner and then head left to the Metro at Alonso Martinez. Hop on the green line and exit at Ópera.

9. From here you may proceed to explore the oldest part of Madrid. Even though you will have a map and directions, be prepared to get lost. The streets are so narrow and winding that it is easy to be walking along, confident of where you are, only to look up and realize you are on a street that you don't see on your map. Relax. As far as we know, no one has ever been permanently lost in Madrid's central city.

10. From the Ópera Metro walk toward the Plaza de Oriente until you find the street Vergara. This is home to one of our favorite leather shops, Granada (No. 12), where you will find the butter-soft leather jackets that you have been searching for, along

with magnificent accessory items, some of which are finished by a jeweler.

11. After leaving Granada, walk uphill until you see Santiago cut off to the left. Follow this street until you end up at the Plaza Mayor.

12. When you reach the Plaza Mayor, you have reached the soul of Madrid. Be prepared to wander in and out of small shops and equally small streets until you drop from exhaustion. The best shopping street is Calle Cava Baja, which looks as if it has remained unchanged for centuries. Shop the souvenir stores along the walled square, but be sure to venture into some of the alleys as well. There will be plenty of cafés where you can stop for a drink, so relax, enjoy, and take your time. When you are too tired to go on, taxi back to your hotel and rest. Remember that everyone dines late in Spain, so dinner won't even begin until 9 P.M.

6▾ TOLEDO BY DAY

Welcome to Toledo

We were prepared to hate Toledo. We thought it would be crass, touristy, and pushy, and generally not our cup of tea.

But we loved Toledo—every trip, every time. We love Toledo even when we aren't there. It remains a shining memory; the very reason why a person leaves home in the first place.

We can't tell you how important it is to see Madrid and Toledo together, so that you get a picture of the depth of Spain. If you don't get out into the countryside beyond this, it's OK. Toledo will fill your senses and flood your soul.

It is a city of art and craft as well as arts and crafts. And it's great for shopping. All those things you have trouble finding in Madrid are readily available here. (Dishes, dishes, dishes.) It is a city of incredible landscape and gorgeous colors and flowers and tile roofs. It is the city of our dreams.

Off to Toledo

Because Toledo is so close to Madrid (about an hour's drive—70 kilometers), most people visit on a tour or take a day trip from Madrid. We've done it both ways: We signed up for a tour at the front desk of our hotel on one of our very first trips to Madrid, and later, we created our own tour by simply hopping on the train at Madrid's Atocha station.

We rate the tour as an OK experience if you want to see a lot in a hurry, have much explained to you (there is a lot to be explained), and be dazzled by the wealth of artworks, but have very little time for shopping. You have nothing to worry about the whole day, since you travel in a herd; you do have to suffer if the itinerary is changed—as ours was. (The sword factory was eliminated in favor of a roadside TT. . . . No vote was taken.) We took the half-day tour (8:30 A.M. to 1 P.M.); taxied from our hotel to the bus company, boarded up, and were back in time for lunch in Madrid. It cost about $30. Painless and quite pleasant.

We were happier on our own, although it does take some organization to be at the right place at the right time. Because the stores in Toledo will close tight for siesta at 1:30 P.M., you want to coordinate your comings and goings in order to have maximum shopping time. This makes it hard to see all the worthwhile cultural sights and shop at the same time, especially before lunch.

Toledo Snags

Going to Toledo is quite easy. We pass on just a few tricks we have learned on our several trips:

▼ If you go by train, please note that the train station in Toledo is not very well marked. We were not the only people frantically falling out the door shouting "Is this Toledo?" Go by your watch and the timetable, and keep sight of a conductor so you have someone to ask.

▼ The train station is outside of the old city, which is where you want to be. It is within walking distance, but it's not an easy walk, and wouldn't be smart with kids. Taxis at the train station are scarce; if there is only one cab there, ask the driver to radio for more cabs. Organize people into groups for the cabs, and order the cabs. You can wait for an hour if you don't do something about helping yourself.

▼ Likewise, if you care to return to the train station during lunchtime, even if you call for a taxi from a store, you are unlikely to get one. Lunchtime is a peak travel time. There are no taxis standing in clusters at the major sights, especially around 1:30 P.M. when the stores are shutting and people are crowding into restaurants. We were lucky enough to have spent several hundred dollars at our last store and to have thus ingratiated ourselves with the owner of the store, who drove us to the station himself after he was unable to call a taxi for us. The phone number for the radio taxi in Toledo is 21.50.50.

▼ Toledo is known for its ceramics. You will certainly be buying ceramics. If you follow our directions, you will be exploring Toledo in a circular route; you should not plan on returning to a certain store—it will be inconvenient to come back for a heavy package. Be prepared to schlepp what you buy. We finally left Toledo not because we were finished with the city, but because we literally could not walk another step due to the weight and bulk of our purchases. Consider bringing your airline wheelies, a backpack, a giant satchel, or perhaps a mule with you.

▼ *One final warning:* On the day we took the tour, as we got off the bus in Toledo, we were handed a brochure printed in four languages that gave shopping warnings ("Never buy wherever someone leads you") and suggestions that you can jump your tour and stay longer in

Toledo, explaining that you can take a bus back to Madrid for about $4 one way, or a train (same price), or even a taxi ($50)—which isn't a bad idea if you load up on ceramics. The brochure was printed by the Association of Commerce of the Artisans of Toledo. While we were never bothered with people trying to lead us into places we didn't want to go (except for our tour director himself), we think the brochure does offer welcome information.

Getting There

We admit that we like fancy hotels, and when we travel we stay in very fancy hotels. So it amuses us to tell you that the concierge and people at the front desk of our fancy Madrid hotels were absolutely appalled that we would consider public transportation to Toledo. They suggested an organized tour (which we took just to compare it to a nontour), or a private car and driver.

Once we were on the train to Toledo, we looked at each other and burst out laughing. The train is incredibly easy to deal with and largely free of pushy tourists. We sat in a car with two nuns, a teenage boy, a farmer and an auto mechanic or two, and a grandmotherly type as wide as she was tall, dressed all in black except for the shawl that covered her head and shoulders. We adored it.

We took the train because we went on a holiday when street traffic was expected to be heavier than usual; under other circumstances the public bus might have been a little quicker and would have taken us right into town— we're told. But we like the train. One benefit of taking the train is arriving at the Toledo train station—one of the best examples of the

Mudéjar style of architecture in all of Spain. And yes, the bathrooms at the train station happen to be clean. They are not in the Mudéjar style, but you can't have everything.

Whether you take the bus or the train, be sure to buy a round-trip ticket, since this is cheaper than two one-ways. On either mode of transportation, round-trip for an adult should come in under $10.

If you prefer the car and driver, you should be able to make a private deal with a taxi driver—or get the hotel to find you someone— for about $100 for the round trip. Fancy limos will cost more ... especially if you want an English-speaking driver.

One final note: The train from Madrid to Toledo stops in Aranjuez, which is where the Royal Palace is located. You may want to visit both cities in a day; you can travel from Toledo to Aranjuez during the siesta to maximize shopping time. You can picnic at the gardens (bring food from Toledo) and then explore. Of course, if you've bought as much as we have, you'll never be able to consider this possibility.

Getting Around

Few cars are allowed in the old part of Toledo, so wear your walking shoes. Taxis are found at the main sights (only when you don't need them), or at the bottom of the hill. Be prepared for the cobblestones.

There are two approaches to seeing Toledo: Get a map, study it, follow the paths; or simply wander. We prefer the second option because basically we're wandering fools, but also because any glance at a map of Toledo will tell you that this city is a warren of tiny streets probably beyond your navigational abilities.

You could figure this out if you lived here for six months; you can't do it all in six hours.

If you believe in a small amount of organization, consider planning your tour in a circle. Start at the Plaza del Zocodover and end at Cardenal, a picture-perfect taverna for a lunch you will never forget. If you make certain to head toward the three or four biggest tourist sights (cathedral, Goya's house, Sinagoga, Church of San Juan de los Reyes), you will automatically see the best of Toledo and pass through the best shopping streets.

Best Buys of Toledo

CERAMICS: Ceramics, ceramics, ceramics. The clay cities are actually past Toledo, and if you have a car, or a car and driver, you can make a nice day out of it—you will indeed get away from the touristy aspects and the Toledo made-for-tourist prices. We generally love to complain about such things, but you will not hear us complaining in Toledo. We understand that the prices are inflated, but we like them just fine. When you can buy an exquisite dinner plate for $12 (actual asking price, no bargaining), a jar for $10, and a monstrous jug (three feet tall) for $60, well, what's there to complain about?

There are two types of basic wares for sale: Toledoware, which is the typically painted faience style made in Talavera de la Reina; and what we call the Archbishop Pattern, because it is made in the city of Puente de Arzobispo, where the distinctive style is painted with yellows, beiges, greens, and browns and always includes a picture of an animal. Some pieces are decorated with people, but animals are much more common.

We don't want to go on at great length

about ceramics, so we simply remind you of the obvious: Both types are earthenware. That means they have a soft paste base, which breaks more easily than bone china. Pack your buys carefully as you schlepp them around during the day, and pack more carefully when you travel—or plan to carry your most precious items on the plane by hand. Buy breakables with your American Express card, or with a bankcard with a protection plan, so that if you suffer breakage, you can, at least, get a refund. And finally, don't count on using your new wares in the microwave (if the plates or mugs run hot in your microwave it means high lead content); don't serve foods high in acids (vinegar or lemon juice included) on painted ware—lead poisoning is not a thing of the past.

DAMASCENE: If we liked damascene, we would tell you it was one of the best buys of Toledo. Unfortunately, as much as we admire the workmanship and the technique, we loathe the fashion statement. If you have the kids with you, they might be interested to see how the gold is implanted in the metal—which can be observed (for free) in many workshops.

SWORDS: You'll be pleased to know that the U.S. Army has its swords made in Toledo; unfortunately, you may not inspect the factory. There are other "sword factories" open to the public—they are like many of the other factories in Spain that are open to the public: Rip-off City. With or without the factory tour, you'll have plenty of opportunity to buy swords at every shop in town. They sell at all different price ranges, and will cause only a small problem when you try to board the airplane to get home.

SCISSORS: The technology that makes swords also produces scissors; they're sold in many sizes, with and without designs.

Hours

Hours are strict; no shops or sights seem to be open during lunch. Stores close at 1:30 P.M. for siesta and reopen at 3:30 or later. They are open until 7 P.M.

Finds

JULIAN SIMÓN: If you shop around town a while, you'll note that the Simón family owns several shops in Toledo. This one specializes in ceramics, but not the usual stuff that's sold everywhere. The pieces here are handcrafted by artisans, signed, and priced accordingly. In some cases, this is one of the few stores in all of Spain where you can buy from this or that particular artist. There is a lusterware called La Loza Dorada that comes with its own pedigree and papers of authenticity. For the serious only; this is not a TT.

JULIAN SIMÓN, Comercio 36

▼

PATIO TÍPICO TOLEDANO: This may be the best find in Toledo if you want ceramics. (Of course you want ceramics.) Because it is in the opposite direction from the sights and the tourists, because you have to go a little out of your way to get here, you will be rewarded with the best prices in town, and one of the best selections. Certainly the setup is charming— an old house, an old man. You enter, walk around the patio, where the wares hang from the brick walls, and then enter two salons. The last chamber is filled with linens and ceramics. We chatted up the owner a great deal (he does not speak English) and in no time at all he offered us a 5% discount. He will not ship, but he will pack for travel. We bought in many shops and we saw some of this merchandise elsewhere in Toledo, but this remains our favorite resource. And out of the two dozen ceramics shops we visited, his prices were the best in town.

PATIO TÍPICO TOLEDANO, Calle de la Plata 9

F. COMACHO: A teeny-tiny ceramics shop that specializes in small items; we bought big fat spice jars in the Archbishop Pattern here at $10 each. Nice gift items and coffee mugs.

F. COMACHO, Nuncio Viejo 1

DE LA PUENTE: For serious aficionados and those with money, De la Puente is not touristy at all, and has very special—read expensive—ceramic crafts. There are tiles, fountains, and decorative wares. This is high-quality stuff and is very, very pricey. Expect to pay $40 for a plate. Even if the prices scare you, please stop by to stare.

DE LA PUENTE, Plaza del Salvador 2 and 3

CASA BALAGUER: This antiques shop is full of serious stuff, much of it religious. It's also a good resource for country style: old furniture, old earthenware containers, etc. A dusty, delightful place.

CASA BALAGUER, Ciudad 12

ARTE ANTIGUO: Another great antiques store, this one almost at the end of the line and quite near the San Juan de los Reyes church. The selection is larger here than elsewhere, the presentation is more sophisticated, and the prices are higher. But this is very good stuff, and you'll love browsing here for everything from old plates to heavy furniture.

ARTE ANTIGUO, Reyes Católicos 10

Toledo on a Schedule

Toledo on Parade: One-Day Tour

1. Begin at the Plaza del Zocodover. Check out its selection of boring TTs (you ain't seen nothin' yet—good TTs are coming). Go to the junction of Calle Comercio and Calle Plata. Calle Plata is away from the Cathedral, but that's OK. Take time out, first thing, to visit Patio Típico Toledano (No. 9), which is one block up, then cut back down to Comercio and head toward the Cathedral.

2. When you are almost at the Cathedral doors, the TTs and fun shops begin. Along the way, catch Jose Herrer (No. 24) for ceramics that are so-so, Julian Simón for swords and damascene in a major and modern TT (No. 50), etc. There are several shops that sell Lladró and Nao figurines.

3. Shop the streets that encircle the Cathedral and then go inside to pay your respects. Emerge and hit the Calle de la Trinidad, which will lead you automatically to Calle de Santo Tomé. This is one of our favorite streets in Spain. Every single building has been turned into a shop; 90% of the shops

are TTs. There are baskets and bushels in the streets, filled with souvenirs. There are people everywhere. There is merchandise galore. Run from store to store as greedily as you can. There is no one best shop here: Check them all out. Only Casa Camino (No. 20) has some unusual handpainted glassware you won't see all over town.

4. Follow the signs toward the Museo de Greco; they will lead you off from Calle de Santo Tomé to more shopping and then to the Sinagoga del Tránsito. Once at the synagogue, you're at the top of Calle de los Reyes Católicos—this is also a street lined with TTs, but they are more modern and crass than the ones on Santo Tomé, and by this time you've bought so much stuff that you're not as amused.

5. As you are approaching the final church of the tour, San Juan de los Reyes, take a detour into the antiques shop Arte Antiguo (No. 10), and then, at the crest of the hill, go to the little house with the plates on the wall at San Juan de los Reyes (No. 2)—the shop has no name. There you'll be able to meet the potter as he handpaints tiles and patiently waits for you to choose from the plates on the wall. He sells both the Mudéjar style with high glaze and luster or the faience styles in both pattern types. A small plate costs $4; the medium size is $6, and the giant dinner size is $10. We buy from this man every time we are in Toledo. And sometimes he takes us to the train station because we are too loaded down to walk.

7▾ SHOPPING BARCELONA

Welcome to Barcelona

You want to talk hot? Barcelona is hot. From now until 1992, you'll hear all kinds of jet-setters talking about Barcelona. Some people will even tell you that Barcelona has more spunk than Madrid.

Barcelona has good atmosphere, it's true. But it's also a strange city. And although it is legally in Spain, you cannot visit Barcelona without understanding that you are in Catalonia (the English version), Cataluña (the Spanish version), or Catalunya (the official Catalán version). We like it here, but you can't compare it to Madrid, one of the world's big-time cities. Barcelona goes for the big time when it hosts the Olympics in 1992 but will always be a big-time small city.

If Barcelona is your only stop in Spain (a cruise possibility), you will not realize how unusual it is, since you will not have a chance to compare it to any other city. If you visit all of Spain, you'll quickly see that in terms of fashion and retailing, Barcelona competes as a city of interest. But the city is nonetheless a loner. It's not a big metropolis like Madrid; it's not as picture-perfect as Sevilla or Granada. And it would not be nearly as much fun as it is if it weren't for the architecture—especially the work of Antonio Gaudí—or the shoes, especially those of Beverly Feldman. In any case, Barcelona is the perfect city for an introduction to Catalán shopping.

The Lay of the Land

Barcelona is the second largest city in Spain, and will grow even more in the next two years as hotels and pre-Olympic edifices are constructed, renovated, and rearranged. There are four principal parts of the city being used for the Games, and these will especially begin to sparkle. But these are not the main shopping areas—yet.

The inner city is built in two cores: the old city (Barri Gòtic), near the waterfront, and the newer ring around the old city, which was built in the Baroque style with some Art Deco and, of course, much Gaudí. These two parts of the city make up the major shopping areas. You can walk from one to the other, although it's a stretch of several miles if you go from end to end.

The main drag of Barcelona is called Las Ramblas, which stretches from the waterfront to the Plaça de Catalunya. The plaza separates the older and newer part of the city, and is surrounded by major department stores, retail outlets, and fast-food chains. Coming off the top of the plaza is the Passeig de Gracia, a Fifth Avenue type of street with the usual high-class stores, airlines offices, and banks. Running parallel to the Passeig is an extension of Las Ramblas, this one called Rambla de Catalunya, which is lined with great shops. See page 195 for our descriptions of shopping neighborhoods and how to get to them.

Barcelona

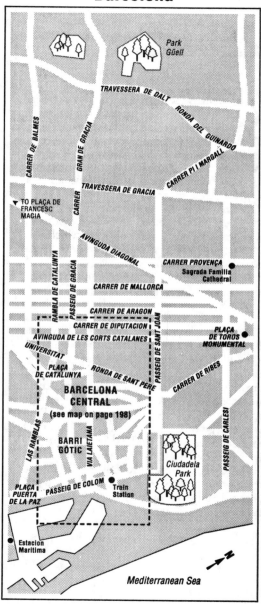

Park Güell

TRAVESSERA DE DALT

RONDA DEL GUINARDO

CARRER DE BALMES

GRAN DE GRACIA

CARRER

CARRER PI I MARGALL

TRAVESSERA DE GRACIA

▼ TO PLAÇA DE FRANCESC MACIA

AVINGUDA DIAGONAL

RAMBLA DE CATALUNYA

PASSEIG DE GRACIA

CARRER PROVENÇA
● Sagrada Familia Cathedral

CARRER DE MALLORCA

CARRER DE ARAGON

CARRER DE DIPUTACION

PASSEIG DE SANT JOAN

AVINGUDA DE LES CORTS CATALANES

PLAÇA DE TOROS MONUMENTAL ●

UNIVERSITAT

PLAÇA DE CATALUNYA

RONDA DE SANT PERE

CARRER DE RIBES

BARCELONA CENTRAL
(see map on page 198)

BARRI GÒTIC

LAS RAMBLAS

VIA LAIETANA

PASSEIG DE CARLES I

Ciudadela Park

PLAÇA PUERTA DE LA PAZ

PASSEIG DE COLOM

Train Station

● Estacion Maritima

N↗

Mediterranean Sea

190

Getting Around

You can walk just about everywhere you want to go in Barcelona but will need a taxi to get to some of the Gaudí sights like the Sagrada Familia Cathedral, or Güell Park, or even the flea market. Taxis in Barcelona have the highest start-up fee in Spain—when the flag goes down to start your ride, you owe $2!

There is a rather extensive Metro system that will get you to main shopping areas and will go to all the Olympic sites. If you are getting around Avinguda Diagonal, you may want to take the bus. The bus is also easy to take around town. Ask your concierge which bus will get you where you want to go. A ride costs under just 60¢.

Booking Barcelona / I

Barcelona Concept, a magazine that offers a snazzy and glossy guide to food, events, and stores of Barcelona, is sold on newsstands for about $4.50. It's much like the American *Vogue.* Although the magazine is in Spanish, it has a pictorial rating system that will allow you to get the general idea in a glance. There is a similar magazine, also sold on newsstands, which is the kind of city magazine we Americans are more used to—*Vivir en Barcelona.* But you're going to need to read Spanish to get the most out of this one.

The tourism people have their own free brochure on shopping in Barcelona that is absolutely adorable—it comes in the shape of a shopping bag and is made of four maps to different parts of the city, each color-coded to pinpoint various shops. We don't know how frequently they update their map, but you can get a basic idea of where you want to be for the best shopping in a quick glance. Stop by the tourist office at Passeig de Gracia 35. The building housing the Patronato Municipal de Turismo is one of the most spectacular buildings you'll ever see in your life. Use your need for the shopping booklet as your excuse to enter this fairy-tale visual delight.

Booking Barcelona/2

RAMADA RENAISSANCE: Ramada is one of the first big American chains to arrive in town; more will be arriving as we get close to 1992, but few will offer all the right ingredients as this hotel does. The Ramada has a fabulous location right on Las Ramblas, within walking distance of absolutely everything. The hotel is nice, not overdone, so you feel comfortable in an American way. It is almost always packed and takes a lot of groups. Obviously travel agents know what we do: This is one of the best bets in town. There is a Club Floor. Moderate. Local phone: 318-6200.

RAMADA RENAISSANCE, Las Ramblas 110 (Metro: Liceu)

▼

ALEXANDRA: This is our personal find and a perfect four-star hotel for those who want to shop till they drop. Located on a side street in the block between the Rambla de Catalunya and the Passeig, the Alexandra has a new and dramatic Art Nouveau lobby. The rooms are not as chic, but they are OK, and the price is right. Moderate. Local phone: 215-3052.

ALEXANDRA, Mallorca 251 (Metro: Catalunya)

▼

HILTON: Hilton has just opened in time to get into the future and has chosen the shopping street Avinguda Diagonal, giving you a third choice of hotel with good location and good shopping. This one is a five-star and more expensive and glitzy in an American sort of way. Expensive. Local phone: 410-8128.

HILTON, Avinguda Diagonal 595 (Metro: Provença)

Snack and Shop

FARGA: When you were a little girl, did your mom or grandma take you to a fancy tearoom for lunch on a special shopping day, for a special meal and sweet? If so, you'll feel perfectly at home at Farga, which is part bakery, part take-out gourmet deli, and part restaurant (upstairs and on the main floor). Located right at the top of the Passeig and on the beginning of the fanciest shopping stretch of Avinguda Diagonal, this is where to be at 1 P.M. with your appetite in place. Prices are moderate. If you're early, you won't need a reservation— but just in case, call 218-3212 (local). Do not confuse with Fargas, which is a candy shop.

FARGA, Avinguda Diagonal 391 (Metro: Diagonal)

▼

BOPAN: This bakery serves pizza, breads, and *buñuelos,* which are fried donut holes with or without filling. (*Relleños* means filling.) You can get a cup of coffee and a snack, but there's no place to sit down.

BOPAN, Rambla de Catalunya 119 (Metro: Diagonal)

▼

MAURI: OK, so we're old ladies who are nuts for tearooms. This one is not dissimilar to Farga, but has even more European style and flair, and is in a better shopping district. Mauri offers an old-fashioned candy counter, with about a million choices in chocolate, but they also have a buffet with baskets of miniature sandwiches and quiche, which you pick up yourself (tongs provided) and munch while sipping a tea or coffee. Best yet, this is an inexpensive way to eat lunch. We feasted on quiche and ham sandwiches for $8 each and thought it a bargain. A true treat. No reservations taken.

MAURI, Provença 241 esq. Rambla de Catalunya (Metro: Diagonal)

Credit Concepts

As we've mentioned throughout this book, it's rare to find stores that welcome all credit cards in Spain. The big famous-name stores and many TTs in Barcelona do take all credit cards, but don't count on little shops being so friendly.

Catalonian Concepts

You don't have to be in Barcelona more than an hour or two before you realize that you are in the Catalonian heartland. All the street signs are in Catalán, the local language, which is a cousin of Spanish and French. (Market is *mercado* in Spanish; *marché* in French; *mercat* in Catalán.)

Likewise if you ask about a particular designer, you are told (and rapped on the knuckles in the telling) that the designer is not Spanish, but Catalán. It is always polite to ask, when you wander into a designer shop that is not familiar to you, if the designer is Spanish or Catalán; then you can't get into trouble. The Catalán people themselves are much more French in temperament than Spanish, and have a rampant national pride that is even stronger recently because it was outlawed during Franco's reign. So mind your manners, forget your Spanish dictionary, and note a few basic Catalán facts: The word for street is *calle* in Spanish and *carrer* in Catalán. Avenue is *avinguda* in Catalán, plaza is *plaça,* and paseo is *passeig.* Guidebooks and some maps will confuse you because they will note some names in Spanish, others in Catalán.

Shopping Neighborhoods

Las Ramblas

We consider this street a neighborhood unto itself, as it reaches from the base of the Plaça de Catalunya all the way to the sea. In the center of the street is a wide promenade around which traffic moves. There are stores on both sides of the street, and stalls in the promenade; on Sundays there is a flea market beginning around the Liceu Metro station. The shopping here is not what you would call posh. In fact, it's almost seedy. Never mind; once you get inside some of the stores you'll have fun. There's a **SIMAGO** (kind of a K mart with a grocery store in the basement level) and a million TTs where you can find all the souvenirs you could ever imagine.

Diagonal

The Avinguda Diagonal is a major thoroughfare that bisects the city at, you guessed it, an angle. It is always referred to simply as Diagonal. (Say "Dee-Ag-o-Nal"). The major shopping on Diagonal reaches from Passeig de Gracia to the Plaça Francesc Macia. Although ECI does have a Diagonal address, it's much farther uptown than you would want to travel, and there are few other stores in the vicinity. Instead, shopping congregates on either side of Diagonal in three distinct neighborhoods:

CASALS: From the Plaça Francesc Macia, if you turn right on Avinguda de Pau Casals, you'll be in a small but chic shopping district where many big-time stores have shops. The street is bisected by Carrer del Mestre Nicolau, with more designer shops on either side of Casals. This is a very tiny pocket up here, but is worth exploring.

AUGUSTA: Also on top of Diagonal, but far closer to the Passeig, is Via Augusta. This street must have been the hot address in town for a while, but apparently something snapped and it never got any further. As a result, you find Armani's **EMPORIO** here, and a few other nice stores, but it's not really worth going out of your way for, and is not as dramatic as one would hope.

RAMBLA DE CATALUNYA: This is the best shopping district in town, and is right below Diagonal, centered around the Diagonal Metro station and running parallel to Passeig de Gracia. From Diagonal down to the Plaça de Catalunya, each side street running the block between Rambla de Catalunya and Passeig de Gracia is a winner. Do not confuse this part of the Rambla with the other part, as mentioned on page 195. While you can walk the whole stretch (and you should), the two are dramatically different.

Barri Gótic

This is the heart of the old city—a maze of streets too narrow for traffic and buildings too old to ruin with neon. The area is just off Las Ramblas (near the Liceu station), and is centered around the Cathedral, going down almost to the waterfront and including the area around the Picasso Museum, which is really its own neighborhood. But you can walk to the Picasso Museum in about three to five minutes (from the Cathedral) and although there's not much shopping along the way, once you get there the atmosphere is identical.

Barcelona Central

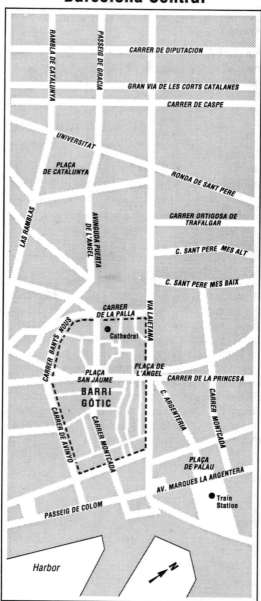

Sunday Shopping

Barcelona is a good city for Sunday shopping: there's a street market on Las Ramblas all afternoon and a few flea markets that are open in the morning. Also, the zillions of TTs that line Las Ramblas are open nonstop. Most of the regular stores may be closed, but you'll barely miss them in a city as alive on Sundays as Barcelona.

COBI Shopping

We'd like to tell you that we are so dumb that the first few times we saw COBI being sold in flea markets across Spain we thought he was merely a bad copy of Garfield, America's popular cartoon cat. Now we know that the '92 Olympic mascot is a personality in his own right. He can be found in plush form, on bumper stickers, on T-shirts, etc. He's the same yellow-orange color that Garfield is, but unlike Garfield, he has a belly button made of the five aligned circles of the Olympic logo.

TTs

If you're looking for tourist traps, you'll find two kinds: the ones owned by immigrants on Las Ramblas and the ones owned by locals near the Cathedral and the Picasso Museum. Our favorite item in any of them was Paloma's perfume! There are several shops around the museum that do a hearty business in Miró T-shirts, Guernica postcards, and all sorts of posters. The shops near the Cathedral sell crafts and ceramics (see page 197); almost all the shops sell some selection of Lladró or Nao—or both. Watch for sales on Lladró and for price competition between TTs. The bullfight posters (see page 46) are most prominent in Barcelona, and least expensive. Prices on these range from $2.50 each to $3, with name included, although some shops sell the poster at one price ($2) and the printing for an additional price (varying from $1 to $2 per name). When you're negotiating, make sure the price you establish includes the printing.

Flea Markets

ELS ENCANTS: This is the Spanish-style flea market, and you really have to get lucky to make a real find here. Vendors place their objects on the ground or on blankets—it is like a tag sale, and a lot of the stuff is astonishingly junky. It's not our kind of market, and you may think it's a total bust. Catch the bus (No. 18) on Las Ramblas across the street from the Ramada or in front of the Ritz; it will take you past one of the city's bullfight rings and give you a small tour of Barcelona as you trek to the edge of the freeway where the market is held. Monday, Wednesday, Friday, and Saturday, 10 A.M.–8 P.M.

ELS ENCANTS, Consell at Dos de Maig near Plaça de les Glòries (Metro: Glòries)

▼

ANTIQUES MARKET: Right at the Cathedral, at the head of the antiques street in the Barri Gótic, there's a small (about thirty dealers) antiques market held on Thursdays. This is not the tag-sale junk you'll find at Els Encants, but much of it is junk of a higher order. There are also big items, furniture, and perhaps a treasure or two. Many dealers will take dollars or credit cards. Thursday only 10 A.M.–2 P.M..

ANTIQUES MARKET, Plaça del Catedral (Metro: Jaume 1)

▼

LAS RAMBLAS: On Sundays Las Ramblas is the place to see and be seen. You'll find everything from vendors selling tie-dyed T-shirts to tarot-card readers. Although most of the stalls sell hippie wares and real junk, you never know what you'll find. We happened upon an artist selling small ceramic trays (probably ashtrays) that we turned into soap dishes as gifts. (Buy Spanish soap—see page 48—and attach to ceramic dish with ribbon.) Each piece was unique, handmade and signed by the artist. He refused to bargain, but we did see his dishes in a shop for 30% more than what we paid in the street, so we felt vindicated. The market is only on Sunday, late morning until dark.

LAS RAMBLAS, Las Ramblas (Metro: Liceu)

Department Stores

ECI: There are two ECI stores of note to tourists. One is conveniently located on the Plaça de Catalunya, the other is a bit on the edge of town, where the shopping ends and the modern apartment houses and high-rise buildings make the streets look more like L.A.'s Wilshire Boulevard than Picasso's Barcelona. This is the suburban Maria Cristina ECI, which you can easily reach by Metro, and it's a winner. It's new, it's modern, it's got more space for display than your usual ECI (which is normally crammed to the gills), and it's the most like an American department store of any ECI in Spain. The Plaça de Catalunya ECI, right at the top of the Rambla de Catalunya, is old and cramped and not too exciting—although they do sell *churros* first thing in the morning.

ECI

Plaça de Catalunya (Metro: Catalunya)

Plaça de la Reina Maria Cristina (Metro: Maria Cristina)

▼

GALERÍAS PRECIADOS: Also two easy-for-the-tourists-to-get-to stores, in locations similar to ECI, but the more upscale of the two is not as far from the tourist core as is the ECI at Maria Cristina. GP is not the better store, at either location, but the uptown store is really OK. The downtown store at Plaça de l'Ángel is very much like a K mart; the uptown store is very convenient to other upscale shopping, and offers you the opportunity to use the passport service and actually get your IVA back if you buy something for 47,000 *pesetas,* or to get an immediate 10% discount on merchandise that is not sold from a store concession. It also has a nice grocery store.

GALERÍAS PRECIADOS

Plaça de l'Ángel (Metro: Jaume 1)

Plaça de Francesc Macia (Metro: Hospital Clinic)

Shopping Centers

B arcelona real estate developers have gone bonkers for shopping centers. These are very European in style, more like the French *passage* than the American mall or strip center. Usually these centers have very small entrances on a main shopping street and then reach deep into the back of the block. While Madrid has its boring *multicentros* that aren't worth your time, almost every shopping center in Barcelona—especially in the high-rent district on either the Passeig or the Rambla de Catalunya—is worthwhile.

EL BULEVARD ROSA: The first time we ran into a Bulevard Rosa arcade we thought, "What fun!" Then we ran into another one and thought, "How strange!" The third time we figured it out. A Bulevard Rosa development is a minimall built into the bottom of an office building, containing small boutiques geared to the busy yuppie class. There is a formula consisting of a coffee bar or restaurant, a jewelry boutique, lots of shoe boutiques, and assorted clothing shops. In the bigger developments, there will be chain stores as well. The Bulevard Rosa development on Passeig de Gracia is the largest in Barcelona. It has four entrances on three different streets, and encompasses the entire first floor of a large office complex. There are 101 shops, most of which are small glass-front boutiques with very select merchandise. Some of the chains include **GLOBE, POLO** (not Ralph Lauren), **TOKIO, CACHAREL, FIORUCCI, SPLEEN,** and **ESCORPIÓN**. Don't miss **MARIA ARAUYO**'s hats in store No. 32. Some shops are open on Sunday and during siesta.

Not far away, on the Avinguda Diagonal in the midst of the shopping section, there is another Bulevard Rosa minimall. This one is not as splendid as the one on Passeig de Gracia, and only has thirty-nine shops, but it does have the Beverly Feldman shoe shop. See page 207 for a full and complete report on Beverly Feldman.

EL BULEVARD ROSA

Passeig de Gracia 53 (Metro: Passeig de Gracia)

Avinguda Diagonal 412 (Metro: Diagonal)

▼

GALERÍAS HALLEY: This one is not nearly as bright as Halley's Comet, or even as good as El Bulevard Rosa (in all its incarnations), yet it's still very, very nice and worth a peek. The minimall is L-shaped and has about forty shops including the usual plethora of shoe shops, an eating area complete with a small fountain, and a good mix of costume jewelry and ready-to-wear shops.

GALERÍAS HALLEY, Passeig de Gracia (Metro: Passeig de Gracia)

▼

LA AVENIDA: This may be our favorite shopping center. It too looks like all the others as it meanders under an office building, but it has a branch of **SPLEEN** (a costume jewelry shop), which we go nuts for. This gallery is made of black marble in several lanes that connect across the courtyard. It's got some chains, like **GLOBE** and **BENETTON,** but it's got some original shops too. At the far corner, the lane leads into another shopping passage called Tiendas Rosellon, a small stretch opening onto the street of the same name. Upscale, with center fountain and café; very refreshing.

LA AVENIDA, Rambla de Catalunya 121 (Metro: Diagonal)

Museum Shopping

PICASSO MUSEUM: The shop is extensive, and probably has more prints, postcards, and T-shirts than there are pieces of art in the museum itself. Some of the shirts can only be bought here, and others are slightly cheaper than in the tourist shops. The museum itself is a stunning example of how an old mansion can be gutted and restructured to let in light, while retaining the integrity of its original charm.

PICASSO MUSEUM, Montcada 15 (Metro: Jaume 1)

Continental Big Names

BENETTON
  Passeig de Gracia 49
  Rambla de Catalunya 121
  Avinguda Diagonal 588
  Vía Augusta 128
DESCAMPS, Passeig de Gracia 75
GUCCI, Avinguda Diagonal 415
LOUIS VUITTON, Mestre Nicolau 8
BRUNO MAGLI, Mestre Nicolau 15
DANIEL HECHTER, Avinguda Diagonal 590
RODIER, Passeig de Gracia 66
FIORUCCI, Passeig de Gracia 76
FOGAL, Rambla de Catalunya 131

CÉLINE, Vía Augusta 5
STEFANEL, Rambla de Catalunya 112
ALAIN MANOUKIAN, Passeig de Gracia 62
   (Galerías Halley)
JACADI, Rambla de Catalunya 79
EMPORIO ARMANI, Vía Augusta 10
PIERRE CARDIN, Passeig de la Concepción 14
[IXI: Z], Provença 270
STEPHANE KÉLIAN, Rosselló 218

Finds

DORY: You might pass up Dory in your rush to cross the street and get to the fine leathers in Loewe, but think again. We recommend that you go to Loewe first, check out the prices, and then go back to Dory. Dory is not as imposing, or as flashy, or as snooty, but they do carry the Enrique Loewe Knappe leather line, which is different from the regular Loewe line! It is exactly the kind of thing you count on us to find for you, since most Americans don't even know about the Loewe brothers' split. (See page 40.)

Be the first in your neighborhood to come home with something unique and special. The purses and wallets are crafted from butter-soft brown and black hides. You can put together whole ensembles of wallets, glasses cases, key cases, and purses that mix and match. A beautiful handbag starts at $125 but escalates to $400 as you get into the high-end stuff. The leather line is sporty, with one color of leather (brown or black) trimmed with natural cognac-colored leather to make a two-tone bag. The quality of the leather is exceptional, as is the craftsmanship, so what you have is a casual bag that whispers money and class.

Inside your handbag, separate from the felt bag that will protect it, is a credit card–like card that is your guarantee of authenticity. This line is not carried extensively around town, and while you will see pieces elsewhere, Dory has about the best selection and can give you brochures on the creator. As far as we know this line is not carried in the U.S. Dory also has a complete luggage line, as well as the Porsche leathers. All major credit cards accepted.

DORY, Passeig de Gracia 33 (Metro: Passeig de Gracia)

▼

BEVERLY FELDMAN: Although this shop is in a Bulevard Rosa development, we think that it deserves its own listing, especially since we feel like we practically own it. One of us bought three pairs of boots and five pairs of shoes; the other drooled and bought whatever fit. We do not suffer from the Imelda Marcos complex. We are just smart shoppers who could not pass up Maud Frizon look-alike shoes selling "two for one" at $75.

Who is Beverly Feldman? An American shoe designer who draws inspiration from Maud Frizon and then adds her own zingy touch to make shoes that are complex, whimsical, and drop-dead chic yet sell at down-to-earth prices! She lives in Alicante, the manufacturing town on the beach, where she makes her fanciful creations with the motto "Too much is not enough" engraved on the sole of each shoe. Even at retail, the shoes are highly affordable ($150); we found them for the same price in Saks Fifth Avenue. (Saks does not have the same selection, however.) This is a shop not to miss. Open during siesta. All major credit cards accepted.

BEVERLY FELDMAN, El Bulevard Rosa, Avinguda Diagonal 472 (Metro: Hospital Clinic or Diagonal)

▼

LOEWE: Loewe is located on our very favorite block in Barcelona. The three finest examples of Art Nouveau architecture are located here, including the one that houses Loewe. Look up from across the street and you will see that the building resembles a birthday cake. The architect, Lluis Domenechi Montaner, built the building as a private residence in 1906. You must enter the business offices of the Patronato Municipal de Turismo de Barcelona (next to Loewe) to really see the interior work. Each room is designed in a different storybook theme, using carved stone, mosaic, stained glass, and molded wood ceilings. Loewe is listed here as a find because the building makes it so special.

Actually, Loewe (and leathergoods) is downstairs, but we know you're going to be visiting Loewe, and we want to make sure you don't miss one of the best treats in Barcelona. Loewe will just have to content itself with being a secondary treat.

And Loewe is indeed a treat. If you are treating yourself to a splurge, you could not find a better place in Barcelona. The spacious store has women's clothing as well as the handbags and accessories in leather and, if you are visiting before the spring or summer season, a beach line that is inexpensive only when compared to the $400 price tag for the leather handbag. All major credit cards accepted.

LOEWE, Passeig de Gracia 35 (Metro: Passeig de Gracia)

▼

GENERAL OPTICA: One of the best optical shops for fashion frames, including Mikli, Valentino, Anne Marie Perris, Fiorucci, Silhouette, and Lanvin is located next to the Hotel Presidente. It is one of a chain of shops, selling trendy looks at fair prices. The Valentino glasses (nonprescription) begin at $190. The shop closes on Saturday at 2 P.M., but is open during siesta on Friday. MasterCard and Diners Club accepted.

GENERAL OPTICA, Avinguda Diagonal 570 (Metro: Hospital Clinic)

▼

JAPAN: We vote Japan hands-down winner in a creative-store design category. Instead of the Japanese copying the Spanish, the Spanish are, tongue in cheek, copying the Japanese. The first thing you notice as you walk into the store is the massive red and black spaceship-cone light hanging over your head. It looks like a bad take on a Hollywood spaceship. However, it does set the tone for the store. If you can get past the picture of the Mona Lisa holding a red half circle containing the words "Japan Barcelona" and look at the clothing, you will see lots of casual, soft, sculpted mix-and-match pieces. The racks are set up on the sides and down the middle. The dressing rooms look like trash cans with cherry-red curtains covering them—with the logo once again printed on the bottom. One thing is certain—even if you never buy a piece of clothing, you will never forget this store.

JAPAN, Rambla de Catalunya 80 (Metro: Diagonal)

▼

ELEVEN: And while we're talking creative stores, you should also see Eleven. Eleven is a shoe store, and the shoes are not anything to write home about. They are nice shoes, to be sure, but the store is so incredibly overbuilt that the merchandise doesn't merit this kind of a home. Step into the glass elevator box, or walk up the runway ramp, to get to the upper level of the store with its extraordinary ramps and catwalks and cutout wrought iron and glass bricks.

ELEVEN, Avinguda Diagonal 466 (Metro: Diagonal)

▼

SPLEEN: We're just fools for costume jewelry (we're fools for serious jewelry too; we just can't afford it) and on any trip to Barcelona can be found with our noses pressed to the glass windows at a Spleen store. About half the line is fashion-inspired (currently that means pieces that mix with the Chanel look), and the other half is purely creative, fun, and different. Earrings begin around $30.

SPLEEN

Bulevard Rosa, Passeig de Gracia 55 (Metro: Passeig de Gracia)

Mestre Nicolau 12 (Metro: Hospital Clinic)

Rambla de Catalunya 121 (Metro: Diagonal)

▼

PAULI VILA: This is a shoe shop right in the high-rent Diagonal district, which carries an amazingly huge selection of shoe brands and has all the wild styles that we associate with Spain that can make you look like you're wearing $400 shoes when in fact they cost under $100. Lots of Maud Frizon–inspired styles, but also classic designs for both men and women. No shoe freak can come to Barcelona without visiting this store. Sara Navarro (page 214) is across the street.

PAULI VILA, Plaça Francesc Macia 1, esq. Calvo Sotelo (Metro: Hospital Clinic)

▼

RAMON SANTAEULARIA: Ramon Santaeularia sells couture finishes. The inside of the shop is divided into three parts. The first section has boxes and bags and bins of buttons, belt buckles, and finishing flourishes. The second section has display cases and drawers of the latest costume jewelry. There are some outright Chanel imitations with Cs on them that are not very good copies, but most of the jewelry is in the style of Chanel or is original, and is excellent. Prices are also much better than at Chanel—earrings cost from $30 to $60. There are a number of handbags on sale here, all made in Spain by Italian designers! They start at about $200. Don't be shy, go through every display case and all the drawers (we did), then go to the back room for the markdown baskets, where you might find a necklace for $5. More expensive and more formal than Spleen, but a good source for the fashion-conscious woman.

RAMON SANTAEULARIA, Rambla de Catalunya 40 (Metro: Catalunya)

▼

CARMINA ROTGER: Still another costume jewelry shop, also offering belts and some handbags. Very sophisticated, very chic, very much the right look for the woman who expects to be recognized for her taste and style.

CARMINA ROTGER, Mallorca 251 (Metro: Diagonal)

▼

GALA: After you've seen enough handbags and enough Loewe imitators, wander into Gala for some totally original thoughts. A small shop, but packed with the kind of style that sets trends across the seas.

GALA, Vía Augusta 29 (Metro: Diagonal)

Spanish and Catalán Big Names

ADOLFO DOMINGUEZ: One of the biggest names in Spanish design is Adolfo Dominguez, who became known to Americans as the man who dressed Don Johnson in the heyday of *Miami Vice*. His Barcelona shop, on the corner of Carrer de Provença, is a wraparound three-level high-tech monument to his understated, simple clothing, shoes, and accessories for men and women. His background is in the classics, but he softens the look with his choice of fabrics and structure. All major credit cards accepted.

ADOLFO DOMINGUEZ, Passeig de Gracia 89 (Metro: Diagonal)

▼

ENRIQUE MUDA: Muda has a few shops around town, and does a nice business in very wearable office suits and dresses. The best shop is on the Passeig in the lower level of a Gaudí building. About $300 for a suit.

ENRIQUE MUDA, Passeig de Gracia, edificio La Pedrera (Metro: Passeig de Gracia)

▼

CARLOS TORRENTS: There is some private label, some Spanish designers, and many European lines like Ermenegildo Zegna in this three-level, high-tech, gray and black shop. Prices are average for imports, with suits starting at $250. Torrents also carries casual clothing and accessories to complement every look. All major credit cards accepted.

CARLOS TORRENTS, Passeig de Gracia 95 (Metro: Diagonal)

CONTI: This store makes us think of an upper-class men's Benetton. There are two stores, one for casual wear and one for formal. The clothing is stacked in blond-wood bins, or hung on racks. There is private label as well as European big names like Nino Cerruti, Girbaud, and Zegna. Spanish designers include Miguel Ibars and others not so well known. Casual shirts begin at $70, suits at $700. All major credit cards accepted.

CONTI, Avinguda Diagonal 512 (Metro: Hospital Clinic)

▼

LOEWE HOMBRE EXCLUSIVAMENTE: Loewe for men? Yes, and only for men. This might be our favorite Loewe shop in the city, because of all the manly charm. We can imagine our fellows dressed head to toe in nautical navy and white, smelling of leather and suede, dashing off to the yacht for a private conference with the head of some major corporation who wants to fund our newest venture. Then a picnic dinner from the Loewe picnic basket, and, in case of rain, shelter under the Loewe umbrella. Finally, off to Marbella with their Loewe luggage. It's a wonderful fantasy. The shop sells everything except the right man to wear all of the goodies. All major credit cards accepted.

LOEWE HOMBRE EXCLUSIVAMENTE, Avinguda Diagonal 570 (Metro: Hospital Clinic)

▼

JOSÉ TÓMAS: One of the up-and-coming Spanish menswear designers is José Tómas. His shop on Carrer Mallorca is all blond wood, with black display racks and huge black-and-white photos of gorgeous men wearing his clothing. The company was founded in 1977 and has been gaining steadily in popularity.

Mr. Tómas's look is casual classic. He chooses to use unconventional fabrics in his suits, shirts, and ties. His tailoring is reminiscent of the 1940s classic slouch, with a lot of attention paid to detail. He also designs a line called Passport. All major credit cards accepted.

JOSÉ TÓMAS, Mallorca 242 (Metro: Diagonal)

▼

GROC: Antoni Miró is one of the leading stars of Catalán design, and Groc is where he show-cases his talent. The store, first opened in 1967 with menswear only, has since expanded into women's wear as well. Miró's most recent honor was receiving the Cristóbal Balenciaga Award for best Spanish designer. He tries to create clothing for the European jet set, but with enough reserve to appeal to the masses. His suits are just structured enough that they don't drape but allow the body to move with the clothing. They are very sexy.

His shop is in a ground-floor boutique that is obvious once you know its location but annoyingly hard to find if you do not. The number of the building and the number of the shop do not coincide. If you walk to the corner of Catalunya and Mallorca and look for the 274 building, you will find the shop. The outside has mahogany squares as shutters, and a tiny sign. There is a complete selection of clothing and accessories for both men and women. If you want to get in on a trend, buy an Antoni Miró design.

GROC, Rambla de Catalunya 100 bis (Metro: Diagonal)

▼

SARA NAVARRO: Sara has a small shop in Madrid, in the ultrachic Mercado del Plaza de Toledo, but this large and elegant boutique in Barcelona makes it quite clear that she has already made an impact on the scene. The store, right on Diagonal at the apex of the shopping district, is very, very white and baroque and grand, and perfectly displays the expensive and luxurious leathers and shoes. Her style is more with-it than Loewe, and we think she offers them some serious competition. Prices are expensive, but this is the kind of talent we spend our lives searching for.

SARA NAVARRO, Avinguda Diagonal 598 (Metro: Hospital Clinic)

▼

ALFREDO VITTALBA: Fresh, original, and exciting, this shop has clothes that are outrageously expensive and slightly outrageous. They are perhaps for the Gaultier fan who wants something unique (not as weird as Gaultier) and special that makes the statement that the wearer is a pacesetter. A pair of earrings cost over $150; chiffon miniskirts start at $200.

ALFREDO VITTALBA, Rambla de Catalunya 88 (Metro: Diagonal)

▼

TERESA RAMALLAL: A store that looks like the tinfoil lining of a spaceship, and creative, innovative clothes to go with. The best fabrics, the best cut in the Euro-Japanese mode. Simple, slightly weird, fabulous. Expensive. Shoes, too.

TERESA RAMALLAL, Mestre Nicolau 17 (Metro: Hospital Clinic)

▼

ARAMIS: One of the old established shops for the gentry, Aramis exudes good taste. When you walk into the shop you smell leather and pipe tobacco. The walls and display cases are painted in a trompe l'oeil tortoise design. The clothing lines are extensive, from casual wear to black tie. Every aspect of dressing is covered. Most of the fashions are from well-known European designers like Ungaro or Zegna, as well as from some Spanish biggies. Even the men's shoes are from the very British Church's English Leather. There are blazer buttons, in case you cannot bear to give up the old comfortable one but need an updated look, or watches to finish off a perfect look. All major credit cards accepted, of course.

ARAMIS, Rambla de Catalunya 103 (Metro: Diagonal)

Barri Gótic Finds

EL MERCADILLO: You will spot this group of shops if you look into a doorway and spy a giant camel looking back at you. As you look up you will see what look like lightning rods in fluorescent colors hanging in an arbitrary pattern along the passageway to the main-floor door. Oh, and you will pass a giant guitar before you go in. El Mercadillo is a group of shops that has formed a minimall of sorts. Each space has its own concession, although all of the styles blend. The fashion look is hip Italian biking chic meets California surfer. There are four floors, which include a garden bar, shoe shop, beauty parlor, and men's and women's clothing and accessories. Some stores do not take credit cards.

EL MERCADILLO, Portaferrissa 17 (Metro: Liceu)

▼

RONIE'S: One of the streets in the old section of town is devoted to wholesale trimmings. We are not sure why, in this tourist-intensive area, these shops sell wholesale only, but we also realize that if you say that you own a shop and are willing to buy by the dozen, you will be welcome. The phrase for wholesale only is *Ventas al por mayor.* Ronie's sells accessories. The last time we visited, the fluorescent craze was hot and heavy. We were able to buy bracelets, earrings, pins, and gadgets for minimal cost by buying a package of each. They made great party favors and gifts when we got home. Our kids thought we were great. All major credit cards accepted.

RONIE'S, Bouqueria 23 (Metro: Liceu)

▼

CASA SARA: A jobber who sells mostly to the trade but will sell to the public without questions, this store has jewelry fixings and sew-on coins, anchors, wheels, harps, buttons, glitter, or whatever will turn a plain pair of jeans into a designer creation. The shop is wall-to-wall packages of bangles and beads. No one bothers you; just plunk your cello-wrapped packages into a small basket that you pick up as you enter. Cash only.

CASA SARA, Call 10 (Metro: Plaça de l'Ángel)

Children

MULLOR: Grandmothers, aunties, friends in waiting, and mothers of all ages, unite and bring lots of money. This is the fanciest, the best, the most exclusive children's shop in

Barcelona, where everything is old-fashioned, traditional, and fit for Princess Caroline's brood. The look is bassinet hung with lace. The handsmocked dresses are perfect.

MULLOR, Rambla de Catalunya 102 (Metro: Diagonal)

▼

TORRENS: Since 1891, Torrens has been dressing children and their parents to look Old World chic. The best selections are the "Mommy and me" dresses and suits that you know need to be hand-laundered. For teenage girls there are Chanel look-alike bags. Dads are not ignored, and there is a special section to make sure that they are suitably attired. One shop is on Avinguda Diagonal, but the larger shop is around the corner on Vía Augusta. This shop is packed full of classic clothing for men, women, and older children. There is a broad range of prices in all styles. Toward the back is a large children's shoe department. We give Torrens a rave review. All major credit cards accepted.

TORRENS
Avinguda Diagonal 576 (Metro: Hospital Clinic)
Vía Augusta 18 (Metro: Diagonal)

▼

CONDER'S: Spain is famous for its wonderful and affordable shoes. And kids are not left out. Conder's carries every variety of children's shoes from baby booties to huge tennis shoes for teens. The largest size is 39, which is quite large. We especially like the many choices in Velcro-closure tennis shoes and dress shoes for boys. For girls, there are tennis shoes with polka dots, bows, checks, glitter, and stripes. Before you leave, check out the bunny slippers that look like donkeys. This is a chain of stores. All major credit cards accepted.

CONDER'S, Portaferrissa 8 (Metro: Liceu)

BEBELIN: A deep shop that has clothes for infants, kids, and moms to be. As you move toward the back you can see the selection is vast. The clothes tend toward the traditional, but it's a good one-stop opportunity to see a lot.

BEBELIN, Passeig de Gracia 39 (Metro: Passeig de Gracia)

Ceramics

PLADELOS: This is actually just a big TT, but it has a very large selection of Lladró and some Nao, as well as some Swedish crystal and a few other knickknacks. (And so-so paintings.) Lladró fans will enjoy the choices. In the Barri Gótic, almost right at Las Ramblas.

PLADELOS, Bouqueria 8 (Metro: Liceu)

▼

PACHECO: This is a shop next door to the Ramada Renaissance, right on the Rambla, that must do a huge tourist business, since they're heavily stocked with pearls, marcasite, Nao, and Lladró. But even though it's geared toward tourists, the selection is awfully good.

PACHECO, Rambla de Catalunya 115 (Metro: Liceu)

▼

LA CAIXA DE FANG: This shop is just a stone's throw from the back of the Cathedral and is a lovely, charming, country-style place selling ceramics and rugs and a few other crafts items, including the glass from Mallorca that we adore. Visually it is so welcoming that you might want to move in. The prices are high, but they are high everywhere in Barcelona, and we are used to street-market prices—which you can't find in Barcelona unless you get lucky or go some distance.

LA CAIXA DE FANG, Freneria 1 (Metro: Liceu)

▼

LA CERÁMICA ARTÍSTICA: This is one of the few shops in all of Spain that sells ceramics from regions all over Spain. The display in the small shop isn't much, and all these different styles don't blend too well together, but if you sort through the piles you'll find a lot of everything. Much of it is not to our taste, but there's plenty we have trouble living without. The small religious fonts are particularly nice, although a good one begins at $100. They don't open until 11 A.M., then hours are standard: 11 A.M.–2 P.M. and 4:30 P.M.–8 P.M.

LA CERÁMICA ARTÍSTICA, Llibreteria 18 and 20 (Metro: Liceu)

▼

GOTIC: This is a TT, no doubt about it, but there are some regional ceramics sold here, as well as some Lladró porcelains. Across from the Cathedral in the TT strip. Not bad if you like to buy plates to hang on the kitchen wall, as we do.

GOTIC, Avinguda Catedral 3 (Metro: Liceu)

▼

1748: Crammed with pottery, ceramics, handicrafts, rugs, and glass; treasures galore for those who love country looks and folk arts. Down the street from the Picasso Museum. Don't miss it!

1748, Placeta de Montcada 2 (Metro: Jaume 1)

Design and Antiques

PILMA: One of the larger furniture showrooms in Barcelona is located on the trendy Avinguda Diagonal, across the street from Vía Augusta. It is housed in the bottom floor of an office complex, but if you look up from across the street on Vía Augusta, you will see the unmistakable sign for Pilma stretched between the two towers of the buildings.

The shop itself carries the best of modern designer furniture from Spain, Italy, and the rest of Europe. Inside the store is decorated in shades of gray, black, and white. There is a ramp leading to the second floor, which contains more furniture and lighting. Downstairs, the vast room is divided into display areas by category. In the front of the showroom you will find the reception desk and sample room displays. The back half of the showroom is devoted to functional objects. There is a display of luggage, pots and pans, plastic and Formica home accessories, and even jewelry. The smaller, more expensive items are protected in glass cases, but otherwise it is very similar to a Pottery Barn setup. Lighting is a large part of the showroom as well, but is so well incorporated into the different settings that you have to look to realize that the lamps are for sale and not part of the fixtures. Very famous designer pieces by Le Corbusier, Ettore Sottsass, A. Castiglioni, Mies van der Rohe, and Aldo Rossi have been re-created. Other more contemporary designers are represented as well. The third level is devoted to carpets, and yet again more furniture. You could easily spend a few hours here. To the trade and public as well. Major credit cards accepted.

PILMA, Avinguda Diagonal 403 (Metro: Diagonal)

▼

VINÇON: Not far from Pilma either physically or emotionally, Vinçon takes itself a little less seriously and is somewhat of a Catalán version of Conran's. The store has two entrances on the Passeig and then one out the back, so you could sneak in from a block away if you knew what you were doing. Along the way there are long, dark halls, showrooms, and a supermarket of china, glassware, and tabletop items. You can buy anything from a vase to an American mailbox. Indeed, about 30% of the merchandise here is American, which is part of the fun of the store, as you can learn a lot about American culture and design just by seeing what appeals to locals.

VINÇON, Passeig de Gracia 96 (Metro: Passeig de Gracia)

▼

HABITACLE: A design showroom geared to the kitchen and home aspects of design, Habitacle offers Sottsass teapots, pots, pans, luggage, gifts, and everyday china with a designer flair. It is a good place to find an unusual gift to take home. All major credit cards accepted.

HABITACLE, Rambla de Catalunya 118 (Metro: Diagonal)

▼

SANTIAG MARTI: One of the more elegant antiques shops in the fashionable area of Barcelona is Santiag Marti. Here you will find very formal pieces of furniture, art, and accessories. We were especially ecstatic over the tapestry chairs, which will of course be gone by the time you get there. However, we are sure there will be other ancient objects to tempt you.

SANTIAG MARTI, Provença (Metro: Diagonal)

▼

ARTESPAÑA: We have seen many of these stores all over Spain, and each one seems to have its own look, although all are geared toward home decor. There are large pieces of furniture, both upholstered and wood, carpets, lamps, and tabletop accessories. We were especially drawn to the handpainted wood candlesticks, picture frames, and clocks that have a fine mahogany lacquer finish. There are also silver and pewter pieces, and some ceramics, although fewer than in other Artespaña stores. All major credit cards accepted.

ARTESPAÑA, Rambla de Catalunya 75 (Metro: Diagonal)

▼

B. D. EDICIONES DE DISEÑO S.A.: B. D. (which you pronounce by saying these two letters in Spanish: "Bey Dey") is the most important furniture and design showroom in Barcelona. It is housed in a landmark building, designed in 1895 by the renowned architect Lluis Domenechi Mantaner, who was at the forefront of the Art Nouveau movement in Europe. Mantaner built the house for Josep Thomas, an innovative art printer. In 1973, when the printworks shut down, the house fell into disrepair. In 1979, B. D. Ediciones de Diseño repaired and renovated the ground floor and basement under the direction of Cristian Cirici and moved their showroom into the space. It seems fitting that the works of great furniture designers should be exhibited in such a great building.

B. D. Ediciones de Diseño S.A. was founded by a group of architects who wished to bring great historic designs to life while at the same time encouraging design of great living artists. Designs from the B. D. collection can be found in museums in both Europe and America. Some of the famous artists whose work is manufactured include Antonio Gaudí, Rudolf M. Schindler, and Charles Rennie Mackintosh. The current designer list boasts the likes of Anna Soler, Ettore Sottsass, Jr., Martine Bedin, Anna Bohigas, Cristian Cirici, and Javier Mariscal.

The showroom is spectacular, from the entry's open stained glass and carved metal railings to the mahogany and glass walls. It is quite a treat to see such beautifully designed pieces of furniture displayed as art. The nonarchitectural works of Gaudí are few, consisting of intricately carved chairs, a gold-leaf mirror, and brass fittings for doors and drawers. Other designers' works fall into every category including lighting, shelving, TV caddies, ceiling cornices, carpets, tables, and chairs. Any student of design should plan to spend a few hours here, at least. B. D. is both a wholesale and retail showroom. There are branch stores in Madrid, Bilbao, Tenerife, Mallorca, Sevilla, Valencia, and Zaragoza.

This shop is just a few blocks from the Passeig, and you can walk to it easily. Don't miss it!

B. D. EDICIONES DE DISEÑO S.A., Mallorca 291 (Metro: Verdauger)

▼

LINARES: We don't know if this is such a common name that everyone in the antiques business happens to have it, or if this is one man with branch stores all over Spain, or perhaps a family of many brothers, but whatever the deal—once again, in the best location in town, there is a Linares shop, and once again it has the same format as all the others. This shop appears to be a major TT, and turns out to have a mix of 50% junk and 50% fabulous antiques. This one's next door to the cathedral.

LINARES, Plaça de la Catedral (Metro: Jaume 1)

▼

COSES DE CASA: This is a small shop that despite its name does not have all the things for the house you might think it would. It carries fabrics—from designer to Souleiado—and you can buy from the bolt or have a quilt made up, which is the house specialty. There are also fabric tote bags and a few other fabric items, but the idea here is to buy one of the ready-made quilts or commission one in fabrics you choose. About $300 for a finished king-size quilt, which is not at all bad.

COSES DE CASA, Plaça Sant Josep Oriol 5 (Metro: Jaume 1)

Other Antiques

A majority of the fun and funky antiques shopping takes place in the old quarter of town, known as the Barri Gòtic. This area extends in and around the Cathedral and the Plaça di Sant Jaume. The two main streets, Carrer Banys Nous and Carrer de la Palla (also spelled Paja) run into each other off the Plaça Nova. Other streets include

Carrer Severo and Carrer Honoratio. All of these are so narrow that a car cannot pass. Walking here is like stepping back in time to a period when the antiques that the shops are selling were new pieces. The shops are in one form or another very similar. Some are fancier than others; some are junky. The majority are somewhere in the middle. We did not find any "incredible" steals. These dealers know what they are selling, and are not willing to give it away. In some cases they are overpriced, in others fair. Bargaining is always expected. Some shops take no credit cards, but will take your personal check. We have never understood why. They would all prefer cash. There are twenty-four dealers who have joined together to form the Anticuarious del Barri Gòtic and publish a map. You can pick it up along the way in one of the member shops. Not all of the shops in the area belong, however.

We have a few favorites:

ESTRADA, Carrer Palla 10A bis, has a good collection of fans; **LIBRERIA ANGEL BATLLE,** Carrer Palla 23, has a substantial collection of old books and new prints; **ALBERTO GRASAS,** Carrer Banys Nous 14, is one of the fancier shops, with beautiful wood marquetry pieces and gold-leaf furniture and mirrors; **ANTI-GUITATS VDA DE SANDOVAL,** Carrer Banys Nous 21, carries a selection of musical instruments, as well as some large Gothic pieces and ceramics; **TANDEM ANTIGUITATS,** Carrer Banys Nous 19, a select doll and fan collection; **L'ARCA DE L'AVIA,** Carrer Banys Nous 20, is the single most wonderful shop in Spain for old linens and whitework, including tablecloths, napkins, collars, shawls, and doll clothing. Some antique costumes, clothes, and a few of the intricately made hand-embroidered shawls ($2,000 and up). This shop is a must. **J. FERRER CASALS,** Carrer Banys Nous 10, is a frame shop where you can buy fan frames for all of the fans that you have collected along the way.

Art Galleries

Since Barcelona is so heavily steeped in its art history, art galleries and museums have taken on a special importance as far as shopping is concerned. Luckily for the shopper, there is one street, Carrer de Consell, between Rambla de Catalunya and Carrer de Balmes, that has a large concentration of galleries representing some of the best of the new art scene. Stop in at **DAEDALUS** (No. 286), **JENESIS** (No. 325), **GALERÍA CARLES TACHE** (No. 290), **GALERÍA RENE METRAS** (No. 329), **GOTHSLAND** (No. 331), **DAU AL SET** (No. 333), and **CENTRO CIUDAD** (No. 294).

Barcelona on a Schedule

Tour 1: Catalonian Core Shopping

1. Now that you have realized that Barcelona is really two different cities joined together, you will want to separate your shopping days into Old City fun and New City adventure. We like to start our Barri Gótic adventure at the corner of Las Ramblas and Plaça de Catalunya. Walk down Las Ramblas toward the water, and enjoy the variety of merchandise that you will encounter in the street stalls and sidewalk boutiques. Las Ramblas has the most intense concentration of tourist souvenir shops in all of Barcelona. You will find the bullfight posters

that you might have passed up in Madrid are even better priced here, while the Barcelona '92 T-shirts are not.

2. When you get to the corner of Carrer de la Bouqueria, take a left into the old town. The streets in this area are mostly pedestrian streets, but the occasional car does come barreling through, so be aware.

3. As you turn the corner look for Pladelos, at Bouqueria 8, for a good selection of Lladró and Nao porcelain. Continue to walk and shop your way down this street, stopping in at the particular shops that catch your eye (there will be many).

4. As the street gets closer to the Plaça de Sant Jaume it will change its name and become Carrer del Call. At this point you will notice that most of the shops are button and trimming outlets. You're now in the wholesale area for bangles and beads. We learned our lesson in the first shop, which asked us to leave, and told the second shop that we owned a store. They happily let us buy packages of trimmings, neon shoelaces, and fluorescent bracelets. Our favorite shops are Ronie's, at Carrer de la Bouqueria 23, and Casa Sara at Carrer del Call 10.

5. Walk into the Plaça de Sant Jaume and take a look at some of the small antiques shops lining the square, then backtrack to Carrer Banys Nous de la Palla and take a right turn. If you are a collector of small antique curios you will adore this street. One shop after another is filled with unusual items. Some shops are fancier than others. Some are really junky. None of them is boring. Be sure to look in at Tandem Antiguitats (No. 19) for dolls and fans and Antiguitats Vda de Sandoval (No. 21) for usual musical instruments.

6. As you get farther along the street, you will see Libreria Angel Batlle (No. 23), which is an excellent source for collector books and prints. At this point you will also be close to the Plaça Nova and the magnificent Catedral.

7. Take time to visit the Cathedral before you hit the souvenir shops in the adjacent square. We especially like Gotic, at Avinguda Catedral 3, for regional ceramics. Behind the Cathedral you should seek out La Caixa de Fang at Freneria 1, if you are a collector of country arts and crafts.

8. If you happen to visit the Cathedral on Thursday, be sure to time your visit between 10 A.M. and 2 P.M., when there is an antiques market held in the square.

9. At this point you will probably be feeling the heat of the pavement and need a rest. However, you can't end your day in the Barri Gótic without a visit to the Picasso Museum. You can either cab it or walk back through the Barri on Carrer dels Comtes (on the other side of the Cathedral) until it intersects Carrer Jaume 1.

10. Here you will want to take a left, cross Plaça de l'Ángel, and continue on Carrer de la Princesa until you reach Carrer de Montcada, where you will take a right to No. 15, which is the museum and shop.

11. The shopping surrounding the Picasso Museum is wonderful. There are art and antiques shops lining the street on both sides. The museum itself is a testament to what a good architect can do to revitalize and restore an old building. The souvenir shop has some unique items.

12. Now cab back to your hotel and relax before setting off again on a night's adventure. Barcelona never sleeps.

Tour 2: Barcelona Gala
Fashion and Art Stroll

1. The Barcelona we keep coming back to is one of wide avenues, intense fashion, and incredible architecture. You can't stroll very far without encountering a building by Barcelona's premier architect, Antonio Gaudí i Cornet, better known as just Gaudí. Be sure on your shopping adventures to look up at the buildings as well as in the windows.

2. Start your tour once again at the Plaça de Catalunya, but this time on the other side of the square. Passeig de Gracia and Rambla de Catalunya are parallel streets that travel away from the Plaça and contain much of the chic shopping that you will find in Barcelona. We like to start on Passeig de Gracia and walk until it intersects Avinguda Diagonal, then return on Rambla de Catalunya. On Passeig de Gracia don't miss Dory (No. 33) for wonderful leather bags and accessories and Loewe (No. 35). El Bulevard Rosa (No. 53) hosts a variety of smaller stores specializing in current hot fashion. Adolfo Dominguez (No. 89) has young, hip, Spanish male fashion, Carlos Torrents (No. 95) presents men's stylish looks, and Centre d'Antiquaris (No. 55) has a variety of antiques shops concentrated in one building.

3. When you get to the top of Passeig de Gracia you can make the choice to turn around or to continue off on Avinguda Diagonal and explore the shops in this area. We do it differently each time. Avinguda Diagonal and the surrounding shopping streets are a mix of furniture and fashion. If you decide to explore in this direction, take a left onto Diagonal from Passeig de Gracia and look in at Pilma (No. 403). Pilma sells one of the best collections of designer furniture in Barcelona. You can

buy a Le Corbusier chair or a vase by Ettore Sottsass.

4. Farther up and across the street at No. 466, stop in at Eleven, one of the most creatively designed shoe stores we have ever seen.

5. When you reach Vía Augusta take a right and explore both sides of the street. Many hot fashion houses come and go here.

6. Now turn around and retrace your steps until you find El Bulevard Rosa at No. 472 Diagonal. Walk inside to Beverly Feldman, our favorite American-Spanish shoe designer. Ms. Feldman lives and works in Spain, creating the most fanciful and fun-to-wear shoes, boots, and bags we could ever hope to buy at a good price. Exit back onto Diagonal and take a right down Rambla de Catalunya. As you walk, be aware of the side streets that cut off the Rambla. Many of them (most especially Rossello, Mallorca, and Consell) have great boutiques.

7. On the Rambla, be sure to stop in at one of our favorite stores, Japan (No. 80), a clothing store that mixes art and fashion in a unique way.

8. Our other "not to miss" store on the Rambla is Ramon Santaeularia (No. 40). Here you will find all of the French fittings necessary to turn your homegrown suit into a couture look-alike. The store carries buttons, belt buckles, earrings, and necklaces that look much better than they cost. Be sure to explore every drawer in the back room.

9. When you reach Mallorca, stop in at José Tómas (No. 242) and Groc (No. 100 bis Rambla de Catalunya). Groc is actually at the intersection and José Tómas is down the street. These are two of the hot Barcelona designers who are making fashion news.

10. When you have walked your feet into oblivion, you can take a taxi to your hotel and sit back with a good cup of tea. You will have earned the rest.

8 ▾ SHOPPING PORTUGAL

Welcome to Portugal

P ortugal is an amazing country. The fact that it is indeed a country and not part of Spain is amazing. The arts, crafts, and handmade items that you will soon be drooling over are amazing. The country and the people are amazing because they combine the hot hustle of Euro big business (foreign money is gobbling up Portugal as the best investment since *grand cru* wine) and the lazy white stucco train stations (complete with inlaid tiles) of a countryside replete with farmers and carts pulled by donkeys.

Portugal may be the last bastion of charm in continental Europe. And while it's not dirt cheap (is anything these days?), it is less expensive than Spain and almost anywhere else in Europe. Portugal just may be the last resort, in all senses of the word.

Welcome to Portuguese Deals

T he thing to buy in Portugal is handicrafts, and Portuguese handicrafts qualify as duty-free under the GSP laws. We will tell you that we paid duty on our *arraiolos* because our Customs agent called it a floor covering and not a piece of art. But better luck to you and yours.

233

Welcome to Lisbon

Your approach to Lisbon is everything.

If you come in by cruise ship, you see the monuments, the incredible architecture, and the fabulous waterfront at the foot of the old city, and you are enchanted.

If you fly into the Lisbon airport (a very nice airport), your taxi will take you across disappointing terrain and through the usual concrete complexes of the outlying suburbs before you get to your hotel, which probably will be in a nice but not fabulous neighborhood of Lisbon. You must then go in search of the true treasures. But they aren't far away, and in short order, you will be enchanted. And broke. Because Lisbon is Needlepoint Carpet City, and even if you don't want a carpet (or need a carpet), we'll bet you are about to buy a carpet.

The Lay of the Land

On August 25, 1988, part of downtown Lisbon was gutted by fire. We mention this immediately because the American press made a big to-do about the fire and led the public to believe that the entire shopping district of Lisbon had been destroyed. We went to check out the damage a week after the fire and, as heartbreaking as any fire is, and as big a loss as Lisbon suffered, we can assure you that the shopping district did not totally burn down. An L-shaped area of fifteen stores did burn. Among them were the city's two department stores. The area is currently being rebuilt, and while it can never be what it was, it will rise (like the phoenix) again. There are still plenty of shopping reasons to visit Lisbon, and when the fire damage is all rebuilt, you'll have a good reason to come back and shop some more.

Lisbon itself is built up and over a bluff overlooking the River Tagus and the Atlantic. The Tagus is navigable at this point, which is one of the reasons why Lisbon became such a major port.

The old city, down near the water, is divided into two parts of yet another hill: There are an upper (Chiado) and a lower (Baixa: say "Baiy-sha") city that can be reached by steps, by an elevator built in the Gustav Eiffel tradition, or by trolley car. Wear sensible shoes.

The basic main square of the city is located a stretch up from the waterfront and is called the Rossio—this is where the main train station is, where all the pigeons congregate, where everyone sips coffee, where the pedestrian streets to the shopping network begin. In actuality, the Rossio is the top of the Baixa area, with Chiado rising to the right—if you are looking at the water. (Or in the direction of the water, since you can't see the water from the Rossio.)

The surrounding hills each have names and house neighborhoods and many landmarks and/or museums. Alfama, the hill on the other side of Baixa opposite Chiado, is the old medieval and Moorish part of town, and home to the Castelo, which you will surely visit. (It's got lots of shops nearby.)

Along the beach, suburbs stretch all the way to Cascais (say "Kaiysh-kaz"), one city past Estoril. Estoril is more famous than Cascais because it was a very chic watering hole for the rich and famous and because various spies and World War II characters hung out there during Portugal's neutrality. It's now an enclave for the British and for those who have retired to the sun. There's not much shopping in Estoril, by the way, so head out for Cascais

Lisbon

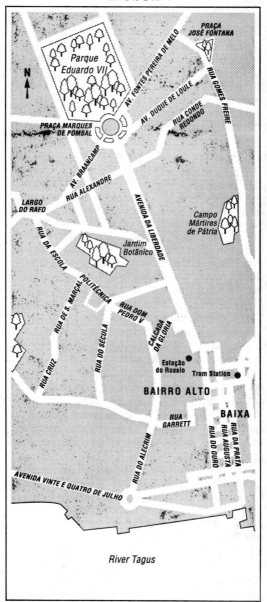

if you want to see the beach scene and shop (see page 265).

Shopping Lisbon

L isbon is not the world's greatest shopping city. Maybe that's why Henry the Navigator sent out all those ships. The city has plenty to see, plenty to do, and lots to buy, but you have to know what you're looking for and where to go in order to maximize your efforts. Despite the charming upper and lower cities in the old part of Lisbon, there is very little hang-together to the city. You take taxis just about everywhere (unless you have time on your side and hooves on your feet) and find yourself bouncing from one part of town to the other. Most of the city closes for siesta, except for the mall and some of the TTs. (See page 239.)

Yet Lisbon is the best for certain types of items:

ANTIQUES: Lisbon's antiques street—Dom Pedro V—is above Chiado (walk or tram up) and allows you an astounding view of the city and the water. While the market in used and antique *azulejos* is limited, there is one fabulous shop here that will make you crazy with desire for everything: **SOLAR.** Dom Pedro V is a two-block length of shops, each one filled with wares—most of them rather high-end, most of them devoted to religious antiques.

ARRAIOLOS: We know you've memorized the Iberian ABCs (page 27) and know all about *arraiolos* carpets already. You will indeed need to learn a little about them if you want to make a smart purchase. There are several top-of-the-line dealers in Lisbon who carry fine examples of the needlepoint carpets (many sizes available); shop only with these. A well-made *arraiolos* should last at least a hundred years. You are buying not only a thing of beauty that you will enjoy, but an heirloom for your family.

TILES AND CERAMICS: We are tile freaks, and we have gone nuts in Lisbon. The fact that tiles are less expensive in Spain doesn't bother us at all. We've bought tiles (and ceramics) in Lisbon and all over the Portuguese countryside. Portuguese designs vary from the Spanish; Portuguese tiles come in different price brackets than Spanish tiles.

Please note that Portugal has a very strong relationship with U.S. buyers and designers: The export ceramics business is highly developed. You will not find much crossover between Portuguese-made goods sold in the U.S. and those sold in Portugal—the best stuff is actually created for those American buyers who come over to Portugal and work in the factories for a few weeks to design unique merchandise for the stores or lines they represent. If you want great (and cheap) Portuguese ceramics, don't forget to shop around the U.S. and to stop by your local branch of discounter Marshall's.

Oh yes, one final disappointment: The flea market in Lisbon is not crammed with tiles or ceramics. You will have to buy these items in the stores and factories that make them, unless you are looking for antique tiles. (Go to Solar.)

Hours

Most stores open at 9 A.M. and close at 7 P.M. They are closed for lunch from 1 P.M. to 3 P.M. On Saturday, the stores usually do not reopen after lunch.

Getting There

Lisbon is a hop, skip, and jump from New York—the flight is under six hours! Two carriers currently fly this route: TWA and TAP. TAP is the Portuguese national airline, and they are busy opening new gateways so that now you can fly nonstop from L.A. and other U.S. cities. You can also get to Lisbon from North Africa: Royal Air Maroc has several connecting flights—you're but an hour away from either world, so look into a package deal.

You can get to Lisbon on a cruise ship or by plane to meet your cruise ship.

Getting Around

Because Lisbon is so spread out (even the touristy parts are far apart), you'll be taking a lot of cabs (quite cheap), riding the Metro (limited appeal since it's not that extensive), and riding the trams, which you will adore. There's also a good bit of walking to do. Commuter trains that haven't been upgraded in decades (therefore adding to their charm) run to the beach communities from the Cais do Sodré train station, on the edge of the waterfront downtown. Trains are a great way to get around Portugal; make sure that you know which station your train leaves from when you head out, as there are several stations servicing trains to different regions. (To get to Sintra, depart from Rossio station in the heart of town; go to the Algarve from Sul-e-Sueste station (Terreiro do Paço) across the Tagus. Get to Madrid or Paris via Santa Apolonia.

The Metro is great if you happen to be going where it's going, which very often is perfect for a tourist—you can get to museums and the bullfights—but not great for a shopper. In the old city we first walk, making a list of the stores we want to hit, then work with a map of the city to form an itinerary, then hop taxis. Traffic can be dense in rush hour, but taxis are cheap.

Don't leave town without riding the tram at least once. You can get a tram in the Alfama district and ride it right to Chiado.

Booking Lisbon / 1

Most American guidebooks to Spain are coupled with Portugal. Michelin's green guide will be helpful, especially with information about the architecture (no shops or hotels included). Your hotel room should have a copy of the *Goldenbook of Lisbon*, a hardbound book of ads, pictures, and editorial matter, with specific listings for museums, shops, etc. *What's On in Lisbon* is published monthly by Publiotel and distributed (free) through hotels. It's in English and lists events, tours, shops, churches, and everything else.

Booking Lisbon/2

Hotels in Lisbon are as scattered as the tourist areas; there's probably no one hotel with the best location. Our hotels are rated expensive (over $150 per night); moderate ($101–$149 per night); and inexpensive (under $100 a night).

LE MERIDIEN LISBOA: The famous French chain of Le Meridien hotels has the reputation in Portugal (Lisbon and Porto) of having the best hotel in town for the chic. A five-star hotel that actually caters to businesspeople from all over Europe, the Meridien has a lobby that is the scene of all the action. While the Ritz, next door to the Meridien, still has a top-of-the-line reputation (go for tea or lunch in the summer), most Europeans prefer Le Meridien. Located across the street from a park, the hotel is within walking distance of many shops and of the big Amoreiras mall. There are some shops in the hotel (also in the Ritz), and several restaurants. Moderate. For reservations in the U.S. call (800) 543-4300. Local phone: 690-900.

LE MEREDIEN LISBOA, Rua Castilho 149

▼

ALFA LISBOA: Located farther from the center of town, but almost next door to the Gulbenkian art museum, the Alfa is a five-star hotel that caters to businesspeople and some conventions. It has several good shops right in the lobby, and a fine restaurant, A Aldeia. Walk one block to the Metro. The hotel is a newish, modern high-rise, but the rooms are total teak and Scandinavian modern. A member of the Occidental chain. Moderate. For

U.S. reservations call (800) 332-4872. Local phone: 722-121.

ALFA LISBOA, Avendia Columbano Bordalo Pinheiro

▼

AVENIDA PALACE: With perhaps the best location of any hotel in town (right on the Rossio), the Avenida Palace is an old-fashioned hotel for lovers of the fabulous but funky. If we had $10 million, we'd renovate this hotel in style. If you have a sense of humor, this could be for you—it's a steal at about $60 a night. Inexpensive. Local phone: 360-151.

AVENIDA PALACE, Rua 1 de Dezembro 123

Snack and Shop

BENARD: It's a take-out croissant stand, it's a bakery, it's a tearoom, it's a great restaurant. Seek and keep seeking when you get to Benard, conveniently located in the Chiado area, right on the main shopping street, Rua Garrett. There are tables and umbrellas in the street. You can walk on with a hot croissant (choose from five tempting toppings), you can sit inside, or—this is our secret to you—you can walk straight back very far into the space until you think surely you've passed the bathrooms, and there a new world begins: an adorable restaurant with yellow stucco walls and ceiling fans. This is called a *tasca*, which is a restaurant and snack bar as well as a *salão de chá*, or tea salon. We eat here several times a week when in Lisbon; it's just that good. And that moderately priced.

BENARD, Rua Garrett 104 (take tram or walk)

A ALDEIA: This restaurant is in the hotel Alfa Lisboa, but the entrance is outside of the hotel, not inside. Decorated with a regional picnic theme, the restaurant has pottery on the walls, rush chairs painted red, and green and white tablecloths. The fare is regional; the selection is huge. If you are frightened by all the unfamiliar choices, just remember that *frango* is chicken and you'll never go wrong. If you are at the Gulbenkian Museum, you're only a block away. Inexpensive.

A ALDEIA, Alfa Lisboa Hotel, Avenida Columbano Bordalo Pinheiro

Neighborhoods

Chiado

We always start a trip to Lisbon in Chiado, for several reasons—we can walk to two other parts of town from here; the street pattern is easy to understand so we don't get lost; and finally, this is where our favorite carpet shop and one of our favorite tile shops are located. Besides, if your taxi is coming from one of the major hotels, you'll get a quick tour of the entire downtown area and a view of the water. The Chiado shopping area is the upper city, and it was built after the lower city, so most of the stores are in Baroque buildings. The Largo do Chiado is the tiny square where you can stop for coffee; the Rua Garrett is the main shopping street. Many of the stores on the Rua Garrett (which is only two blocks long) aren't the kind of stores where you're going to buy anything, anyway, but just the kind of stores where you can look at the storefronts and enjoy their beauty. Just look at **OURIVESARIA ALIANÇA** (No. 50) with its carved wooden swags, brass medallions, and brown wooden lion's head over the door. Other stores, as good inside as out, include:

CASA QUINTÃO: Founded over 100 years ago, Casa Quintão is the most famous source of *arraiolos* in Portugal, and for good reason. We'll save you a lot of time and aggravation by admitting right up front that we spent a week traveling in and out of little villages and tearing the countryside apart to find a better deal than what you get at Casa Quintão, and couldn't. We found a few designers who do private account work, and we'll tell you about them, but if you want a fine carpet, with guarantees, and if you want to do business with people who speak English, who know what they are doing, and who are honorable—this is the place.

Casa Quintão does not look impressive from the outside, or even from the inside, where it looks like a furniture shop. But go upstairs to the mezzanine floor, where you will need the smelling salts. The walls are hung with magnificent needlepoint carpets; the showroom floor is devoted to five or six mounds of carpets, all separated by size. You express interest in a certain size and move to that mountain with your salesman. He, with the help of another salesman, begins to peel back the carpets at the halfway point so that you can see half of each carpet you are shown. Should you express serious interest, they remove your designated carpet and put it on another part of the floor or at the top of the pile. Prices per size range are usually similar, although each carpet in a size group may not be the same size (these are all handmade, so they differ by a few inches each way), and the work may not be as intricate on one carpet as it is on another.

You may bring a swatch of your own fabric with you, and commission a carpet to be made. You should not have trouble finding carpets from the vast selection, but some people prefer custom work. Most U.S. designers who order custom *arraiolos* do so from Casa Quintão. (Not all, just most.)

You can buy your carpet right then and there, and the salesmen will roll it into a small package for you and tie it with string so you can easily pack it in your suitcase. Try not to unroll this package before you get home, because you'll never get it back as small as it was. If you want to have the carpet sent to you in the U.S., you simply waive your VAT return, and that amount (13%) pays for the shipping. If you take the carpet with you, the store will process VAT refund papers for you. You will have yours stamped when you leave the country (you must show the carpet to the Customs agent to get your papers stamped) or when you arrive in the U.S. (a U.S. officer may stamp the papers) and then mail it yourself—from the U.S.—to Casa Quintão. Within a few weeks (ours took two weeks!) you receive not only the proper refund, but the money in U.S. dollars!

Carpets are measured by the metric system in Portugal, but because Casa Quintão does so much work with Americans, the dimensions of each carpet are also written in feet and inches. Just for your own information as you shop around, you should know that a meter is 39 inches. Carpets are shown in more or less standard sizes: 3 feet by 5 feet; 4 feet by 6 feet; 8 feet by 10 feet; etc. Although prices can vary, a ballpark figure is $450 for the 3×5; $1,000 for the 4×6; and $2,000 for the 8×10. Any carpet dealer will quote you a per meter price.

Casa Quintão takes all credit cards; your refunds still comes in dollars—they do not do credit-card refunds. They are closed on Saturday afternoon after 1 P.M., and all day Sunday.

CASA QUINTÃO, Rua Ivens 34

▼

SANT'ANNA: Lisbon has two tiles-cum-ceramics workshops that are famous—and very different from each other. One block from Casa Quintão, you get to visit the wonders of Sant'Anna. This is a small shop, but it is crammed with merchandise; if you want to go to the factory you must ask at the shop and make an appointment. There is no outlet shop at the factory, but you can see the tilemaking process firsthand.

Sant'Anna makes tiles for Country Floors, a company with showrooms all over the U.S. that is famous as a distributor of the best international tiles. Because of their relationship with Country Floors, Sant'Anna will not sell certain tile patterns to Americans. Not to worry. There's still plenty to buy. Tiles cost from $3.50 to $10 each, and while this is very expensive, these tiles do cost more in the U.S. The shop has panels of scenics and individual tiles in boxes. If you are interested in a certain style, ask if there are more in the back. There is a small selection of tiles framed with intricately bent wrought iron that forms a sort of picture frame—these make great gifts, and cost about $10 each.

Tiles are a small part of the stock at Sant'Anna. The rest is ceramics—everything from tiny gift boxes ($10) to umbrella stands to chandeliers. Plates and all dishes, whether in sets or single units, are available. A large vegetable dish costs about $60. The designs are unique to the Sant'Anna style and are easily recognized—there are Persian touches to the motifs, which are small geometrics and animals. Open during lunch!

SANT'ANNA, Rua do Alecrim 95
SANT'ANNA factory, Calcada da Boa Hora 96

▼

VISTA ALEGRE: Vista Alegre is the finest porcelain made in Portugal, and competes internationally with names like Limoges. They have shops all over the country, with several in Lisbon. We are sending you to the main shop because some of the other shops we looked at did not compare. There is a factory store in Ilhavo (near Aveiro) that is better stocked than any of the boutiques (no seconds).

Vista Alegre makes a very fine bone china. This is the serious stuff, folks, with gold borders and heavy-duty regal patterns, and it is very well priced. Bad news: They won't ship. Vista Alegre is not only sold in the U.S., but they also do private-label work for Tiffany & Co., the Metropolitan Museum of Art, and many other clients. They will not offend their customers by shipping less expensive merchandise.

But would a little thing like that deter us? With dinner plates at $11 each (not all patterns, mind you) we felt compelled to buy a dozen and pack them in our suitcases. They survived perfectly.

Most Vista Alegre shops also sell Baccarat glass at prices that we find to be the least expensive in all of Europe.

VISTA ALEGRE, Largo do Chiado 18

▼

ANGULO: Right above the Largo do Chiado is another small square called the Praça Luis de Camões. It has shops on either side. Angulo is one of many stores here. We like it because they sell bed linens. Not only do they have Missoni and Bassetti, but they have new versions of antique Victorian whitework. It's a modern but elegant shop with competitive prices on the white tablecloths, place mats, and bed linen.

ANGULO, Praça Luis de Camões 8

▼

PÓRTICO: This is a decorating and furniture store for locals that provides gift items, wedding registry, and a ton of brass. It's a good place to find gifts. The shop seems to have two personalities. Downstairs is sort of old-lady fancy, while upstairs is crammed with lamps and shades and brass and copper. There is a china department where we saw patterns of Vista Alegre we never saw anywhere else, except at the Vista Alegre factory in Ilhavo. You'll pass this shop if you walk from Chiado to the antiques street.

PÓRTICO, Rua da Misericórdia 31

Antiques

The antiques area of Lisbon is on the Rua Dom Pedro V, which is above Chiado. You can walk—it's not very far, but it is straight up—from the Rua Garrett, with the water at your back and the Largo do Chiado to your right, up Rua Misericórdia until it becomes Rua Alcantara, which becomes Dom Pedro V. You'll know you're going right, because about halfway up—when you're praying for oxygen— you'll see a parklike viewing area, where you can get a view of the city and the sea. (And catch your breath.) Steps before you get to the park, you'll notice on your right-hand side that the tram ends right into the wall that becomes the street you are standing on. Very interesting, these hill people. Once you pass this parklike area, the street becomes Dom Pedro V, and you'll be in antiques heaven. All these shops are closed during lunch. You can browse both sides of the street without needing to know the names of any shops, and be perfectly happy. The most important address on the block is Solar, which you have to visit when you are in Lisbon (if you are a tile freak), or you have not done the city properly. Stroll and enjoy:

SOLAR: Because a tile can last for hundreds of years, especially when it's in the wall of a building, and because a tile has to be physically pried from a wall to be removed, there just aren't a lot of antique and old tiles hanging around. Those that are available are on sale at Solar, which looks rather a nice enough shop when you enter but turns out to have several secret chambers complete with buried treasures.

The tiles are in piles throughout the shop, with handwritten signs giving the century in Roman numerals. One alcove is entirely devoted to Art Deco tiles. If the tiles are pieces to a scenic they are stacked together. Tiles are organized by centuries and patterns. The oldest available are about 300 years old.

Back around to the side is a room filled with ecclesiastical antiques. We went nuts for the wooden candlesticks. (We had them shipped; no problems.)

If you go to Solar, allow yourself at least an hour to be lost in time. The shop has levels, with steps going up a few or down a few, and is dark and damp in the rear parts. This all adds to the charm.

Of course, by now you're asking yourself what to do about these gorgeous tiles. Well, here's our trick. At any TT we buy birthday numbers for a certain friend (40 is our favorite). Two number tiles when placed together create a tile that is almost four by four, the size of a regular square tile. Then, at Solar, you buy one spectacular 4-inch square. (About $12–$15.) When you get home, you glue the tiles together to form a hot-plate trophy (40 on one side; the antique on the other) and then glue grosgrain ribbon along the edges. We bought tile for the edges, but that was expensive and hard to fit (Solar has a wide selection of edges and borders in the Art Deco chamber). When your friend turns forty or (whatever) you explain that when considered next to something that's 300 years old (the other tile), forty looks awfully good.

SOLAR, Rua Dom Pedro V 70

Other antiques shops worth looking at include **XAIREL,** Rua Dom Pedro V 111, country and religious antiques; **LUIS L. LEAL,** Rua Dom Pedro V 59, Russian icons; and **SALÃO DE ANTIQUEDADES,** Rua Dom Pedro V 31–37, mostly religious and heavy stuff like big pieces of furniture.

Baixa

Baixa begins with the Rossio with its giant square, and moves right down to the water and the Praça di Comércio, where all the giant Customs buildings and statues are. Much of the area is closed to vehicular traffic; furthermore, many of these streets are named for what they sell. While these are medieval names that may not apply today, the Rua do Prata is still filled with silver shops. The main street of Baixa is Rua Augusta, which runs in a straight line from the Rossio to the water. If you are walking toward the water, to your right is the Rua do Carmo, where you get the elevator up to Chiado. A block from there you can see the fire damage and the cranes that are rebuilding the city. Most of the clothing stores here are for locals only, so what you want to do is just wander and take in the charm. **FOGAL** is at Rua Aurea 294, but there are not a lot of big-name shops here.

ANA SALAZAR: This is a local big name, and one you'll want to memorize after you've seen the shop and the couturelike clothes. Some of the styles have a bit of a costumey look, but much is high fashion. The shop is all modern architecture and tony decor, looking almost out of place in this old-time neighborhood. A winner.

ANA SALAZAR, Rua do Carmo 87

▼

CASA MACÁRIO: Count on us to lead you right to the chocolate and the coffee. This shop, founded in 1913 and unchanged physically, is a step back in time. The dusty bottles of wine include many from vintages you can't find elsewhere. There are teas, coffee, candies of all sorts, and many wines, ports, and liquors. Great good fun.

CASA MACÁRIO, Rua Augusta 272–276

▼

CASA VIANA: This is a smaller and even funkier version of the above shop. It specializes mostly in coffee and is a treat to smell, to shop, and to see. Founded in 1864, it has not been decorated since. No one speaks English, by the way, but who cares? Bring home beans for everyone you love.

CASA VIANA, Rua da Prata 61–63

▼

JOALHARIA FERREIRA MARQUES: The most famous silver shop in Lisbon, this is another of those 100-year-old wonders. You have to ring to get inside the shop, and they sell only sterling, no silver plate, but the green velvet walls and the dark woods and the incredibly crafted silver make you realize that those days are gone with the wind. There is also a shop in Porto. Some jewelry, but mostly tabletop. There is not a more impressive shop for a house gift. If you can afford it.

JOALHARIA FERREIRA MARQUES, Rossio 7–8–9

Castilho Meridien

The Rua Castilho runs in front of the Ritz and the Meridien hotels and houses most of the city's TTs in the block right before you get to the hotels. Obviously, you can walk from these hotels. We're not sure that you have to make a special trip here, but if you are on a city tour, you might be brought here. If you are looking for a good, solid TT, there are better ones near the Castelo (see page 254). But these are a good source for basics and will help you see what's available in the market and get an idea of prices.

CENTRO DE TURISMO E ARTESANATO: This shop, which distributes brochures to the hotels, claims to be a shopping center of hand-icrafts. While they do have a lot of handicrafts, it is such a serious TT that we have trouble telling you to go wild. But if your shopping time is limited, this store has a selection of everything you can imagine. Ignore their *arraiolos,* except to learn what not to buy, and concentrate instead on the little rooms filled with charming ceramics. There are crèches here, as well as plates and numbers for your house (or your birthday). There are national costumes, dolls, Madeira linens. But know your quality and prices if you insist on the very best. They ship all over the world, and are open during lunch!

CENTRO DE TURISMO E ARTESANATO, Rua Castilho 61B

▼

DIVINARTE SHOP: Where there's one TT, there has to be another, so Divinarte is your chance to compare prices and wares. This is a smaller shop that is also well stocked but that concentrates on ceramics and tiles. We found them to be about $1 less than the Centro, but they do not have nearly the same amount of stock. They also pack and ship.

DIVINARTE SHOP, Rua Castilho 67B

▼

GALERIAS RITZ: This is a shopping center attached to the lower level of the Ritz hotel, with its own entrance on Rua Castilho; it does not connect into the Ritz itself. There are a few shops here, including a fancy antiques shop and an art gallery, but the best is the ATRI Travel and Cargo Agency, where you can bring your goods to have them shipped back to the U.S.

GALERIAS RITZ, Rua Joaquim Antonio de Aguiar

▼

AMOREIRAS SHOPPING CENTER: Also in this Castilho neighborhood, but several blocks uphill (of course) from it, is the Amoreiras Shopping Center, which although it is no longer new is still the talk of Lisbon. This American-style center is a combination of the Pompidou Center in Paris and the Beverly Center in L.A. It is where all of Lisbon shops, especially the young people. The mall is open during lunch and until midnight, and has a branch of any successful store that's ever opened in Portugal. It also has a giant grocery store (called Sugar Loaf—Pão de Açúcar) that you will enjoy. There are over 350 stores; there are restaurants and a fast-food court; there're movies; there's parking. Just pitch your tent. Among our faves: **LOJA DAS MEIAS** for the Ann Taylor look with makeup; **CREARE** for T-shirts, tiles, and some crafts; **A LOJA DO VINHO** for wines and ports; **SUPER CON FEX** for K mart-high fashions for all ages and sexes; **CARROLL,** a branch of the French source for sweaters and knits; **MR. WONDERFUL,** a branch of the best men's store in Rio; **MIMOS,** a toy shop with American toys; **CORREO DA MANHA,** adorable kids' stuff; **ALTAMIRA,** high-tech furniture with rag rugs; and a fabulous tourist information office.

AMOREIRAS SHOPPING CENTER, Avenida Eng. Duarte Pacheco

Castelo

Perhaps our all-time favorite neighborhood in Lisbon is Castelo, that area surrounding the Castelo São Jorge, which was built by the Moors and held as a fortress by various conquerors. The Castelo and grounds are very nice, and you get a great view of the city below, but because they are the number-one tourist attraction in town, they also boast an enclave of TTs. Your tour bus will undoubtedly take you to any of these. **A BILHA** is one of the best TTs we've ever been in. The building itself is old and covered with tiles, so you actually want to go inside. The inside has two floors jammed with stuff, clean bathrooms tiled in the best blue and white Portuguese tiles, and a little bar area (more gorgeous tiles) where you can have a Coke. If you come on a tour bus, you may even get a free Coke. The specialty of the house is handicrafts, so you'll find lots of ceramics downstairs. The upstairs sells mostly Madeira linens and Almorábida (factory name) *arraiolos.*

Flea Markets

FEIRA DA LADRA: The so-called Thieves' Market is a bust. If you're used to a good flea market, you can just forget it now. OK, so you don't believe us. Good. Just don't be disappointed, and then everything will be fine. The market couldn't be better located—it's in the Alfama district—but is really a mess of new (cheap) clothes, army gear, bootleg tapes, and junk. We like junk. The buy of the fair seems to be used brass picture frames, but they weigh a ton. If you are used to flea markets in Spain, this is in the same genre. If you are used to something better, this is a sad day in shopping history. The market is held 10 A.M. till sunset, Tuesday and Saturday.

FEIRA DA LADRA, Largo de Santa Clara

▼

FEIRA DO RELOGIO: It doesn't get any more real than this. No tourist has ever been here, we're sure. The smell of fast-frying fish may overpower you, but this is the real world, and it's very colorful. Mostly factory overruns are sold here—we lucked into some Benetton—in mounds on the ground. Every weekend.

FEIRA DO RELOGIO, Aeroporto

▼

FEIRA DO AZEITÃO: This is a monthly fair that is held on Sundays across from Lisbon just before Setúbal. It rotates with the nearby villages of Pinhal Novo, Coina, and Moita, so you'll have to ask around to find out which week is the right week to be where. This fair is a little more fun than the one in Lisbon, although it's not paradise. There are lots of shoes, however, and some potteries. About 1,000 vendors sell here, and this is a big do for locals.

FEIRA DO AZEITÃO, Via Nogueira de Azeito, 20 miles south of Lisbon

▼

FEIRA DO SÃO PEDRO: Held in Sintra on the second and fourth Sundays of each month; take the train from Lisbon for about a half hour to this picturesque hill town famous for its views, its charm, and its antiques! The perfect Sunday treat; far more upscale than the others.

FEIRA DO SÃO PEDRO, Sintra

Finds

CRISTALISSIMO: This is the shop for Atlantis crystal, which is made in Portugal. There are actually several shops—one is in the Meridien hotel, another is in a tiny shopping center next door to the Sheraton hotel. Atlantis crystal, a stately cut crystal, is considered one of the best buys in Portugal. There is an independent Atlantis shop in the Amoreiras Shopping Center.

CRISTALISSIMO
Imaviz Shopping Center
Le Meridien, Rua Castilho 149

▼

VIUVA LAMEGO: If you have time to go to only one shop in all of Lisbon (poor you), this is it. The store specializes in ceramics and tiles. Despite the fact that it is not in a shopping neighborhood (although it's not far from Baixa), you'll quickly recognize the building, since it is entirely covered in tiles—with life-size portraits of 18th-century dandies. The company, which was founded in 1849, does a huge export business and is famous in the international design trade. Wander into the studio through the wrong door and you are in the shipping department, where case after case of tiles is stacked ten feet tall, with FRAGILE stenciled on each box.

No other store in town has these designs, which are much more Spanish and Mexican than Moorish or Persian. We're talking bolder strokes and more use of white space; brighter colors and bigger patterns than at Sant'Anna. Selection is huge: plates, lamps, bowls, planters, candlesticks. (Candlesticks!) Small tiles cost $1 each; a pair of knockout candlesticks is $50.

Here's the bad news (there's lots of it): a) the sales help is less than polite; b) the store doesn't take any credit cards whatsoever; c) they will not ship.

Who cares?

VIUVA LAMEGO, Largo do Intendente 25

▼

H. STERN: With jewelry shops all over the world, of course Brazilian gem king Hans Stern has also opened in the motherland. The shop in the Meredien lobby is small, but the glamour is not. Brazilian and local stones.

H. STERN, Le Meridien, Rua Castilho 149

Linens and Lace

OS VILOES: Down the hill from the castle is a little shop that is as much fun to look at as it is to shop in. Os Viloes specializes in embroideries and linens from Madeira. The outside of the shop is covered in handpainted tiles, decorated in murals that depict life on the island. One tile mural shows the ladies of Madeira sewing the linens by the sea. Another mural depicts the island, its wine, and the beautiful seacoast. Inside the shop, samples of the beautiful linens are displayed behind glass cases. The drawers are filled with options of good things to buy. You can bring home a lace hankie, an apron, coasters, or a complete set of linens. The varieties are endless; prices are on the high side.

OS VILOES, Rua Bartolomeu Gusmão 15–17

▼

MADEIRA SUPERBIA: This shop is not on a heavily trafficked tourist street, which leads us to believe that it sells as much to the locals as to the tourists. It is located in the vicinity of the Sheraton hotel, but it's an easy cab ride from just about anywhere. You can walk from the Meridien, but it's kind of a hike, and most of the walk you'll wonder if this could be the right neighborhood. (It is.)

Inside the shop, the walls are beautifully paneled in wood. There are baby christening dresses, women's blouses, table runners, table-cloths, banquet cloths, and the usual place mats with matching napkins. The quality of these items is better than anywhere else in town. In fact, we're talking Bergdorf-Goodman quality. The overall prices are comparable to other shops, although there is a wider selection of the expensive, better-quality items here.

MADEIRA SUPERBIA, Avenida Duque Loule 75-A

▼

A BILHA: The largest tourist shop on the hill to Castelo São Jorge is also our favorite. Yes, they see every tour bus that hits the city. Yes, their prices are often higher than elsewhere. But you will not go home empty-handed if you are looking to buy a gift. The quantity of selection makes it almost impossible not to buy. On top of that, they carry some linen items that we saw nowhere else. We happily bought every linen poinsettia coaster we could find, and then negotiated the price. In fact, once we started buying, the prices kept coming down. Remember that this is a store that is used to seeing guides bring busloads of tourists in. They understand deals.

A BILHA, Rua do Milagre de St. António 10–14

▼

MADEIRA HOUSE: This is the best-known shop for Madeira linens, and is in the busy shopping area, Baixa. Madeira House is the perfect tourist haven, with just the right prices and selection of merchandise to please everyone. There are drawers and drawers of place mat sets in every color and stitching style. If you want a tablecloth, just ask, and they will be pulled out and displayed in the middle of the store for you to see. There are tourist souvenirs along with beautiful handkerchiefs . . . something for everyone. Prices are as high as elsewhere, although you can negotiate if you pay cash. Madeira House will honor the tax-free system, but don't believe them if they say that you can ship your purchases home and still get your tax back. You can't. We tried and were soundly reprimanded at the airport by a Customs official who thought that we were trying to cheat. If you want your tax back, you have to produce the goods at the airport to prove that you are taking them out of the country. By the time we finally got our goods, we had spent $168 on shipping, and it had taken two months. Technically, no VAT should have been charged on items for export, but the store personnel assured us that they were experts in this and that they were right. Who were we to argue? Next time we will pay cash and carry!

MADEIRA HOUSE, Rua Augsta 131–135

More Antiques, and Old Books Too

While the traditional antiques street is Dom Pedro V (see page 248), there are a few antiques shops and antique book and print dealers located in Chiado. They are all near the Largo de Luis Camões, and many are just about adjacent to the famous tilemaker Sant'Anna.

CASA QUINTÃO: We know that everyone is coming to Casa Quintão to buy carpets—but don't overlook the furniture, lighting, and tapestries. As a matter of fact, when you walk in, the store looks more like a furniture showroom than a carpet shop. The entire first floor is covered with antique repro furniture and Belgian tapestries. Some are good, others not. It's worth a look.

CASA QUINTÃO, Rua Ivens 30

▼

A. M. SALGUEIRO BAPTISTA: This small shop has only the finest selections of china and furniture from all over the continent. The prices are on the high side, but so is the quality.

A. M. SALGUEIRO BAPTISTA, Rua do Alecrim 87–89

▼

REGENCIA: Located just up the street from Baptista, Regencia has a mixed selection of European and Asian quality pieces of furniture. Most are large, and would be hard to transport, but where there is the desire . . . We saw a magnificent Coromandel screen that we would have carried home by hand if we hadn't already bought too many tiles across the street at the Sant'Anna showroom.

REGENCIA, Rua do Alecrim 64–66

▼

LIVRARIA CAMPOS TRIDADE: Old books and prints in a nice, old stacked-books-on-the-table-and-library kind of shop where you feel compelled to touch everything.

LIVRARIA CAMPOS TRIDADE, Rua do Alecrim 14

▼

CENTRO ANTIQUARIO DO ALECRIM: Specializes in the pages of old books, many of which are hand-colored and suitable for framing.

CENTRO ANTIQUARIO DO ALECRIM, Rua do Alecrim 48–50

Carpets

ROSINDA DOS SANTOS: After you've touched every needlepoint carpet in Lisbon and decided that your needs are superior to the supply, you are ready to graduate from retail to special-order. You're also ready to go to a wholesale supplier and artisan directly. We have the artist for you, and the price will be right, but you're going to have to go out of your way on a wild adventure that will take half a day and may require your renting a car and learning to speak Portuguese. But you get what you search for, and this is one quest that will truly pay off.

We discovered Rosinda dos Santos through

our friend who is the public relations director of the Meridien hotel. The Meridien, competing as it does to beat the Ritz as the best place in town, often uses its mezzanine space for art shows, and the public relations director prides herself on being on top of everything. So a few years ago she gave a show of *arraiolos* (carpets) and invited only prizewinners to show. This is where she met Rosinda, who had just won the equivalent of the Academy Award for needlepoint carpets. This honor is so serious in Portugal that a picture of the statue is printed on Rosinda's business card. Furthermore, she was chosen by the Portuguese government to make the carpet that Portugal presented to Queen Elizabeth II.

Rosinda designs and executes all her carpets herself. Her style is more traditional than most, with Hispano-Moresque influence. Many of her carpets are geometrics that have a sort of Navajo-Turkish feel. She does do flowers, of course. And she will customize a carpet for you. You must call Rosinda and make an appointment—if you do not speak Portuguese, get your hotel concierge to help you. The cab to her studio (in a suburb of Lisbon) will cost about $50, so consider renting a car. She takes cash or traveler's checks in dollars, but prefers not to take dollars, and will not take a U.S. check. Believe it or not, you can communicate with pencil and paper and mime pretty easily, so an interpreter is not essential.

This is a real insider's source, perhaps best for those in the trade.

ROSINDA DOS SANTOS
Office: Rua D. Antonio de Chatilon 28, 2830 Lavradio (Local phone: 204-9324)
Shop: Rua da Bélgica 12 A-B, Lavradio (Local phone: 204-1777)

▼

CASA QUINTÃO: We've already listed this shop earlier in the book (page 244), since it is the standout of the Chiado district. We suggest that any proper carpet-buying expedition begin at Casa Quintão in order to see the most, get an idea of prices, and work with the people best equipped to deal with American tourists. If you discover that your needs are more specialized, or you want to touch every carpet ever made, then you'll go to other shops in town and also visit other parts of Portugal before you buy. We did this, and still ended up buying at Casa Quintão.

CASA QUINTÃO, Rua Ivens 30

▼

TRICANA: Located near the Sheraton hotel, but on a residential street, Tricana caters to a mixed clientele. On the street level, where you enter, the shop has a waiting room reminiscent of a commercial carpet shop. Nothing very special. There is a sales counter, lots of carpets on the floor, and people milling about. Through a video screen, you can see the downstairs salesroom, where individual customers are shown carpets. Sometimes the wait to get downstairs can be an hour, depending on who is ahead of you. We suggest that you go here first thing in the morning to look and check prices. The designs are a mixture of stock and better quality. Prices are slightly lower than at other shops.

TRICANA, Avenida Praia da Vitoria 48-A

▼

TREVO: The carpets that you will find at Trevo are vastly different from those that you will find at Casa Quintão. The Moorish influence is much more heavily represented. Quasi-Moorish designs include geometric shapes, medallion carpets with cartouches, and carpets with animals in the borders and backgrounds that surround central medallions and vines of arabesques.

The shop is in a residential area (not far from the bullring), and somewhat hard to find. We suggest taking a taxi the first time. As you walk in, you will be ushered back to two low-ceilinged rooms where the carpets are displayed on the wall and in stacks. If you want a floral, your selection is limited. In fact, depending on the time of year or the luck of that season, the stock can be quite low. But they will make a custom design for you. The prices are very fair; quality is high. There is a catalogue (in English), and they will ship. This is a small shop with an intimate atmosphere that offers a different type of shopping experience than Casa Quintão or the other carpet shops.

TREVO, Avenida Óscar Monteiro Torres 33A

▼

ALMORÁBIDA: If you are sick to death of overdecorated carpet places and fancy stitches and perfection that you consider overbearing, perhaps you will be happier looking at the Almorábida selection, which is far more informal —the carpets are much more peasanty in design. Most of them have fringe, which is the local traditional but which many American designers do not like. Many of them are in the bigger stitch that is not acceptable to designers. Almorábida is for the customer who isn't looking for the carpet of a lifetime, but wants something nice in the souvenir category. A midsize (4×6) throw carpet, perfect for the den, begins at $500. They also make round carpets, which are not shown elsewhere. Furthermore, there is an office in New York (call 212-689-3307) and a factory in the village of Arraiolos, where the carpets are made. You can go to Arraiolos and visit this factory (and others) and buy directly from the source. Have plenty of cash, and bargain like mad. Styles are in both geometric Moorish patterns and florals. Make sure the carpet lies flat and there is no bunching in the stitches. We priced a floral that measured 10 feet by 7 feet at $1,200, after some bargaining. There is a showroom in the A Bilha shop near the Castelo.

ALMORÁBIDA at A BILHA, Rua do Milagre de St. Antonio 10–14

ALMORÁBIDA FACTORY, Avenida Nova 9, Vimieiro, 7045 Arraiolos, (Local phone: 066-461-74)

Day Trips and Tours

Estoril and Cascais

The famed beach resorts of Estoril and Cascais are the destinations of many visitors to Portugal. If you are staying in Lisbon, however, fear not. Estoril and Cascais are but a train ride away. The train station to find is Estação Cais do Sodre, on the water next to Baixa. Trains leave on the hour for Cascais and Estoril. All you have to do is walk in, buy a ticket, and be on your way. The ride along the seashore is beautiful. Before you know it you have arrived. Cascais is where all the shopping is, so we suggest that you start there. It is also the farther destination of the two, and the end of the line.

1. Walk or taxi to the Cais do Sodre and buy your round-trip ticket. (A round-trip ticket saves you ten *escudos*.) If you have to wait a while for the next train, there are snack bars and newsstands in the station. Read the board and listen to announcements for the proper track.

2. As you exit the train station in Cascais, walk straight ahead, cross the street, and try to

spot the tiled sidewalk with the wavy lines. This is the main drag, and the pedestrian shopping walk. (Or just follow the throng.) Along the way you will see myriad shops selling T-shirts, pottery, beachwear, sunglasses, and tiles. It is fun to just wander in and out. The shopping district is not so large that you can't do it in two hours, have lunch at one of the sidewalk cafés, and be back on your train and in Lisbon in time for dinner.

3. While you are strolling, be sure to stop in at the two stores that make this trip extra worth doing:

J. A. S. AMORIM: In some honesty, this should be classified as a TT. But since it specializes in ceramics and tiles, we call it a find. Go up the stairs and discover two showrooms of tiles with a porch hung with even more stuff. Ceramic chandeliers are about $100, and a steal. Tile scenics begin at $75. It's all here: the plates, the house numbers, the umbrella stands, etc. Prices aren't drop-dead cheap—after all, you are in a seaside resort—but they are competitive with Lisbon and less than some of the fancy Lisbon shops. They also have copper, pewter, lead crystal, and tableware. They are open during lunch. They'll ship.

J. A. S. AMORIM, Rua Frederico Arouca 43 (upstairs)

▼

ISTO E AQUILO: One block from the main walking street is this tiny square with a white stucco Portuguese potter's atelier and shop that reeks charm. They sell a few tiles, a good bit of pottery, and some quilts and rag rugs, as well as linens and doodads. Each piece is exactly your fantasy of what Portuguese craftsmanship should be. There're coffee mugs in blue and white ($5 each) and dinner plates handpainted with pictures of fishes ($15); cachepots cost $15. They do not ship, and you'll have a problem lugging too much weight on the train. Perhaps you should rent a truck and load up now.

ISTO E AQUILO, Largo da Misericórdia

4. As you finish your stroll, you'll wind up on the beach. After taking in the view, and maybe a little swim, you can walk a half block to Beco Torto and have lunch at Le Bec Fin (Beco Torto 1), which has French and local food in a charming indoor-outdoor café.

5. Wander back toward the train station, this time first exploring the Rua Visconde da Luz. Don't miss Casa Torrado (No. 13A), a huge TT that sells a lot of everything. What they lack in charm they make up for in stock.

6. You may be tempted to take a taxi or the local bus (we took the local bus and got lost for an hour) to Estoril, which is only a kilometer or two away. Estoril may have the rep, and if you've got a cottage there, enjoy it—but it doesn't have a lot of shopping. They are building a shopping center. But locals now go to Cascais. Return by train from either Estoril or Cascais and explore more of Lisbon. The train leaves you close to the Museum of Folk Art, which you may now have an even greater appreciation for.

Lisbon on a Schedule

Tour I: Lisbon Chiado Day

1. Lisbon is such a sprawling city that to get from one area to the other requires the use of taxis, the tram, or the Metro. We prefer the taxi system when in a hurry.

2. Start your day tour in Chiado, the upper city. Ask the taxi driver to drop you off in the Largo do Chiado, which is the central square.

3. Rua Garrett is the main drag, and all of the good streets intersect it. Some of the nicer stores are here as well. While getting your bearings, stroll up one side and down the other. If you haven't had your morning coffee, or want to plan for afternoon tea, the main square is the best place in town to stop.

4. From Rua Garrett find Rua Ivens, which will cut to the right as you are walking toward the fire-damaged part of the street. Here you might want to allocate lots of time to one of our favorite *arraiolos* shops, Casa Quintão (No. 34). Trust us, you will not find a better selection or prices than you will here. We tried.

5. When you have finished at Casa Quintão, go back to Rua Garrett, take a left, and walk past the square to Rua do Alecrim, where you will take a left and walk to No. 95, Sant'Anna. This is one of the two infamous tile shops in Lisbon, and our very favorite, because they ship. Sant'Anna makes the wonderful Country Floors tiles that we drool over, and you can buy look-alikes. We stocked up on Christmas presents.

6. When you can't carry any more ceramic goodies, wander up Rua do Alecrim and look in all of the design and fabric shops. This is decorator row.

7. When you have reached Rua Garrett once again, turn right to reach Largo do Chiado 18 and the Vista Alegre shop. There are many Vista Alegre shops in Lisbon, and each one of them seems to sell a different variety of the line, which is why we suggest visiting as many of them as possible.

8. Turn around again in the direction you came from, walk on Largo do Chiado to Rua da Misericórdia, and take a right turn up the hill. Look into Pórtico (No. 31), a decorating and furniture store that also has lots of pretty gift items.

9. As you keep walking up the hill, notice the small craftspeople's shops and grocers along the way. When you reach Rua de San Pedro de Alcantara, you will be almost at the top of antiques heaven. Take a look to the right for a spectacular view of the Baixa section of Lisbon and the Alfama on the opposite hill. Check out the tram in case you need a ride down after you finish shopping.

10. When you finally hit Rua Dom Pedro V, you are home free, and you should browse the antiques shops until you cannot look another old tile in the face. The very best shop on the street for tile and ecclesiastical artifacts is Solar, at No. 70. Plan to spend many hours there.

11. At this point we know your feet will need a rest, and we suggest a taxi down the hill to your hotel, and a good cup of tea.

Tour 2: Lisbon Baixa and Alfama Day

1. The two older sections of town are right next to each other, but because of the hilly topography they might as well be worlds apart. Plan your day with lots of walking in mind.

2. Start your tour by the train station, Estação do Rossio, which is next to the main square, Praça Dom Pedro IV. With your back to the station, walk toward the water on Rua Augusta, the main drag. Before you head down the street, however, check out one of Lisbon's famous silver shops, Joalharia Ferreira Marques at Rossio 7–8–9, one of the oldest and finest in the city. You will feel like you are in a museum.

3. Now stroll down Rua Augusta, taking time to make side trips down the streets that run perpendicular. You will notice that many are named for the products that they once sold, as in a true market village. Our favorite street parallels Rua Augusta, and is called Rua do Ouro. Along the way, check out the many linen shops. We like Madeira House at Rua Augusta 131–135 for sheer selection (see page 259).

4. When you have tired of shopping in the small streets and alleys, and are ready for some touristy fun, grab a cab (you can walk if you are in great shape), and head up the hill to Castelo São Jorge, located at the top of the Alfama. The taxi driver will let you out in the square in front of the Castelo. Before you get distracted by all of the tourist souvenir shops, be sure to walk around the grounds and look out over the city. The view is breathtaking.

5. Now that you have seen the sights, you can feel noble about indulging in a little TT shopping. This is the best area for doing that, as all the way down the hill you will

find shop after shop selling ceramics, carpets, lace, linens, and swords, not to mention postcards. We have a favorite shop along the way that seems to have it all. A Bilha has two floors filled with touristy items, all of which are overpriced. The good news is that they will bargain, and have a tremendous selection. You will find them at Rua do Milagre de St. António 10–14.

6. Also on the way down the hill from the Castelo, you will see a shop that is covered on the outside with handpainted tiles depicting life on the island of Madeira. The shop is called Os Viloes, Rua Bartolomeu Gusmão 15–17, and specializes in lace and linens of the best quality. Prices are higher here than many other shops, but so is the quality.

7. When you get tired, or reach the bottom, hail a taxi and ask the driver to take you to the "other" famous tile shop in Lisbon, Viuva Lamego at Largo do Intendente 25. Plan to have a wonderful time looking at all of the selections of vases, tiles, and knickknacks. Then plan to be totally frustrated when you realize that they do not ship and do not take plastic. We still love it here.

8. After Viuva Lamego, you will need to taxi back to your hotel with all of your purchases, and figure out how to pack them safely in your suitcases. You might need to buy a new suitcase at this point.

Size Conversion Chart

WOMEN'S DRESSES, COATS, AND SKIRTS

American	3	5	7	9	11	12	13	14	15	16	18
Continental	36	38	38	40	40	42	42	44	44	46	48
British	8	10	11	12	13	14	15	16	17	18	20

WOMEN'S BLOUSES AND SWEATERS

American	10	12	14	16	18	20
Continental	38	40	42	44	46	48
British	32	34	36	38	40	42

WOMEN'S SHOES

American	5	6	7	8	9	10
Continental	36	37	38	39	40	41
British	3½	4½	5½	6½	7½	8½

CHILDREN'S CLOTHING

American	3	4	5	6	6X
Continental	98	104	110	116	122
British	18	20	22	24	26

CHILDREN'S SHOES

American	8	9	10	11	12	13	1	2	3
Continental	24	25	27	28	29	30	32	33	34
British	7	8	9	10	11	12	13	1	2

MEN'S SUITS

American	34	36	38	40	42	44	46	48
Continental	44	46	48	50	52	54	56	58
British	34	36	38	40	42	44	46	48

MEN'S SHIRTS

American	14½	15	15½	16	16½	17	17½	18
Continental	37	38	39	41	42	43	44	45
British	14½	15	15½	16	16½	17	17½	18

MEN'S SHOES

American	7	8	9	10	11	12	13
Continental	39½	41	42	43	44½	46	47
British	6	7	8	9	10	11	12

INDEX

About the Authors

SUZY GERSHMAN is an author and journalist who also writes under her maiden name, Suzy Kalter. She has worked in the fiber and fashion industry since 1969 in both New York and Los Angeles and has held editorial positions at *California Apparel News, Mademoiselle, Gentleman's Quarterly,* and *People* magazine, where she was West Coast Style editor. She writes regularly for *Travel and Leisure;* her essays on retailing are text at the Harvard Business School. Mrs. Gershman lives in Connecticut with her husband, author Michael Gershman, and their son. Michael Gershman also contributes to the *Born to Shop* pages.

JUDITH THOMAS is a designer who began her career working in the creative and advertising departments of Estée Lauder and Helena Rubinstein in New York. Previously she was an actress in television commercials as well as on and off Broadway. In 1973 she moved to Los Angeles where she was an art director for various studios while studying for her ASID at UCLA. She later formed Panache and Associates, a commercial design firm. She is currently involved in developing and marketing new trends in building design for MPS Systems. Mrs. Thomas lives in Pennsylvania with her husband and two children.